John Da

On Hope, Evolution and Change

Selected essays

Hawthorn Press

ISNB 0 950 7062 – 72 (Philosophy)
Typeset in Baskerville by **Artmark** Nailsworth, Glos.
Printed by Billing and Son Ltd., Worcester
Cover design by Margaret Shillan represents the Järna flow form as pioneered in Britain
by John Wilkes.
Book format, research and editorial work by Judith Large

Hawthorn Press gratefully acknowledges the help of Gudrun Davy and Owen Barfield with this
book. Appreciation is also extended to Roger Franklin and the Mercury Provident Society for
their assistance.
Thanks for kind permission to reproduce articles go to Adam Bittleston of the Golden Blade, to the
Anthroposophical Review, The Observer, The Times Educational Supplement,
Resurgence and the Teachers College Record.
Thanks also to Douglas Sloan and Margli Matthews for their advice and support.

Table of Contents

Foreword

What is a journalist? *Jour* is French for 'day', so the very derivation of the word suggests a shallow mind eagerly swallowing the events and opinions not of the week, not of the month, not of the year, not of the centuries, not of the millennia, but just of today and possibly yesterday. There they are, those journalists, every night on television jostling each other to poke the blind mouths of their microphones nearest to the face of someone who is very likely in deep distress and who in any case was never heard of yesterday and will have been forgotten tomorrow. Scratch a journalist, I have often thought, and you find a quidnunc.

To this rule, if it be one, there are notable exceptions, and it may well be that there has never been a more notable one than John Davy. 'Journalism', he once remarked in an interview (where he was for once the interviewee), 'is a peculiar sort of job: you are always a bit of an onlooker at what other people are doing. But on the other hand, you can go and meet more or less anyone whose work interests you.' John Davy was 'interested' in other people and in what they were doing, not because it meant a scoop or a story, but because of his own outgoing and affectionate moral imagination; and he was interested in their work both for its own sake and as a manifestation of vaster currents in the depths beneath it. It is in this last respect that he differs most markedly not only from the quid-nuncs but also from other exceptions to the quidnunc rule. It was perhaps the former quality, his genuine and participating interest in other human beings, and thus in the people themselves with whom his work brought him into contact, that produced an element in his character on which many have remarked. I mean a certain unas-sumingness, a total absence of any sort of brashness or self-conceit born of the awareness (which must nevertheless have been there) of his own penetration being rather deeper than that of his interviewee.

That such penetration was an outstanding feature of his intellec-tual make-up is clear from the essays and articles that follow. They also leave us in no doubt that he owed its development in him, a development for which 'wisdom' would perhaps be a better name, in large measure to his lifelong familiarity with the teachings of Rudolf Steiner. It was with their help that he acquired a mind that surveys the ages. Thus, it is no accident that the contents of this book are twofold: on the one hand Davy's articles in the *Observer* and elsewhere displaying his sensitivity to numerous and varied ripples of contemporary thought, both scientific and social, and on the other hand his contributions to anthroposophical publications. What is so distinctive is the readiness with which the two divergent approaches fuse; and that fusion, effective in many of them, culminates to my mind with especial force in the brilliant essay entitled *Scientific Progress and the Threshold.*

However accommodatingly he may have adopted the other man's terminology when interviewing scientists like Crick and Watson or behaviourists like Professor Skinner, Davy remained quietly convinced that the intellectual materialism characteristic of our age is a passing phase. 'It is odd,' he remarked in the interview already referred to,

> 'that we should so easily accept the idea that for some thousands of years, people had stupid, erroneous or superstitious ideas about the universe, and then, quite suddenly, from the Fifteenth Century onwards, the true facts suddenly begin to enter our heads.'

He had realised at a fairly early age that the total heterogeneity between matter and spirit first formulated by René Descartes in the Seventeenth Century was the foundation on which modern science is erected, and further that it is a false foundation if taken as a statement of fact, though a sound one if taken as describing the right *method* for investigating inanimate phenomena. And no doubt it was not long before he came to realise also that the barrier, the 'threshold', between matter and spirit, which has been densified by our growing habit of thinking in that mode, is correlative to the 'Threshold' which Anthroposophy, and indeed some other schools of thought, depict as severing man's daytime consciousness that is dependent on the senses from a higher consciousness, to which alone a knowledge of the spirit is accessible.

He perceived modern science as a *phase* – and an important one – in an age-long evolution of consciousness and of the world; an important one indeed, but for all its technological achievements, important *as* a phase rather than for any claims it has to understanding and knowledge of reality. He perceived also that that evolutionary process involves the severance of human consciousness from the spiritual world that underlies both nature and itself. It is to be followed by a re-union with that world in the future; but meanwhile it is to the severance – the threshold between matter and spirit – that we owe our *self*-consciousness, and thus our very existence as autonomous individual spirits. Davy saw, with Steiner, the age of the 'Consciousness Soul', beginning in the Fifteenth Century and extending for some two thousand years – our own age therefore – as a crucial turning-point in that evolution, since it includes both the culmination of the severance and the first stirrings in the direction of re-union. For this reason he detected in relatively recent developments in science and elsewhere symptoms, however faint, of a coming break-through from the cramping bonds of materialism. Yet, though he was far from ignoring it, he was not one of those who excitedly exaggerate the significance of quantum theory and the principle of uncertainty; his perspective was longer than that, so that the 'recent developments' included such phenomena as the discovery of electricity (with its need to cope with forces imperceptible to the senses) and a psychology of the unconscious. For the same reason he was interested in any symptoms, in his own time, of a changing attitude to death and the possibilities of a Life extending beyond it.

But above all, I think it was his keen awareness of science as the engine of the severance, and for that reason the first to begin stumbling against the fatal illusion embalmed in it, that gave the science correspondent of the *Observer* a fellow feeling with almost anyone genuinely engaged in scientific research, no matter how widely his philosophy differed from theirs.

It is not only in the realm of thought and knowledge that the Consciousness Soul reveals itself. Steiner sometimes pointed out that, in the whole conduct and experience of life, a single human being at that stage of his development tends towards universal rather than departmentalised self-expression. This is not always beneficial. One recalls Matthew Arnold's complaint in *The Scholar Gipsy* that ours is an age wherein 'each half lives a hundred different lives'. Perhaps it calls for especial strength of character to surmount the fissiparous temptations, and thus make it a positive rather than a negative element in a man's biography. I would say that John Davy, having that strength, was a true Consciousness Soul man. Though journalism was the field in which he laboured longest, he was far from being *only* a journalist. There is enough in the Biography that supplements these essays to make that plain. But I feel that, apart from the circumstances of his life, this 'universalism', if the term may be allowed, is something that comes through in the essays themselves – partly by way of the comprehensive, yet solid, interest they reveal in so many different departments of life and thought, and partly in other and more indefinable ways. What might all this have led to, had he had another twenty or thirty years of life? Davy himself had no doubts whatever of the reality of 'Karma'. When one surveys the combination in his life of achievement and promise, it is difficult not to believe that there was some purpose, beyond the comprehension of most of us, in his early and unheralded death.

Owen Barfield
South Darenth
Kent
May, 1985

Biography of the Author

John Charles Davy was born on 8th August, 1927 in London. He was the eldest son of Charles and Doris Davy, both distinguished journalists. A second son, Richard was born two years later. John had a happy childhood and fondly remembered their London garden, the little pool his mother had built with her own hands and the walks in Kensington Gardens. The family moved to Chelmsfield in Kent some years later where John attended a small preparatory school. John was a very keen learner, and the story goes that one day, when still in the nursery class, he picked up his chair, and moving it to the next room to the older children, declared: 'I am ready to read now'.

At the beginning of the war the family moved to Leeds where Charles Davy worked for the *Yorkshire Post*. John began boarding school at Abbotsholme in Derbyshire, a school offering long hikes, crafts and music as well as academic subjects. He was later grateful to his mother for choosing an alternative to traditional public school.

In 1944 John had a 'spare' year before being called up for military service. He detested the idea of staying on as a 'Prefect' at Abbotsholme and working for higher examinations. His own choice instead was to join the Rudolf Steiner School, Michael Hall, since the war evacuated to Minehead in Somerset. John thrived during this year. It was a great change to suddenly be in a co-education school and he became deeply engrossed in all the drama, art, and music there. He later claimed jokingly that he had never worked so hard in his life as during this year at Michael Hall.

In 1946 John was called up for military service and by joining the Intelligence Corps was spared a lot of military training. Instead he ws sent to Vienna to help with interviewing refugees from the Balkan countries. It was an interesting time but John felt later that he had been 'too asleep' to make full use of the opportunities offered him there. On the one hand there was all the post-war misery before him, on the other it was easy to enjoy almost every night performances by the Vienna Royal Ballet. For packets of cigarettes John could obtain lessons on the cembalo from one of the leading Viennese concert performers.

In 1948 John was free to take up his studies at Trinity College, Cambridge. He had toyed with the idea of becoming a medical doctor and later often wondered what would have happened if he had. But a biology teacher at Abbotsholme and his own mother's passion for nature inspired him to take up Natural Science instead.

John had many other interests and was gifted in many ways. Music and poetry played a great part in his life but he equally enjoyed using his hands for woodwork and gardening. He was perhaps most interested in meeting people. Cambridge offered plenty of opportunities for all of these interests. John also began to read Steiner. He had read *Occult Science* in Vienna and what was related there did not present any problems to him. It rang true and was worth exploring further. So John and one of his friends started a small study group on anthroposophy at Cambridge. John found Steiner's writing 'door openers' to life.

In the summer of 1951 after obtaining his B.A., John attended an International Conference of the Christian Community near Shrewsbury. There he met his German future wife, Gudrun zur Linden. The mutual recognition was instantaneous. He followed her to Germany, working first as a woodcutter in northern Germany and later teaching at a Steiner school in Stuttgart in order to be near her while she studied at the University of Heidelberg. The next year they both transferred to the University of Freiburg. John had been granted an exchange scholarship for a research year.

It was at Freiburg that John received a letter out of the blue from David Astor, then editor of the *Sunday Observer* offering him a job as a science reporter. Charles Davy was working at that time on the *Observer* as Assistant Editor. It was only in the early fifties that so much was happening in the world of science and technology that it had to become a specialised newspaper subject. John was intrigued, fascinated and honoured to be asked to try his hand as first Science Correspondent of a paper he much respected. So John and Gudrun were married in Germany at the end of their Freiburg year and John took up his work in London after three months of training at the *Manchester Evening News*.

The sixteen years of commuting from Forest Row, Sussex to London Fleet Street began. The computer age was in its early stages and so was space travel. Interesting biological discoveries were made and John went to many laboratories to talk to the scientists concerned. He looked back on this time with immense gratitude that life offered him the chance to become an observer and interpreter of so many exciting developments.

He saw the first take-off from Cape Canaveral and went on interesting journeys to Israel, Africa, and even the South Pole. But John was equally interested in what went on in the field of psychology. From short reporting pieces he soon wrote long articles after interviewing people like Ronald Laing, Professor Skinner, Ivan Illich and many others. In the field of biology he was very excited to meet Crick and Watson to learn and report their discovery of DNA. Fritz Schumacher wrote for the *Observer* before he became well-known and John soon recognised his voice as a very important one.

John's lively and lucid writing was soon recognised by the world at large. He won several prizes as 'the best science journalist' of the year and in 1965 he was awarded an OBE by Her Majesty the Queen for his 'services to science'.

In the meantime, at home in Sussex three sons and one daughter were born in the course of these years. John took a special delight in very small babies and whenever he was home took a very active part in the care and upbringing of the children. At the same time his interest in and study of Steiner's anthroposophy had increased steadily, so that John soon became the chairman of the local group and also was elected to the Council of the Anthroposophical Society of Great Britain.

During the last two years of his *Observer* time John began to feel restless. He felt that the time was approaching when he might want to devote himself more fully to work arising out of Steiner's ideas. At that time he was already lecturing occasionally to the small 'Emerson College' which had moved from the Midlands to Forest Row. Francis Edmunds, the Principal had long had his eye on John, and in 1970 John left the *Observer* to teach at the ever growing College. Emerson College is a very international adult education college, based on the work of Rudolf Steiner. At first John taught only part-time as he was hoping to follow up some research into methods of testing the quality of water. But soon he was needed more and more at the College and had to drop the research reluctantly.

Fourteen busy years followed. John soon became the Acting Principal of the College and was in charge of the Foundation Year. At the same time he became General Secretary of the Anthroposophical Society which involved him in a lot of work in London and twice yearly trips to Dornach in Switzerland. Apart from all this John was very much in demand as a lecturer and writer to very diverse groups of people ranging from academic circles to so called 'New Age' explorers. John enjoyed bridge-building and hated any form of sectarianism. He also took on several assignments for the *Observer*. One of them was the series on *Life after Life*, which took him to America. He was deeply moved by his encounter with Elizabeth Kübler-Ross and felt she was one of the truly great people of our century.

His last few years became increasingly busy: regular lecture tours to the States, Canada and Europe, teaching, administration and endless conversations with students at the College, writing and advising many people who sought him out, and the work for the Society filled his time. To his great regret this left him little time for his family and his beloved garden. He remarked several times that it seemed to him that he had to pack three lives into one.

In the spring of 1984 John returned from a lecture tour to Canada and the United States very satisfied but also extremely exhausted. It turned out to be more than that. Soon he was diagnosed as suffering from a malignant brain tumour. He had only five more months to live.

It was characteristic of John that he was quite open about his illness but not deterred by a 'life sentence'. He said he would prepare himself for a short, long or medium time and bring life into healthy movement and development. Suddenly he was released from the constant demands the world had made on him and could be for a bit master of his own time. He put down his thoughts on the future of the College and went with his wife on a holiday to his beloved Tintagel.

On 28th October John died in his own home, surrounded by his family and close friends. He was mourned all over the world for his way of being, his warmth and his clarity of thought.

Gudrun Davy
Forest Row
Sussex
May, 1985

John Davy *(Photo: Malcolm Powell)*

"Thank God our time is now
When wrong comes up to meet
           us everywhere
Never to leave us till we take
The greatest strde of soul
Men ever took.
Affairs now are soul size
The enterprise
Is exploration unto God.
Where are you making for?
It takes so many thousand years
           to wake.
But will you wake
For pity's sake?"

Christopher Fry

THIS LIVING EARTH

Wisdom and the Life of the Earth

The deepest experience which astronauts appear to bring back from their space journeys is not their encounter with the moon, but their new vision of the earth.

The moon, whose silver light graces the earth's nights, becomes for the astronauts, at close quarters, a giant cinder, a wasteland of dark rock, a fossil of past cosmic dramas. The lunar landscape inspires awe but not affection. There is nothing there for man but emptiness and desolation.

In contrast, the earth hangs in a dark, star-pricked space like a giant water drop, a shining blue jewel in a black and white universe. The mathematical fact that two thirds of the globe is covered with water becomes direct perception. The continents are seen as a kind of bone structure in dim greens, dull browns, dusty yellows embedded in the brilliant blue sphere of the oceans. Both oceans and land are often veiled in vast streamers and vortices of vapour, the great weather systems which unfold where water and air flower as clouds in the light of the sun. This seems to have been an overwhelming experience for many astronauts, but especially for those who have travelled far enough into space to look back on the earth from the region of the moon. It is then borne in on them, with all the force of a religious experience, that the earth is man's proper home, the only place in the material universe where he truly belongs and which holds a future for him.

This experience of man's home as a kind of living water drop contrasts in a curious way with the experience of those terrestrial explorers who set forth in ships at the beginning of our modern age, who felt they had come 'home' when they stepped once more onto dry land. The upright citizen is designed to live on *terra firma*. But the astronaut standing on *luna firma*, well supported on solid rock, looks back and experiences his true home as a shining watery sphere. And it is the oceans of the earth which first receive the American astronauts when they return from their space journeys. Coming home is not a stepping onto dry land but a 'splashdown'.

It seems to me that there is here an image, in miniature, of a new relationship to the earth which is beginning to emerge among human beings. It is a remarkable fact that, coinciding more or less with the moon voyages, whole communities and even nations have started to discuss the problems of conservation and pollution.

Industrial activity is based on transforming the physical body of the earth. But we are now realising that this activity is threatening the water and air of the planet. Water is the great life-bringer – where it is present, living processes can unfold; where it is not, we have physics and chemistry, but no biology. Air mediates, in many subtle ways, between the earth and the sun, forming weather and climate which shape so strongly the patterns of life and vegetation on the earth's surface. All over the world, water supplies are beginning to be dangerously strained, both in quantity and quality. In arid countries, the need to conserve water is part of every person's awareness. But industrial cities first grew up in temperate regions, where water appears to be cheap and plentiful. So even today, it is not realised how near to the limit we are even in some parts of England, an island whose citizens spend part of their time lamenting the abundance of rainfall, and another part nurturing their uniquely green lawns which the rain makes possible.

The simple fact is that cities and city dwellers have to flush themselves with enormous and growing quantities of water to keep themselves clean. In itself, this is admirable. Running water and main drainage are now taken for granted by most people in this country, but it is not so very long ago that the gutters of many London streets ran with sewage all day long. The first step was to channel it all into drains, which eventually emptied into the nearest river or sea. But this turned the rivers into sewers, and the fish died. The next step was to build sewage disposal plants to process the wastes first. This is still going on, at considerable cost. But there are some visible improvements: conditions in the Thames have improved recently, and fish have been seen near London Bridge for the first time since the last century.

All this helps – but the problem remains formidable. To begin with, increasing amounts of water have to be taken from rivers and underground reserves to pump through the cities and flush away the wastes. A great many modern industrial processes consume water on a grand scale, and may produce effluents containing chemicals and other wastes which cannot be digested by ordinary sewage plant. There are now a considerable number of rivers whose flow would shrink to a trickle in summer if they were not fed with effluents from sewage plants. These effluents may be relatively clear and inoffensive, but they are likely to contain a lot of dissolved salts, and to bear little resemblance to the fresh water which originally cut the river channel in which they run. Furthermore, this degraded water is now increasingly recirculated, via chemical purifying plants, to provide water for communities further downstream. There are townships in the American Middle West where water is recirculated some twelve or thirteen times before it escapes to freedom along the river bed.

To meet these problems, increasingly ambitious water collection and distribution schemes are being prepared. There is an idea for a kind of 'water grid' which would eventually collect water from the northern and western parts of Britain, where there is still a surplus, and distribute it to drier regions in the south and east. On the North American continent, vast schemes are being discussed to divert whole river systems which now run into sparsely inhabited northern territories, so that they will water the cities and more arid lands to the South. These schemes are on such a scale that some scientists are asking whether such a massive redistribution of water might not affect the climate, in unpredictable ways. However this may be, in all industrialised countries, a natural and free circulation of water from hills, through streams and rivers to the sea, is gradually being replaced by a man-made grid of reservoirs, pipes and processing plants.

Yet despite all these efforts, there are growing signs of a major water crisis within a few decades. It may well be the impossibility of sustaining a sufficient supply of usable water that will put a limit to the explosive industrial expansion which has characterised 'advanced' societies in recent decades. As for many less advanced communities, they are already in deep trouble. Cities like Calcutta, which are ringed by nauseous slums, are the result of exposing a peasant culture to a western-type industry and economics which has evolved over centuries. All the social and economic forces which create large cities are released quite suddenly into such societies without providing any of the resources or experience needed to keep them habitable. The result is the creation of centres of chronic social and human catastrophe. All over the 'developing' world, European technology is creating rural unemployment; the unemployed flock to the cities, which cannot house, feed and employ them. There are growing up unbelievable expanses of shanty slums for which no solution is in sight. In Lima, Peru, for example, 1,000 peasants a day are arriving on the city's outskirts, and nobody knows what to do with them.

The water crisis is accompanied by growing concern about the atmosphere. Here again, much has already been done to control the crude black smoke generated by coal-burning, a legacy of the nineteenth century's industrial revolution. The problem of the twentieth century is the combustion of oil and petroleum,which releases acrid sulphur and nitrogen compounds from chimneys, carbon monoxide and complex poisonous chemicals from car exhausts. To give only two examples: there is evidence that fumes from the British Midlands, carried by prevailing south-west winds, are contributing to acrid rainfall which is stunting forest growth in Scandinavia. And some recent studies have shown a dulling of mental alertness among drivers inhaling exhaust fumes in traffic-filled streets.

On a more global scale, there is a good deal of scientific discussion about the effects of the vast amounts of dust and carbon dioxide which are being poured into the atmosphere, with effects now detectable all over the globe. The earth's atmosphere has been measurably darkened during the past 50 years, and this could lead to far-reaching climatic changes. The carbon dioxide level has also measurably increased – perhaps fortunately, for it could offset the effects of the dust: carbon dioxide helps trap the sun's warmth in the atmosphere; suspended dust reflects sunlight back into space.

*   *   *

Many of these problems have been visible to those interested for twenty years or more. What is remarkable is the quite sudden way in which large numbers of people all over the world have become aware of the issues. It is as though some new kind of global consciousness were in the making, a consciousness which knows that in the end, every human individual on earth is involved with and dependent on every other. This is in sharp contrast to the essential attitudes which made the industrial revolution. This revolution was made, in great part, by the entrepreneur, the pioneering industrialist, who went his own way, the self-made man. Such men took hold of the solid substances of the earth and bent them to their individual wills. One can recognise in the developments which led from the fifteenth century, through the industrial revolution, up to the twentieth century, a kind of schooling for individualism which brought men into a new awareness of the solid earth and of themselves. This belongs centrally to what Rudolf Steiner called the Consciousness Soul, a phase in the evolution of human consciousness in which man becomes aware of himself as an Ego, independent of 'Nature'. Every man becomes an island, standing on his own inner 'rock'. Technology has been a crucial aid in forming this consciousness. But if we are now becoming aware of the shadow sides of the industrial age – egotism, self-centredness, brutality, disinterest in the wider effects of one's actions on others – it may be because we are becoming ready for a further step.

In certain spheres, a good deal has already changed. In the early parts of the last century, millowners strode blindly past the coughing and exhausted child workers in their mills. The cities were filled with a huge, degraded proletariat, living and working in appalling conditions. But as time went on, groups of liberal reformers began to struggle for change (Charles Dickens was one). The remarkable thing is that from such small groups, a new consciousness spread. It is no longer necessary to argue, as those groups had to, that child labour and sweat-shops are humanly intolerable. We have acquired a new, shared standard of humanity, based on a capacity to venture out from our enclosed personal islands, and enter with imaginative sympathy into the life and work of others. There may still be a long way to go: both unions and employers still negotiate on the assumption that labour is a commodity to be bought and sold. But at a purely physical level at least, our whole feeling for what we owe to the dignity of human life has changed, and is still changing.

I think that a similar change – or perhaps the same change manifesting in a wider sphere – may be beginning to show itself in this new awareness of the environment. We now begin to see that each individualistic enterprise has its repercussions throughout the globe. Continued for much longer, such individualism could devastate the whole planet. We need a new, more 'oceanic' kind of awareness, spread out over the whole world and over the whole community of men, in order to develop a wiser relationship to the earth and its resources. Such an awakening out of the isolated Ego consciousness, a dissolving of the rocks of Egotism by the waters of imaginative understanding for our surroundings, is described by Steiner as the particular problem and task for the future development of the Consciousness Soul, in preparation for a more truly 'social' order.

To pursue this theme further, we may ask whether similar problems and changes are discernible in other spheres of human life. I think they are. The environmental crisis concerns, essentially, the bodily life of man and of the earth, and the health of both. But Steiner asks us to understand man also as a spiritual being who enters into a relationship with a physical body in order to experience the earth. As a spiritual being, he is a creative individuality, capable of bringing new things into the world. But in experiencing the world and his fellow human beings, he develops a soul life, a rich interchange of inner and outer experience. In more familiar language we could say that man has a creative intellectual life and also a social life. And here too, there are profound changes and an element of crisis.

In the spiritual, or intelectual life of man, there has developed what is now called the 'information explosion'. Just as industry generates a barely manageable tide of goods and services, so the human intellect has become, in a certain way, almost uncontrollably productive. Particularly in science, but also in other fields of knowledge and scholarship, great mountains of data are accumulating at increasing speed in books, journals and the memory stores of computers. Many laboratories are now really fact-factories, equipped with apparatus which allows unbelievable productivity in recording and accumulating new observations.

This situation is increasingly experienced by scientists themselves as a kind of environmental crisis within the spiritual life of man. There is a kind of pollution by undigested and unprocessed facts. It is not merely the difficulty of analysing any particular body of data. The industrialisation of research generates a competitiveness and haste which make it increasingly difficult to find the time and inner quietness to think what data should be gathered next or how they should be evaluated and understood.

The spiritual capacity which orders and relates such fragmented data, which enables them to grow into an ordered whole, is imagination. As water unites all physical parts of the body of the earth and brings dead substance to life (so to speak), so imagination gives life and meaning to dead data. Recently, many scientists have begun to see this, and there is a deep new interest in the human imagination as the faculty which can bring wholeness and healing into the fragmentation of knowledge.

The third 'environmental crisis' which I think is now confronting us is more difficult to describe, because it concerns the environment of the soul. And the soul life of man includes all his instincts, prejudices and passions. Yet I think it is significant that recognition of the environmental crisis and concern about the information explosion have developed along with profound social changes which we have come to call the 'permissive society'. Sexual behaviour – both normal and abnormal – has become a matter of public discussion, comment and display. These changes have been seized upon and commercially exploited with great energy by the entertainment and promotion industries. Sex has been made a kind of obsession.

A great obstacle which hinders a clear perception of the real issues is that sexual 'liberation' has been widely associated by progressive people with the battle for freedom. This idea goes back to Freud, who believed that as we grow up, the 'free expression' of our 'natural' being is inhibited and frustrated by external authorities and abstract rules. Society implants in man a 'Super-ego', a kind of spectral schoolmaster constantly wagging an admonitory finger at every urge of the Id.

This picture has appealed deeply to many people because it seems to describe an important experience in most people's lives, the time especially in adolescence and early adulthood when the idealism and vigour of youth meets rigid and uncomprehending attitudes and rules of an old society. As a result, creative spiritual capacities and ideals of freedom become linked with sexual capacity, sexual freedom and youth, while tyranny and prejudice become associated with sterility and age.

There is indeed a link between sexual vigour and creative idealism. But the great confusion of the Freudian tradition is its failure to see that where the fire of the individual human will becomes bound to the vigour of the living physical body (as in part, of course, it must), it becomes *instinct* and therefore un-free. Least of all are we free in our sexual instincts – their very power resides in their capacity to drive us to sexual behaviour. But Steiner sees the individual will as an expression of the spiritual being of man, born out of spiritual worlds, and finding its connection with that world on earth in striving for the great spiritual ideals of truth, beauty and goodness. These ideals do not impel us in the same way as the appetites of the body. The decision to seek them lies in ourselves, and it is a free decision.

This search, for the spiritual worlds which we almost forget when we are born into a physical body, has risen up in all kinds of images and pictures in different times of human history. But I think that today, behind the scenes of the permissive society, so to speak,one may discern a delicate process going on, which is part of this search, and which is expressed in the words 'communication', 'community' and, quite simply, 'love'.

A great many young people know, or soon discover, that sexual behaviour *on its own* contributes nothing to human relationships. One physical body simply uses another to assuage, temporarily, a biological appetite, thus emphasising rather than diminishing the separateness of the bodies involved, and of the human souls who live in them. But out of this recognition there is growing a more subtle interest in the intercourse not of bodies, but of souls.

In discussing these questions, one phrase crops up again and again: someone will say that in order to truly understand another person, you must 'open yourself to him' receive something of his being into yourself. And a further comment may be added to the effect that you soon discover that the biggest obstacle to achieving this lies within your own soul. It does not need much thought to see the truth of this. Social relationships are all too often polluted by a dragon of self-seeking or prejudice, which seeks to dominate, exploit or dazzle the other for its own satisfaction. There is no freedom for either party in such a relationship. But if the dragon can be stilled, and one soul opened to another, then the true spirit, the ideal being, of one person, may speak in the heart of another. This is what 'free love' should really mean. It is an ideal which is struggling to find expression in the social life of many people today. But it is easily obscured by a social environment polluted by so many appeals to instinct and appetite, and particularly to sexual appetite.

*   *   *

In the permissive society, the word 'virgin' has come to have a very limited, purely biological meaning. But I believe that uniting all the phenomena I have been describing is the beginning of a new discovery or striving for something which is virginal, in a much deeper sense, in the soul and in the world.

We could not be aware of an 'environmental crisis' unless we also had a sense for an unpolluted nature, an ideal which speaks through language particularly when we have to do with water. We still talk, for example, of a 'virgin spring', and we can easily feel that fresh, unpolluted water bubbling from such a source is a kind of physical embodiment of all that we feel to be the ideal of purity and self-sacrificing goodness.

It is perhaps less easy to see that the second crisis of which I spoke, the fragmentation of knowledge, also involves a search for a virginal quality, this time within the human mind. The modern scientist seldom opens his powers of cognition to nature; instead, he imposes certain forms of thought upon her, and imprisons her. It is of the essence of modern experiment to subject nature to measurement – and the information explosion is essentially an explosion of measurement.

The thoughts we embody in measurement are only applicable to dead phenomena – for measurement means dividing up into units which can be counted, and no living thing can be thus fragmented without dying. It is a form of thought entirely appropriate to the inanimate world, but quite inadequate for apprehending life. We do not ask often enough how we come to think dead thoughts of this kind. According to Rudolf Steiner, we can do this by drawing on an unconscious experience of the dead and dying parts of our own body – the mineralised bones and the nerves. The Consciousness Soul could only develop through taking hold of these death forces, and using them to acquire an intimate knowledge of all that is dead in nature. But it should not be surprising if a technology based on such knowledge brings death to living nature. Today a quite new step is needed. Human beings must learn to draw upon the living forces of their organisms, with the full strength of their Egos, and create a faculty for understanding the true life of nature. The beginnings of this faculty are already familiar in the life of imagination, that aspect of the inner life of man which so deeply interested the Romantic movement.

Today, scientists are already beginning to see imagination as the faculty which can heal and order the fragmentation of knowledge. But Steiner speaks of a further development, an imagination so purified of all that comes from the physical world, so permeated by the spiritual activity of the Ego, that a new faculty is born, an organ of spiritual perception for the formative forces in man and nature which Steiner called Imagination. This faculty must be the basis for a new ecological wisdom in the future.

Finally, in human social relationships, the sexual obsession needs to be metamorphosed into a perception of a drama which takes place in every meeting between two human beings. An individual may live in a male or a female physical body, and can never have more than a one-sided experience in a purely physical relationship. But in the social sphere, every person is both male and female, both giver and receiver. Within each soul is a knight, who rides out to adventure. But each soul is also a virgin, who can receive the individuality of another in true social understanding. And each soul is a battleground, where dragons would imprison the soul in prejudice and transform the knight into a self-centred entrepreneur.

Thus the environmental crisis, together with the other crises which I have mentioned, reflect back to man a moral question, a challenge to development in his own nature. When speaking of paths of meditation and spiritual development, Rudolf Steiner often stressed the need for three steps of moral development for every step in spiritual experience. In doing so, he is pointing to the need for the knightly sun-filled Ego forces of each individual to free his own soul nature from the grip of egotism and untruth, before a new spiritual child can be born in the soul. In more technical anthroposophical terms, it is the task of transforming the astral body so that the Spirit Self can be born.

I think that the twentieth century, for all its apparent darkness, violence and corruption, is bringing events and experiences which are gradually educating many human beings to a deeper and truer experience of this situation. It is as though many people were coming to stand, not necessarily in full consciousness, but in a kind of dream, before the picture which confronted St. John as he wrote the twelfth chapter of Revelation – a woman clothed with the sun, the moon beneath her feet, upon her head a crown of stars, and near her, the Archangel Michael battling with the great dragon who would destroy the child to whom she will give birth.

It is a picture which is renewed in Steiner's account of Michael's battle in the present age to help man find again in his own soul, but in full personal freedom, a deeper more living wisdom with which to transcend the dead knowledge which now threatens to destroy him. This wisdom will lead him once more to a living connection with the spiritual worlds out of which he has descended and into which he must now be re-born. Steiner has described how this wisdom can be experienced as a spiritual being, related to Sophia, the Goddess of Wisdom in whom the Greek philosophers felt all their knowledge to be harmoniously embodied.

Today this Being approaches man not from without, as the Greeks experienced her, but from within, when she is freed in the purified soul by the sun-filled powers of the individual Ego. There man, the Anthropos, will meet the Sophia as the bearer of a wisdom renewed and rejuvenated, personal yet universal. From this meeting, a heavenly wisdom can find a way again into the world through man. This is the picture behind the word 'anthroposophy' which Rudolf Steiner chose to describe his life's work. Anthroposophy exists to serve Anthropo-Sophia.

When they come to the moon, the astronauts find no new wisdom, no life, no future for man, but only a dead relic of the past. They look back and see the earth as a living whole, desperately in need of a wisdom which cannot be born out of exploration of the physical spaces of the planetary system, but only within human souls. They return and find crisis and disorder on every side. But the crises are working as an educative initiation force within human life which is gradually dissolving the veils which are still obscuring the Virgin Sophia.

1971

A. Dürer

Man and the Underworld

Quite large numbers of people in the West now have the sense that we are living in a 'new age', an age in which some form of spiritual awakening is taking place. In the U.S.A., there is even a 'New Age Journal'.

At the beginning of this century, Rudolf Steiner also spoke frequently of the end of a dark age, the Kali Yuga, and the twentieth century as the beginning of a new age which can receive strong new spiritual impulses.

Some of the most powerful new impulses in this century have come from science. Physics, in particular, has penetrated into quite new realms. What kind of journey is here being undertaken? This is the question I want to explore in this essay.

In 1975, a young Vienna-born physicist, Fritjof Capra, now working in California, published a book which became a best-seller,[1] in which he describes the journey of physics as essentially a spiritual journey. And he argues that it is now penetrating into the *same* realities as were known and described in many ancient mystical traditions. His conviction springs not only from the study of these traditions, but from a personal experience which he describes in a Preface. He had previously experimented with peyote, and become interested in meditation. Then one day he had a spontaneous vision:

'I was sitting by the ocean one late summer afternoon', he writes, 'watching the waves rolling in and feeling the rhythm of my breathing, when I suddenly became aware of my whole environment as being engaged in a gigantic cosmic dance . . .'. He had been steeped for some years in the ideas of modern physics: 'As I sat on that beach, my former experiences came to life; I "saw" the atoms of the elements and those of my body participating in this cosmic dance of energy; I felt its rhythm and I "heard" its sound, and at that moment I *knew* that this was the Dance of Shiva, the Lord of Dancers worshipped by the Hindus.'

He goes on to describe and discuss the thought-world of twentieth century physics, and its resemblance to the worlds described in several ancient spiritual traditions. His fundamental assumption is that both paths, the mystical and the scientific, are leading to the same spiritual realms. It is a thesis which has enormous appeal to seekers of the 'new age'.

But there is a problem which Capra does not face: As thought, as 'pure' science, as theory, modern physics may reach into realms of great mathematical beauty, harmony and elegance. But as technology, as applied science, these thought forms are releasing into our lives new forces which we experience not as light but as darkness: Our 'new age' is having to face the possibility of its own extinction when it has barely begun, through its inability to manage the forces it has released. We cannot ignore this experience. The birth of new light is evidently being accompanied by the emergence of new darkness. This was clearly foreseen by Rudolf Steiner, but is rarely to be found at all clearly in the many current 'new age' voices.

So I want to look more carefully at the paths of science and technology in recent times, and then consider how they can be illuminated with the help of Steiner's work.

*   *   *

Our current assumptions about the world, which in the West are fundamentally materialist, have been shaped by the experience of the first phase of science, from the fifteenth to the nineteenth century, during which 'classical' physics developed. This was the physics of matter, of solid inanimate bodies moving in a fixed three-dimensional space and a uniform flow of time, which has given us such enormous confidence and skill in manipulation of the physical world, in the making of physical structures and machines.

This purely physical world was conceived as activated, as brought into movement, by energy, work, force, heat. We less often realise that these concepts were all clearly abstracted from our own experience of physical activity, of the work of moving and manipulating physical things. Because this is so, the world of classical physics is one in which we can feel at home, secure and confident. I shall return to this phase of physics later. But towards the end of the nineteenth century, a 'new age' began to dawn for science.

The doors into new worlds were really opened by electricity. An electric shock is like meeting a mysterious foreign will which tries to seize our muscles and limbs, and shakes and contorts our bodies to make inhuman movements. It is not a force with which we feel 'at home'. It has an occult quality, emerging from hidden depths of nature, full of tension and buried violence.

Very rapidly, it prompted both new technologies and new forms of theory. In technology, it made alliances with other curious and uncomfortable phenomena – with magnetism, and with the vacuum. Electric motors and dynamos, which are the basis of the exploitation of electricity for power, derived from Faraday's discoveries of the links between electricity and magnetism. Electric light became practical just a hundred years ago, when Edison arranged a delicate carbon filament in an evacuated glass bulb. The play of electricity in vacuum tubes led on to the discovery of radio waves and X-rays, and eventually into the realm of atomic physics.

The twentieth century has seen an extraordinary journey into the interior of matter. With the discovery of radioactivity in 1898, the secure world of classical physics, already made uneasy by electromagnetism, began to dissolve and change, both in its concepts and in the phenomena with which it began to work.

Electricity can still be directly experienced as a force, even if it cannot be adequately understood with concepts taken from familiar experience. (Words like 'potential', 'tension', 'current' and 'field' already point to a world of mobile active forces, very different from the world of classical physics with its solid objects moving in a secure three-dimensional space). But the radiations of the atomic world are more hidden. As with Edison's light bulb, they emerged into direct physical appearances as a new light – but a light of terrifying intensity and power that spread across the desert of New Mexico in July 1945 when the first experimental atomic weapon was detonated. For those present, the light indeed signified the dawn of a 'new age', the birth of a death-bringing light. One of the most remarkable stories of this moment is the experience of Robert Oppenheimer, the scientific director of the project.[2] He was in a bunker observing the fireball spread across the desert. A phrase from the Bhagavad Gita came into his mind: 'I am become Death, the shatterer of worlds . . . '. I shall return to this story later.

A direct and tragic experience of the death-bringing qualities of nuclear radiations had occurred earlier in the development programme. Louis Slotin, one of the physicists at work in Los Alamos, made a mistake with two hemispheres of uranium. A brilliant blue light shone out before he tore them apart. He felt nothing, but died of 'radiation sickness' in great agony nine days later. The new age of physics has led us into an encounter with forces which we cannot perceive directly, but which can work into the life processes of our bodies like a kind of poison.

These events have been accompanied by profound changes in scientific theory, and in the idea of science itself. The first pictures of the hidden atomic world were modelled from classical physics: particles in orbit round a nucleus, like planets round a sun. But in the first part of the century, Einstein began to conceive matter as a manifestation of energy, its solidity transmuted into force. And the 'models' of atomic structure, and more recently of the structure of 'fundamental particles' themselves, have gradually ceased to bear any resemblance to phenomena of the familiar physical world. Capra describes some of these concepts in his book. We are led into a world of elaborately interwoven patterns and fields of energies.

But equally far-reaching is the realisation that the relation of the scientist to his work can no longer be conceived as it was. The classical physicist believed himself to be a 'detached observer', an 'onlooker' at events taking place quite independently of his own thoughts, feelings and intentions. His aim was 'objectivity' and he produced a science of 'objects', of bodies moving independently in otherwise empty space. Then the 1920s brought what is often called the 'revolution in physics'. This was much more than a matter of making some new discoveries or propounding some new theories. One of the most significant aspects of this revolution is the 'indeterminacy principle' propounded by Werner Heisenberg (and independently, and in a slightly different form, by Erwin Schroedinger). I will only paraphrase it, rather loosely, here: It can be seen as a consequence of a science which was no longer an 'onlooker' at perceptible phenomena, but which was learning to manipulate 'occult' forces and energies. So physical science was becoming dominated by experiment, using increasingly elaborate machines and instruments; and the *theories* of science were becoming mathematical tools which allow the machines to be built and the experiments to be performed. The detached observer was being replaced by the manipulator of hidden forces. The results are a consequence of these manipulations.

Thus the sub-atomic world cannot be described separately from the experiments through which it becomes manifest, nor from the theories which shape the experiments. In the 1920s, some experiments were suggesting that the world within matter should be imagined as wave-like; others were suggesting it should be pictured as corpuscular. Heisenberg made it clear that we must cease to ask what this world is like *independent of how we imagine it*, since we can only know the experimental consequences of how we conceive it. The famous dichotomy between mind and matter, observer and observed, subject and object, propounded philosophically by Descartes in 1637, and forming the habitual basis for scientific thought ever since, was thrown into question. In some way, the physicist is no longer a detached observer, but a *participant* in the unfolding drama of sub-atomic physics.

*　　*　　*

It is an extraordinary journey, which is still far from concluded. What is its appeal for the spiritual new age movements? What resemblances does Capra find between the new physics and ancient spiritual traditions? Principally the fact that solid matter has been replaced by interweaving patterns of energies, and that the human being is no longer a detached observer, but *participates* in these patterns. Yet the comparisons remain rather superficial. As a conceptual world, pure physics may seem to be describing harmonies and patterns similar to those of certain forms of spiritual experience, But as phenomena, the forces released by the new physics are cold and terrifying. In no way do they speak to us of the spiritual home from which we have come, and into which we shall pass at death.

To explore further, we must look more deeply into the inner experiences out of which science has emerged. As a basis for this exploration, I want to include here several passages from the very last letter written by Rudolf Steiner to the members of the Anthroposophical Society, which was published after his death, and bears directly on our theme.[3]

The first part of the letter indicates how the soul lives as will unconsciously connected with the forces at work in the physical body: *'Man connects himself with certain earthly forces, in that he gives his body its right orientation within them. He learns to stand and walk upright; he learns to place himself with arms and hands into the equilibrium of earthly forces.*

Now these are not forces working inward from the Cosmos. They are forces of a purely earthly nature.

In reality, nothing that man experiences is an abstraction. He only fails to perceive whence it is that an experience comes to him; and thus he turns ideas about realities into abstractions. He speaks of the laws of mechanics. He thinks he has abstracted them from the connections and relationships of nature. But this is not the case. All that man experiences in his soul by way of purely mechanical laws, has been discovered inwardly through his relationship of orientation to the earthly world (in standing, walking etc.) . . . By far the greater part of that which works in modern civilisation through technical science and industry – wherein the life of man is so intensely woven – is not nature at all, but sub-nature. It is a world which emancipates itself from nature – emancipates itself in a downward direction . . . Man needed this relation to the purely earthly for the unfolding of his Spiritual Soul. Thus in the most recent times there has arisen a strong tendency to realise in all things, and even in the life of action, this element into which man must enter for his evolution. Entering the purely earthly element, he encounters the Ahrimanic realm. With his own being he must now acquire a right relation to the Ahrimanic.

But in the age of technical science, the possibility of finding a true relationship to the Ahrimanic civilisation has escaped man. He must find the strength, the inner force of knowledge, in order not to be overcome by Ahriman in this technical civilisation. He must understand sub-nature for what it really is. This he can only do if he rises, in spiritual knowledge, at least as far into extra-earthly super-nature as he has descended, in technical sciences, into sub-nature. The age requires a knowledge transcending nature, because in its inner life it must come to grips with a life-content which has sunk far beneath nature – a life content whose influence is perilous . . . There are very few as yet who even feel the greatness of the spiritual tasks approaching man in this direction. Electricity, for instance, celebrated since its discovery as the very soul of nature's existence, must be recognised in its true character – in its peculiar power of leading down from nature to sub-nature. Only man himself must beware lest he slide downwards with it . . .'

I have quoted this letter at length, because it raises several questions we must pursue further: That we meet the purely earthly realm inwardly when we learn to walk; that electricity leads into 'sub-nature'; and that to deal rightly with sub-nature, we must achieve an equivalent knowledge of 'super-nature'.

In the first paragraphs of the letter, Steiner also refers to the 'laws and processes of nature as they work in colour, sound etc.'. These laws, he says, have a cosmic, not a terrestrial origin. The mechanical laws alone are purely terrestrial. These remarks, which are extremely condensed and aphoristic, point back to the origins of classical physics, and particularly to Galileo. He distinguished the 'secondary qualities' perceived by our senses – colour, warmth, sound, taste, smell – from the 'primary' qualities of mass, motion, position, etc. which can be subjected to calculation. Only these, Galileo believed, can be regarded as real properties of 'external bodies'. He thus eliminated a good deal of ordinary human experience from the purview of science. Yet he does not seem to have realised that the primary qualities also derive from sense experiences, notably from those senses that bring us awareness of our own bodies: Touch, movement, balance, and the generalised somatic awareness which makes up the 'body schema'. These senses enable us to know directly the position and movement of our physical organism in three dimensional space. Without these senses, we could not learn to stand and walk, nor develop a science of bodies.

We are also now much more aware than was Galileo that we 'know' a good deal of classical physics intuitively, long before we can grasp it abstractly. We learn it empirically in early childhood. Two boys on a see-saw are exploiting laws of leverage long before they can understand how to calculate how far from the fulcrum the fat boy should be positioned in order to balance the thin one. As we learn to walk, run, tie shoe-laces, climb trees, manipulate sand and water and dough, we are acquiring an intimate practical experience of the purely physical world.

Such an experience, of course, has been part of human life for thousands of years. We can well understand that in standing upright, as Steiner says, we begin to meet the realm of mechanical forces. But why was physics not born in conceptual form much earlier? The mathematics used by Galileo would have been perfectly comprehensible to the Greeks. So why did they not anticipate him? It is clear that one major obstacle was how to think about moving bodies. The movements of the planets or of falling stones were discussed in terms of our own experience of movement. We move because we will it, or desire to reach some goal. So it seemed that all moving bodies in nature must be moved by beings, or by their own desires. Not until Galileo was the idea conceived of an inanimate body in motion without an immediate mover.

This points clearly to a changed awareness of the body by the soul. The formulation of abstract laws of motion depends on a capacity for a detached relationship to the experience of movement in one's own body, so that the body itself can begin to be conceived as a *thing*. Contemporary with Galileo came the first systematic dissections of the body in medical schools in Padua. Long before this, armies had surgeons – usually conscripted butchers – who had a detailed practical grasp of human anatomy. But a detached scientific study of the corpse (although anticipated by Leonardo da Vinci) was an achievement of the sixteenth century.

Steiner described these developments as manifestations of a new quality of consciousness – the Consciousness or Spiritual Soul. It awoke when the human soul met inwardly for the first time, as a deep but almost unconscious experience, that aspect of the body which is truly inanimate – the skeleton, constructed as it is from hard, crystalline and mineral substance. In Greek times, the soul had drawn from experiences of the life (or etheric) body. Greek philosophy participates, so to speak, in this life. Abstract science is born only when the soul can draw into consciousness its inner encounter with that realm of nature which is 'abstracted' from life, the mineral realm where 'detachment' is at home. (A living plant cannot be detached from its soil; a stone is indifferent).

This is soon reflected in philosophy. With Descartes, the first truly abstract thought begins. Mind is explicitly detached from matter. This opens the way to seeing the body as a mechanism. The Renaissance was much preoccupied with imaginations of death and the skeleton, and of automata.

We cannot prove that the birth of mechanistic science awoke, historically, through a deeper incarnation of the soul, an inner encounter with the skeleton. But once we recognise that we have direct sense perceptions of our bodies as objects – as masses moving in space – we can begin to realise that the beginnings of modern science must have depended on a new capacity to draw into consciousness the experiences of the senses concerned. It is then not surprising that classical physics should be essentially a science of bodies – inanimate bodies moving in impersonal space. From such a physics, the idea of a universe consisting of 'fundamental particles' emerges inevitably.

The period from the 15th-19th centuries is the time of our deepest inner entanglement in the purely physical realm, especially as regards developing forms of thought. But during the 19th century, a mysterious, though mainly unconscious, process begins, which Steiner calls 'crossing the Threshold'. It is essentially the same Threshold we cross at death – and the symptoms include the beginnings of a loose connection of the soul with the body. We can see many cultural symptoms of this. In art, the world of solid realism is quite rapidly replaced by attempts to paint forces rather than things: Turner, a master of realism at the start of his career, gradually dissolved his landscapes into pure colour. Soon the Impressionists began to try to paint the pure laws behind the surfaces of the world; the Expressionists delve within, bringing to the surface buried and dynamic levels of inner life into which psychoanalysis is also trying to explore.

This is also the time, as has already been described, when the solid materialism of science begins to dissolve into a world of hidden forces and activities, when even space and time begin to lose their fixed and stable character. Here, too, we must ask whether we are looking at straightforward intellectual and experimental discovery, or at expressions of deeper changes in consciousness, as Steiner maintains.

All around us, in the twentieth century, we can also see manifestations of a search for a world of more living qualities, for that faculty of Imagination which will reveal the living formative elemental realm of the etheric or life forces, the realm of 'super-nature'. This realm, as Steiner describes it, is one of constant change and activity. It is also a realm in which there is no separateness, no possibility of detachment. All is interconnected. There is a reflection of this world in our dreams, where we do not usually feel detached, but are swept along by the tide of images and feelings. The current interest in dreams, mythology, in the experiences of schizophrenia and in older cosmologies, reveals a dawning awareness of a region which is now nearer to the surface of consciousness than it was in the nineteenth century. Some sense of this realm lives, widespread but just below the surface, in the language and interests of many 'new age' movements.

But we can also recognise how, as the soul is a little freed into the world of life forces lying 'above' the physical, where it is a participant, not an onlooker, it can also reach down, below the physical, into a realm which, in Rudolf Steiner's words, 'emancipates itself in a downward direction'. Steiner did not refer explicitly to this realm very often. But in a reply to questions after his lecture on *The Etherisation of the Blood* *, he does describe a realm of 'fallen' ethers, and refers to electricity as 'fallen light ether'.

We should thus expect the world into which nuclear physics is penetrating to have certain features in common with the 'unfallen' etheric world – notably 'constant activity' and 'interconnectedness'. We should also expect to be related to it not as onlookers but as participants, as Heisenberg showed. The 'resemblances' discovered by Capra to forms of spiritual experience become comprehensible, but acquire a different and more problematic aspect. It may be that Capra has had authentic glimpses of the realm of 'super-nature' — a 'dance' of constant harmonious activity. But the interpretation of such experience as another aspect of sub-atomic physics could prove dangerously misleading. A good deal will come to depend on whether we identify nuclear forces with super-nature, or see them as belonging to a world which is a sub-earthly reflection of the world of cosmic life, a realm in which the forces at work have qualities of anti-life.

We must then ask what determines the nature and degree of our participation in sub-nature. If classical physics is a consequence of a new inner power to bring up into consciousness deep inner experiences of mechanical forces at work in the physical world, so the birth of the new physics must point to a capacity to bring to consciousness experiences which lie *below* the Threshold.

In a curious way, science itself has begun to become aware of this, in its descriptions of its own methods. Classical physics is abstracted from familiar experience. But electricity made it necessary to picture forces for which we have no sense organs. Such pictures can be shaped into tools with which we operate in hidden realms of nature. But where do the pictures come from? During the nineteenth century, scientists began to put increasing emphasis on the role of 'hypothesis'. In this century, the most generally accepted formal description of the scientific method starts not with observation, but with what is essentially an act of imagination, the formulation of a hypothesis which is to be tested by experiment.

It is well known that crucial hypotheses often appear unbidden in the mind, emerging from the unconscious like genies out of a bottle. Once out, they can't be put back again. But this means that science can no longer be described as a purely 'rational' activity. It depends on the 'unconscious' – a realm which a writer on psychoanalysis once called *The Savage and Beautiful Country.*[5]

It is, on the face of it, very curious that we can imagine things which turn out to have some direct relation to hidden realities of nature (or sub-nature). Yet it is not so odd if we follow what is really implied by some of the ideas of psychoanalysis, namely that in our unconscious we participate both in a personal and in a more universal realm of nature forces. If we begin to take this seriously, the implications for science are considerable. Since Descartes conceived the detached observer, a scientist's personal life has seemed to have little relevance to his science. If you imagine yourself outside the universe looking in, what is at work in your personal soul will seem quite irrelevant to what is going on in the world you are observing. To undergo a scientific discipline, it is in no way necessary to follow a moral discipline.

This is not to say that science does not include a certain code of conduct: It is generally agreed that you must not fake results or steal those of others; you must publish truthful accounts of your work, and be prepared to be proved wrong with a good grace. But as long as these commandments are observed at work, your moral life in other spheres is regarded as irrelevant.

It was not so with the spiritual disciplines which preceded those of science. Pathanjali, in his *Aphorisms of Yoga*, is emphatic that pupils must *begin* with Yama – the overcoming of violence, theft, covetousness, lying, incontinence. This is equivalent to Steiner's equally emphatic advice that any step in spiritual awareness should be accompanied by three steps of moral progress. In the past, a spiritual path was often supported by the discipline of a religious order. Much of Steiner's work in this field consists of advice for an equivalent ordering of personal life which the individual will need to attempt for himself. What is the reason for all this?

Quite simply, it is because, as we cross the Threshold, the distinction between personal soul realities and world realities ceases to be clear-cut. We become participants, not onlookers, and what we are as human beings becomes part of what we behold. This is already obvious in dreams: Intimations of archetypal realities are entangled with dramas generated by our own 'hang-ups' and even by indigestion from last night's supper.

As long as science was working with the purely physical, and concepts were reflections of this realm of detached reality, the scientist's soul could function as a mirror, cool, clear, immobile. But the need to grapple with more 'occult' forces summons an activity of fantasy from below the mirror. Here we have to look more deeply at certain rooted but hardly conscious habits of mind.

If there is one habit universally cultivated in science, it is *reductionism*. An automatic response to any puzzling phenomenon is to take it apart and seek simpler elements. To the living world, this brings death. Nuclear physics, with its expectations of fundamental particles and its atom-smashing machines, entails an intensive practice of the reductionist habit. Habits have their basis not in the physical but in the etheric body. Here we are also participants in a wider 'unconscious' world. Every deeper habit of soul brings a relationship to the beings and forces of this world.

There is a dramatic pointer to this in the story told of Robert Oppenheimer which I mentioned above. The phrase "I am become Death" is not the language of the detached observer, but of participation. We might imagine this phrase expanded: "In my thinking, I have practiced imagining the sub-physical world in terms of disintegration and death. I have *become* death in unconscious realms of my soul, whence I draw my hypotheses. Can I wonder that I have thereby offered beings, whose activities and nature are to bring death and destruction, an invitation to embody themselves, with the help of my imagination, into the experiments and devices which give them entry into the physical world?"

Does this seem far fetched? Only as long as we persist with the myth of the detached observer, and the conviction that the inner life of human beings exists quite apart from the life of the universe. Steiner once attributed to science a certain laziness of soul. We allow ourselves to dream our way into the world 'behind' nature. So we hand over to a play of fantasy thrown up from parts of ourselves where we are not properly conscious (and can therefore not be properly responsible). Here, where we are still very much unredeemed beings, we can be open to promptings of Ahrimanic beings in whose world, at these levels, we also participate.

Perhaps this can go some way towards understanding the questions raised by Capra's book, and to offer a different way of seeing the 'resemblances' between the new physics and the spiritual interests of the 'new age' movements. When Steiner wrote of the great tasks unfolding for us in these developments, he emphasised that we would not be able to cope adequately with sub-nature unless we could also ascend in awareness to discover the realities of 'super-nature' – to begin with, the world where the upbuilding, life or 'etheric' forces are at home.

To explore the way into this realm for science would need another essay. I must confine myself to a few general remarks. The issue centres on the development and use of our own faculties, notably the faculty of imagination. If the habit of reductionism leads us into sub-nature, how are we to school our imaginations towards 'super-nature'?

As we have seen, the way we experience nature is at present dominated by thought-forms which are themselves shaped by our perceptions of our own physical bodies as physical objects in space, mediated by the senses of touch, balance, movement etc. So when we look at the surrounding world, we see separate objects in space – trees, rocks, animals. We feel ourselves to be looking *at* the world, and thinking *about* the 'objects' it contains.

It is not too difficult to notice that these concepts are simply not appropriate for a lot of what we see in nature. The whole plant kingdom cannot be adequately understood as a collection of objects, for much of it appears and disappears with the seasons. This kingdom of nature invites us, not to look *at* it and think *about* it, but to think *with it* (and perhaps also *feel* with it: the colours and scents of a rose are as much revelations of its nature as its form and growth). The plant world asks for a schooling of the imagination not towards 'objectivity' (the grasping of objects), but towards participatory movement (thinking with *processes*). In an elementary way, we can all quite easily follow the development of a plant *in time*, and make one of Goethe's first discoveries, the rhythms of expansion and contraction that run as organic law through plant growth.

We can also notice that these processes are linked with processes in the *whole surroundings* – the changing seasons, the rhythms of light and dark, warmth and cold. Here we can take seriously the use of those senses which reveal what Galileo categorised as secondary qualities having no real existence. Possibilities of conscious participation in nature are immediately at hand, without demanding special states of awareness, or a plunge into our personal subconscious. If we attend in the right way, we can see all around us in the manifestations of life, a realm whose reality is to be found in constant activity, in wisely organised harmonious rhythm, in interconnectedness. Nature herself offers us the schooling for those faculties which are available, still mainly undisciplined, as fantasy and imagination, but which are the germs of new, entirely 'scientific' (i.e. knowledge-bringing) faculties for the future.

To attend properly to nature in growth and movement, we have to learn to keep our attentiveness clear of all the images, associations, random thoughts and feelings, which bubble up inwardly out of memory and less conscious personal realms. Anyone who tries to practice a clear and open living with the processes of nature will find himself often thrown back into an inner struggle with prejudice, wishful thinking, a disordered feeling and will. Once any regular attempt is made to think *with* nature, the need for an inner 'Yama' to accompany this 'Yoga' becomes immediately clear.

But if we can in effect continue what was the original way of science, and ask nature to be our teacher, we shall begin to realise that we are being invited to follow a path which leads in the opposite direction from reductionism. Any vivid and clear following of the emergence of leaves and flowers in spring and summer can only bring a sense of mystery, of an invisible realm with which we live inwardly, though not yet fully awake, as we follow what is happening. It becomes obvious that we shall not understand the plants by looking into their constituents as objects. They are born out of an invisible reality in which the whole plant world, the life of the whole planet, exists as a living dynamic unity. We can begin to realise that this world of life is itself an invitation to seek further, not for fundamental particles, but for fundamental *Beings* whose living activities we are beginning to recognise.

Such a relationship to nature we actually practice, more or less instinctively, when we meet other *human* beings. If we enter a room in which someone has lived, we look at the arrangement of the objects in it as a consequence of how a person *lives*. We want to meet the living being. We experience another person at first as a living moving picture, dressed in certain colours, with certain features, moving around in a characteristic way. So we want to go further and meet a deeper expression of the being: We want to open a conversation. So we embark on a path of knowledge which calls on new faculties in ourselves at each step: We look *at* the objects in the room; we 'think with' the living appearance, and 'listen into' the living language.

The few centuries in which science has practiced a 'detached' relationship to nature have suppressed any expectation that our journey of knowledge could lead towards meeting a being or beings. Nature has no face for us, no expression of any inner reality other than the impersonal entities and forces imagined along the reductionist road. But thinking *with* nature, with the rhythms of growth and the seasons, brings a different experience. It is a first step towards 'super-nature'. We can begin to look at physical nature as the completed work of a creative spiritual world, and to seek for a realm above the physical, a world of constant living activity, which we can know as the working of spiritual beings in harmony with the spiritual worlds out of which we ourselves are born.

Thinking *with* nature demands a definite effort, a summoning of more vigorous inner life. In contrast, the way into sub-nature has a curious passivity. First, a looking *at* the world, then withdrawing into mere reflection. Soon, in a kind of dream, 'hypotheses' may surface from unconscious depths. Without an inner activity to awaken a free and directed attentiveness, guided by the real phenomena of nature, we cannot expect to distinguish clearly the world of super-nature from its sub-earthly reflections.

It is evident that there is today a dawning awareness of realms of reality beyond the purely physical, especially among 'new age' spiritual movements, but they are still approached in a kind of dream. It is in the need for an awakening that we can begin to hear the voice of great Being: Rudolf Steiner spoke often of the urgent need to hear this Being if we are to grasp the essential tasks of the new age. We need to hear the voice of Michael, who since the last part of the nineteenth century has become the guiding spirit of the times. He took office, according to Rudolf Steiner, in the very year that Edison's new but sub-earthly lights began to shine. Michael is the Archangel of the sun. His light can only shine into the soul that makes its own free effort to awaken to the world, to think *with* the world. Such an awakening reveals nature as the veil of a mystery, and the earth as the temple where we can tread a free path of knowledge.

Michael has traditionally been pictured with the dragon beneath his feet. There is today little sense of triumph and excitement about the advances of science and technology, and a growing unease and even fear at the forces we are releasing into our midst. A particular dread surrounds the forces of nuclear energy, which speak much more immediately of the world of the dragon than of a world of heavenly harmony. But it is part of the new age, of the crossing of the Threshold, that we must also begin to look into sub-nature. The great question is whether we can adequately understand what we see, and find the strength to meet it. This insight, and this strength cannot be found within sub-nature itself. But they are offered by Michael, who is also the Archangel of courage, if we will wake up to see the living questions put by nature herself, and seek the living answers in the living thoughts these questions awaken in our souls.

1980

[1] *The Tao of Physics* by Fritjof Capra (Fontana).

[2] Described by Robert Jungk in *Brighter than a Thousand Suns* (Gollancz).

[3] *Anthroposophical Leading Thoughts*. Letter of 12 April 1925. (Rudolph Steiner Press).

[4] Basel October 1st 1911.

[5] See the book thus entitled by Alan McGlashan (Chatto and Windus).

True and False Flames
Reflections on the Energy Crisis

The 'energy problem' is treated in most discussions on two levels – physical and political. The physical questions include the depletion of fossil fuel reserves, the development of 'renewable' energy resources (sun, wind, water, wood), the hazards and potentials of nuclear energy. The political questions focus on the tensions of supply and demand, notably the relations between the main oil suppliers in the Middle East and the main consumers in the industrialised West.

The political issues show very clearly that we are dealing not only with 'extensive' energies bound up with physical resources, but also with 'intensive' energies of a different kind, which exist within human beings. Two such energies are recognised, explicitly or by implication, in the debate: Egotism and fear.

The fundamental focus of modern politics, both Marxist and non-Marxist, is on material consumption: Human nature 'demands' goods and services; the first responsibility of political management is therefore to meet these demands as far as possible. The problem is not the absolute supply of physical energy for survival, but the fact that we have made a way of life based on economic growth, and fears that any major frustration of economic demands, and still more, any substantial reduction in material consumption, would release unmanageable social and political unrest. Internationally, we find the same convictions writ large: In the last resort, will nations fight for the earth's dwindling oil reserves?

The nuclear debate is permeated with the same egotisms and fears: The drive for nuclear weapons is energised by nationalism, the need to ensure self defence, to deter enemies and to exert power. The need for nuclear power is debated in terms of the demand for energy, its disadvantages in terms of fear of nuclear accidents, pollution, terrorist raids, the spread of nuclear weapons, and the conviction that society is not careful or responsible enough to look after nuclear wastes for long periods of time.

A very little reflection on these facts shows that these inner 'energies' are far more potent and fundamental than the physical energies with which they are at present concerned. This is not to say that our need for physical energies is not real: Culture grows out of the mastery of fire, and our culture expresses this on a very large scale. But the problems of distribution and management of the earth's resources would be relatively easy to cope with were it not for the enormous and problematic inner energies at work in human beings and human society. The energy crisis is thus as much an inner as an outer question.

So much might be generally agreed. Yet the energy question has developed in a culture whose habitual framework of thought is materialist. So the forces at work in souls are regarded as epiphenomena of physical and biological processes. They express 'laws' of human nature, which cannot be changed.

The energy process with which we are most familiar is combustion. Kindle a piece of wood: It burns to ash, giving off light and heat. The energy stored as potential in the wood is dispersed and cannot be reassembled. From this develops the scientific picture of the whole universe as a kind of combustion process, which will eventually disperse as cold dust and vapour – the 'heat death' of the universe. One notion is that the universe oscillates, contracting the dust into a minute point of almost infinite energy, which then explodes as a Big Bang to inaugurate a new cycle.

It has been widely remarked that living things appear to defy this universal combustion process. They build matter into complex arrangements rather than breaking it down. But the usual response is that the building up is achieved only locally, at the expense of the universe as a whole. The living world draws its energy from the sun, which is regarded as an immense combustion process due eventually to burn itself out.

How are the energies of human beings, and indeed of life in general, regarded in this context? Here we meet a curious situation. All living things feed. Nutrition is seen as a kind of combustion: Living things must be constantly stoked with food, or the flame goes out. But what about desires, and 'demand'? Animals and human beings not only eat food, they demand food – they have appetites. These are the psychic equivalent of the up-building life processes. We do not simply burn out; we take active steps to acquire more fuel.

We are here at the edge of one of those open secrets which science at present has no means to unlock. The energy processes of the universe are seen as a kind of dying; so there is no clear view of the inward counterpart of the energy question, where 'energy' becomes *intensive*, as life, as desire, as will.

In a curious way, we can see a picture of this secret in the simplest and most familiar combustion phenomenon, a candle flame. Understood as physics, the flame is a by-product of a chemical process of oxygenation of wax vapour, giving carbon dioxide and water. The energy released excites the vapours so that they give off light and heat. When all the wax is burned, its energy is dispersed, the flame goes out.

As a picture, though, the flame speaks to us of other qualities: It seems to have a kind of life. As it consumes fuel, it may grow, spread, move and 'reproduce' (kindle new flames). It is highly sensitive to its surroundings and we easily describe its behaviour with figures of speech: A flame 'springs to life', 'dies down', 'licks hungrily' at a piece of wood, grows to a 'raging inferno', is 'frustrated' when it reaches a river. Flames are like beings of light and warmth which manifest when we create an appropriate physical situation, and then vanish again. But while our idea of energy is purely extensive, we do not ask 'where does a flame go when it goes out?'. And when the inner flame of life, consciousness or being, goes out, we regard it as extinguished.

Yet light and warmth are qualities which, in our language and our feelings, live in two worlds which we do not know how to relate. Extensive light makes visible the extensive world, and needs expenditure of energy. Intensive light – the light which dawns when we find the answer to a riddle, which lives in an illuminating remark – is not a reality for science. Nor is the intensive warmth of a warm welcome, a heartfelt greeting, a heated argument. These are figures of speech for a science which can grasp dying but not living. So there has developed a profound understanding and control of extensive energy, its expenditure and conservation. But we have no notion of energy 'inpenditure', of working with intensive energies which renew, create, build up.

The same open secret is shown by the sun. We assume that its heat and light are only extensive, and that this is what is used, somewhat mysteriously, by the plants in the up-building process of photosynthesis. We are told that although the plant world stores each year vast amounts of solar energy as complex combustible substances, the sun itself has died a little more: The solar energy irrevocably expended very much exceeds that accumulated. So the plants simply conserve the sun's expended energy for a while, as a reservoir holds up the flow of a river as it rushes to its death in the sea. This energy is then released, slowly in decay, rapidly in combustion. Our culture is simply living on subterranean energy reservoirs, created by living nature accumulating solar energy in the past. These reservoirs we can expend more or less rapidly. The appeal of using solar energy direct is that the sun can be expected to go on burning for a very long time. 'Renewable' resources simply mean 'renewed by the sun'. The sun itself, though, is not conceived as renewable but, like all stars, as dying.

Rudolf Steiner spoke often of warmth and light as phenomena which live at the threshold between the extensive dying world explored by science , and the intensive up-building world to which we are related through inner experience. Yet our science has persuaded itself that inner experience is subjective, an illusionary by-product of extensive energy processes. Similarly, it has no place for the thought that the planets themselves may respond not only to the sun's extensive light, but also to an intensive creative light which builds rather than breaks down; that intensive energies could be at work on a further level in the desires of animals (and the 'demands' of human beings), and on yet another level in the creative 'fires' of individuals.

Yet if such energies exist, they belong in the discussion of the energy question, particularly in its social aspects. What are the energies of egotism and fear? They potentiate each other, and their consequence in the extensive world is to accelerate energy expenditure and consumption, and the exhaustion of the earth's resources.

*   *   *

In creating a picture of a dying world, science has also made an impersonal world. In pre-scientific times, the ultimate realities of the universe were always regarded as Beings. Now they are pictured as fundamental particles and forces, subject to impersonal laws. In pre-scientific times, the first question to be asked about any energies or laws was: Of what Being are they an expression? *Whose* energies? *Whose* laws? Today, physics and chemistry are completely impersonal, biology almost so. There is a lingering sense of the presence of Being in the animal kingdom (we have some reluctance to cause suffering). Our sense of the Being in human beings is increasingly precarious.

Yet in the language of politics and economics, some sense of Being survives in the notion of 'demand'. This energy is not extensive, but intensive, an inner flame licking hungrily and insatiably at goods and services. Unlike extensive flame, it may grow fiercer if deprived of fuel. But if we now ask '*whose* flame?', we are told: 'The animal in man, intent on its own survival.' It is thus of some importance to know the nature of these energies. Are they the essential energies of the human soul? For Freud, they were. The Id embodies the essential energies of biological man. The biology is a matter of hormones, and the hormones are a matter of chemistry.

It would change the debate profoundly if we were to seek the primary origins of intensive energies, not in the physical world, but in the activities of Beings. At the end of his life, Rudolf Steiner described briefly four levels of awareness through which human consciousness has passed during evolution.[1] At first, long ago (although still surviving as tradition and in some tribal cultures as what we call 'animalism'), there was a direct, intuitive apprehension of Beings of the Hierarchies and their servants in the Elemental worlds. Then, like leaving home, human beings still heard the manifestations of Spiritual Beings, their language, but no longer knew their immediate presence. Later still, there was a knowledge only of their living activity in the world, as we might watch the hands of a potter shaping a pot, without knowing his mind or his being.

Finally, today, we know only the 'finished work' of Beings, the end results of a creative, up-building activity.

In Steiner's description, we can begin to see a certain profound but partial truth in the ideas of physics. In so far as we deal with an extensive world, a finished work from which the immediate activity of the spiritual beings has withdrawn, we are indeed dealing with a dying aspect of the universe. So, too, when we burn fossil fuels, or even consume Uranium-235 in a reactor, we are merely making visible and usable certain energies which were once inner spiritual energies, existing as creative utterance, but which have now died into coal fields, oil fields, uranium ores, matter itself. Since the early part of this century, physics has known that what we call matter is really energy. Only a tiny fraction is released in any processes we have yet invented (we do not yet *control* nuclear energy in any fundamental way; we simply exploit a curious natural phenomenon of fission. If we ever truly control the forces involved, to the degree that we can now control electricity, our present powers will seem quite limited).

We can then begin to seek the Beings who are the origins of all extensive and intensive energies. In physical matter, according to Rudolf Steiner, we find the end result of a tremendous sacrifice – the outpouring by the Thrones of a portion of their own substance as primeval spiritual warmth. Here is the earliest cosmic energy process with which we can be concerned – but an energy still wholly inward. Within this warmth, other beings could then unfold their own creative deeds. So we are not asked to envisage a Big Bang, an explosion into a dying process, but the birth of a warmth which nurtures and up-builds. So, too, with all the making of the cosmos, the earth, the kingdoms of nature. Only relatively recently, in our cosmos, has a dying process begun[2] – and with it, processes of the kind now understood in physics.

So what we now call fire is indeed a gift of the Gods, which becomes extensive when their activities in soul and spirit are expended into the realm of finished work, dying into physical flames and combustion. Even in physics itself, there are phenomena which we could learn to see as open secrets, speaking of warmth living at a threshold between extensive and intensive worlds. (These are explored in Steiner's so-called Heat Course).[3] But in the open secrets of living nature, sentient animals, and creative human beings, we could find doorways into the intensive energies of living, working manifestation of Being, and creative Being itself. To grasp these energies, these qualities, scientifically, we shall need new forms of inner perception. Living thought, strengthened to what Steiner calls Imagination, can open the way to the world of living working, in which the intensive and extensive realms interweave. Intensive awakened feeling can give access, as Inspiration, to the intensive energies of soul, the manifestations of Being. And intensive awakened will, as Intuition, can bring immediate experience of the creative essence of Beings themselves.

Yet without the development of these higher faculties, the world of intensive reality can be glimpsed in our own ordinary experience. For we are also spiritual beings, engaged in manifesting our Being, in living and working in the world, in making finished works. And here we can notice some very familiar but deeply interesting phenomena.

A creative idea is born in inner warmth. It brings a sense of light, of revelation, and a stirring of inner vitality. We are fired with an idea, see a golden opportunity, are enlivened with a creative impulse. These intensive events may pass over as physical events into the organism, as movements and utterance ('Eureka!'), increased pulse and respiration, etc. But no-one in his senses imagines that a good idea can be generated by leaping out of the bath or by heavy breathing. The physical energies released are ripples from intensive events, becoming extensive through the mysterious gateway of warmth.

A creative idea needs not only the inner warmth of its progenitor, but a corresponding warmth in others, if it is to be hatched out into the extensive world of manifest activity. Ideas need enthusiasm, a warm welcome. But this warmth, this energy, does not depend on combustion of fuel. It may prompt the body to an enhanced metabolic rate, in preparation for physical action. But in the soul, creative energies live intensively. Their 'energy crisis' comes not from using up the stored energies of a Big Bang, but from the inactivity of the Being who is their source – in this case, the human being, understood not as a combustion device but as a spirit.

In the activities of Beings, energies are not consumed, they are created. The universe becomes more, not less, than it was. Spiritual beings are indeed a bit like flames – but *intensive* flames which dispense up-building warmth and light. The extensive flames of physical combustion show us a picture – but only a picture – of the activity in which the dying universe has its origins.

*   *   *

Let us now return to those very potent energies in the human soul with which we began, egotism and fear. *Whose* energies are they? Are they really the essential human energies? Or are they showing us the working of other Beings in the human soul?

The great wooden carving created by Rudolf Steiner near the end of his life, he called 'The Representative of Humanity'. It shows not one Being, but several. We are shown a whole, within which several qualities of spiritual activity, of Being, are at work. Beings have names. The energy we know in our souls as egotism would be revealed to awakened spiritual perception as the activity of Lucifer, Fear as announcing the presence of Ahriman – Lucifer, the bringer of a consuming personal flame, Ahriman as the Lord of Death who ties the flame to the physical world, until it burns itself out.

We inherit Lucifer as part of our nature from the past, living in our desires in such a way that we live at odds with the wise order of nature. As self-centred flames we are then faced with a meeting with ageing and death, and we fear the future as a cold threat to our flames.

But Rudolf Steiner's carving includes a central figure, Who we can look upon as the inwardness of the Sun. This Being lives since the Mystery of Golgotha united with the dying earth, but bringing a warmth and light of Resurrection. Within the extensive world, there is a seed secret, an 'energy', which shines now not out of the past but from the future, a new Sun.

The fires of egotism and fear live in the soul as intensive fuels for the extensive destruction of the earth. Yet within the activities of science and technology themselves, there is also hidden a flame of a different quality. In the past, human beings sought the renewing fire for their lives, their moral ideals and guiding ideas, beyond themselves in revelation. Cultures were inwardly and outwardly kindled through Initiates, who stood at the threshold where the intensive and extensive worlds met.

With the birth of science and scientific technology, many human beings began to explore, un-called and unguided by Initiates or wisdom from the past, into mysteries of the physical world. There awoke remarkable new inner energies, a free and independent search for insight, a creative practice of experiment and invention. The path of this initiation has led deep into the dying world, into the finished work of the divine creation. In this world, there are Beings who would entrap and extinguish these newly kindled flames. So we see ouselves only as processes of combustion, dependent on consuming energies from the past. The future looks dark and cold, and we are filled with fear and uncertainty.

This fear will only be transcended if we can find a different flame, the light and warmth which constitute the True Flame of humanity. Within the dying processes which dominate a materialistic culture we can seek a 'golden opportunity', which calls us to a new responsibility. This is not only to conserve the energies from the past – although this must be done wisely. It is to awaken to the work of transmutation, the renewal of insight and of culture.

Because the new Sun shines from beyond death, when it reaches into the world through human souls it begins to create a new intensive life, a seed realm leading into the future. So far we know little of this redemptive fire directly. Yet there is a sphere we know more intmately and can begin to work in more consciously. We can't change human nature with physical energies. But the True Flame of mankind can bring a transmuting light and warmth into our egotism and fear. The heart of the energy crisis is whether we find some glimpse of the reality of this new Sun in ourselves and in one another.

Speaking of the way between the intensive and extensive aspects of human nature, Rudolf Steiner once described how true moral ideals reach with a transforming activity right into our physical bodies.[4] He included as physical our warmth and our air, as well as our fluid and our solid. Awakened spiritual perception, he said, sees how such ideals bring a renewing warmth into our warmth, a renewing inner light into our air, a renewing music into our fluid, a renewing life into our solid organisation. These 'energies' live hidden and seedlike for the future.

We cannot yet develop a real science of these mysterious processes. Yet we can to some degree feel them. When we are fired with true creative impulses, we may indeed feel warmer, lighter, more harmonious and more alive.

We shall need to seek such experiences and phenomena as we move more deeply into the growing crisis of the extensive energies.

I realise that these reflections do not contribute immediately to many questions. What shall we do, now, about nuclear power, about natural resources, about the immediate and pressing problems of the physical world? They are real problems, and are likely to bring much tension and suffering. But I do not think that the crisis will be met without a deeper exploration of the intensive energies at work in the human soul, and a recognition of the Beings whose activities they represent. The sources and the redemption of the crisis are alike in the world of intensive realities, and we shall not find a solution in conservation alone. We need the light of deeper insight and the fire of moral ideals. The crisis is calling for us to seek the new Sun, which now lives as a light and warmth of Resurrection, within the dying inheritance from the past, showing the way into the future.

1980

---

[1] See *Anthroposophical Leading Thoughts* (Rudolf Steiner Press).

[2] In Steiner's terminology, from the middle of the Atlantean age. See *Occult Science*, Chapter 4 (Rudolf Steiner Press).

[3] In print only in German: *Gesamtausgabe Bibl.* No. 321 (Rudolf Steiner Nachlassverwaltung).

[4] Rudolf Steiner: *The Bridge between universal spirituality and the physical constitution of man*. Lecture 2, Dornach, December 18, 1920 (Anthroposophic Press, New York).

CONSIDERING SCIENCE
Bacon, Rudolf Steiner and Modern Science

The centenary of Rudolf Steiner's birth has helped to make his name and work better known. Nevertheless, the body of teachings that he called Spiritual Science is still very far from being widely accepted or understood.

This makes a curious contrast to another 1961 occasion – the four hundredth anniversary of the birth of Francis Bacon. Although Bacon lived three centuries before Steiner, his work makes a direct appeal to the present age. Centenary articles and lectures about Bacon have all emphasised his astonishing *modernity*.

How is it that Bacon can speak across four centuries in a way which meets with instant comprehension in the 1960s, while many people find Steiner, who died as recently as in 1925, strange and difficult?

The answer is connected with the evolution of human consciousness, about which Steiner spoke so often and with such emphasis. In a lecture given in 1920 (Dornach, 1 Feb. 1920), Steiner described Bacon as the "inaugurator" of the modern age. There is an obvious sense in which this is true, since Bacon was one of the earliest advocates of science, and it is the ever-spreading power and influence of science, above all, that distinguishes our age from earlier ones.

It is almost uncanny to find in Bacon passages which sound almost like leading articles in today's technical and scientific journals. We find him urging that there should be more scientifically qualified people in Government, expressing anxieties about the shortage of scientific manpower, and emphasising that applied science is the key to prosperity.

Bacon's central achievement, though, was to define and describe the modern scientific method – and above all, to emphasise the importance of impartial observation and experiment. Much of what he says seems commonplace now, but in his day it struck an entirely new note – so much so, that only a few of Bacon's contemporaries were really stirred by his ideas. Nevertheless, thirty-six years after his death, his *Novum Organum* inspired the founders of the Royal

Society, and to-day the seed that Bacon planted has sprouted into luxurious growth.

* * *

But when Steiner called Bacon the inaugurator of the modern age, he was referring not only to the age of science, but to the age of Consciousness Soul. Modern science has arisen because of a change in human consciousness. During Greek and Roman times the form of consciousness which Steiner called the Intellectual Soul was developed. Greek science remained essentially an intellectual activity, in which physical experiment never played an important part.

A new stage in the evolution of consciousness began in the fifteenth century, the beginning of the age of Consciousness Soul. Bacon was one of the first individuals in whom the new outlook began to express itself strongly.

A characteristic feature of the Consciousness Soul (or Spiritual Soul, as Steiner also called it) is that each individual clairvoyance of earlier times, with its experience of participation in a world of spiritual beings, has gone. Awareness has withdrawn into the fortress of the skull, where the ghosts of the older perceptions flit through the consciousness in the form of thoughts. At the same time, awareness of the world revealed by the senses has increased enormously in importance. Eyes and ears have become windows communicating between 'inner' and 'outer' worlds which in earlier times were not sharply distinguished from each other.

In this way, man's original unitary experience has fallen apart into two halves. Modern man no longer feels himself to be a participant in nature or in a spiritual world; he has become an onlooker.

* * *

How is this change reflected in modern science? The early development of science was still much influenced by an outlook characteristic of an earlier age; still imbued with many attitudes and habits which really belong to Greek and Roman times, to the Intellectual Soul. Even to-day, this is still true to some extent. One example of this is the dichotomy between 'pure' and 'applied' science.

The ideal of 'pure' science is knowledge for its own sake. The purpose of experiment is to aid the understanding, to throw light on a puzzle presented by nature. It is designed to enrich man's inner life. Applied science, on the other hand, is concerned with the external world, with doing rather than thinking, with increasing material rather than spiritual wealth. The emphasis is on controlling rather than understanding nature, on power rather than knowledge.

The pure scientist, though he may be a creative thinker, is in one sense a consumer, while the applied scientist is a producer. The pure scientist consumes sense impressions and digests them in his mind. The applied scientist uses the concepts that result to produce effects in the world of nature. Pure science is specially connected with the senses and the head, while applied science is an activity which finds expression through the will.

Obviously, there is no such thing as a purely pure scientist, any more than there could be a wholly applied one. Any form of scientific observation involves some activity of the will – particularly when an experiment is set up – while no applied scientist could start work unless he were first able to from concepts about what he proposed to do.

Nevertheless, a dichotomy exists, and is reflected, for instance, in the universities, where there was – and still is to some extent – a strong prejudice against admitting applied sciences such as electrical or chemical engineering into the syllabus. The 'redbrick' universities, which have grown up near industrial centres, have less of this prejudice, but the attitude persists at Oxford and Cambridge, with their powerful classical traditions.

This indicates, I think, how 'pure' science is still coloured by the outlook of the Intellectual Soul. It is expressed, too, in the use of Latin and Greek for scientific terminology and even, until comparatively recently, for scientific theses.

This is just what Bacon wished to overcome. He lamented the overpowering authority of Aristotle, the constant looking back to the past, that characterised the learning of his day. He wanted the slate to be scrubbed clean of tradition, and scientists to start to fill it in anew, basing everything on careful observation and experiment. But the most characteristic thing about him is that he was not really interested in knowledge 'for its own sake', but only in what could be done with it. "The real and legitimate goal of the sciences," he wrote, "is the endowment of human life with new inventions and riches" (*Novum Organum*, Bk. 1.). Thus Bacon was not only the first scientist, but the first *applied* scientist, in a quite modern sense.

It is really only in this century that a deliberate effort has begun to apply science to industry and agriculture. The 'industrial revolution' made very little use of science in the strict sense. Most of the new machines were designed and built empirically, by inventors rather than by scientists. Little or no theory was used.

With the discovery of electricity, the situation changed rapidly.

It is possible to handle steam power, and put it to work, with the help of a few rules of thumb derived from experience. But the use of electricity calls upon scientific theory at every step.

Since then scientific theories have been put to work on a steadily expanding scale. Chemicals, plastics, electronics and radio, atomic energy and aeronautics are now completely dependent on highly evolved concepts.

There is a sense, then, in which science has only just become truly Baconian. From Bacon's time right up to the end of the nineteenth century, the Consciousness Soul was still not fully developed. A powerful legacy from the Intellectual Soul age tended to keep science in the universities, making it a contemplative, almost monastic activity. Applied science had far less status. Of course, many scientists realised the potential power of science. But the traditions of learning for its own sake were still very strong, and it is only in the last few decades that the 'scientific revolution' has really got going.

But Bacon's outlook is maturing today in a deeper sense than is often realised. For the basic attitudes which inspire applied science are gradually colouring pure science as well. The concept of knowledge for its own sake is gradually losing its meaning, since it is becoming increasingly difficult to define the word 'knowledge'.

Bacon's conception of knowledge is characteristic: "We . . . rear a holy temple in [man's] mind, on the model of the universe, which model therefore we imitate" (*Novum Organum*, Bk. 1). The human mind is for Bacon a kind of building site on which 'models' of the outside world are erected through the activity of the individual. The word 'model' is significant, because it is in constant use by physicists today.

For a nineteenth-century scientist, a theory was rather more than a model. It was a picture of the real world existing outside the observer. Thus atomic theory pictured minute billiard balls as the ultimate constituents of matter, and it was taken for granted that if the theory were correct, such balls actually existed.

Since then, the situation has become far more complicated. A whole series of 'models' is now used by science to deal with matter. Thus an atomic 'particle' may be treated as a kind of billiard ball, but also as a kind of wave, and as a kind of electrical cloud. One 'model' for the nucleus of the atom is a series of concentric shells; another is a kind of 'liquid drop'.

Some of the 'models' being used, especially in physics, cannot be 'visualised' in any direct way at all, but only defined mathematically. They no longer have any content which can be related to sense experience. They may still be 'models' – but they are no longer 'pictures'.

It is clear, therefore, that atomic billiard balls cannot 'really exist' in the simple sense. You cannot dissect matter down to tiny indivisible material objects. In fact, when you get into these realms of the very small, the whole concept of 'matter' becomes difficult to define. The atomic physicist no longer deals with 'things', but with 'forces' and 'events'.

All this has compelled philosophers of science to take a closer look at what is meant by words such as 'theory' and 'model'. But I do not want to go into the philosophy of science in detail – partly because the majority of modern scientists are not philosophically inclined. I am more concerned to describe what scientists today actually do – even if they make philosophical mistakes.

The most characteristic feature of the outlook of modern scientists is its pragmatism. A theory is not used because it is 'true', but because it is 'useful'. The main test of the truth of a theory is whether it *works*. As experiment has come to dominate science, theories are coming to be treated more and more as mere tools, as provisional working models. They are no longer revelations of what 'nature' is 'really like', but implements for conducting experiments and uncovering further effects.

In this way, 'pure science' is gradually becoming, in effect, a kind of applied science. 'Knowledge' is less a matter of understanding the world of nature than of learning how to produce various effects. The actual phenomena in which science deals are now largely man-made. New theories are built up on the basis of phenomena which reveal themselves only under the most elaborate experimental conditions – which themselves embody elaborate theories. Numerically, far more scientists are now involved in experimental work than in theorising. An establishment such as the European Centre for Nuclear Research at Geneva, with its giant 'atom smasher', exists to advance 'pure' science. In practice, the majority of the staff are involved in keeping the great machines working, building up elaborate measuring instruments, and negotiating with contractors for new equipment.

*   *   *

If one now stands back and looks at this progress from Greek times to the present day, the transformation from the Intellectual to the Consciousness Soul age emerges clearly. Particularly striking is the gradual withdrawal of human consciousness from its dependence, first on revelations from the spiritual world, then from the authority of the past, and finally from the authority of 'nature' as perceived by the senses. The scientist is no longer a 'knower' – he has become almost entirely a 'doer'.

The world we live in today we have shaped for ourselves. Not only the things but many of the ideas we use are the outcome of our own activity, and owe little to tradition. We feel free to think what we like, to experiment almost without limit, and science is being used to transform the world. The ideals of Francis Bacon seem to be coming to realisation in the most thorough way.

It is also clear, though, that this process of withdrawal is in danger of going too far. In everyday life, people still contrive to keep their feet on the ground, so to speak, and to relate their thoughts to the world revealed by their senses. But science is becoming increasingly esoteric, dealing in forces and entities which are not accessible to the senses, and in concepts which are inaccessible to all but a few who have gone through the necessary mathematical discipline.

At the same time, this very esoteric activity is having the most drastic exoteric effects. New inventions and discoveries pour in upon the world, and society can barely digest the effects of one scientific discovery before it is faced with another. Why is this?

It should be clear by now that the power of science derives from its 'models' – from the concepts which are then embodied in material form, as electronic computers, atomic reactors or supersonic aircraft. The question is: where do these models come from? They cannot be derived entirely from the sense world, since they are often, so to speak, non-sensical: they contradict normal sense experience in all kinds of ways.

There are several cases on record where new 'models' have flashed into a scientist's mind as a kind of inspiration. One of the best known is the experience of Kekulé, who was riding on a London bus when he suddenly saw, dancing before his mind's eye, the now familiar benzene ring, six carbon atoms holding hands in a circle, with hydrogen atoms attached. This model proved to be the key to a vast section of organic chemistry and showed the way to making all kinds of new synthetic substances.

Not all scientific inspirations are as dramatic or well-defined as Kekulé's. Yet I believe that a very large proportion of scientific advances, if traced back carefully to their origins, would be seen to derive from similar moments of sudden insight.

According to Steiner, such inspirations often come from, or are strongly influenced by, Luciferic and Ahrimanic beings. In this connection, it is interesting to read how he describes some of the characteristics of Ahriman, for example in *Die Geistige Hintergründe der Menschlichen Geschichte* [1] (Dornach, August and September, 1916), Lecture V:

One of the main characteristics of Ahriman is that he is quite unaware of the direct relationship to truth that man has when he lives on earth. Ahriman does not know this direct relationship to truth in which one endeavours to establish truth simply as the agreement of a concept with something objective. Ahriman does not know this. He is not concerned with this at all. Through the whole position which Ahriman has in the world, which I have often described, it is entirely a matter of indifference to him whether, when a concept is formed, it corresponds to reality. The kind of truth which he is concerned to build up – we would not call it truth in the human sphere – is entirely concerned with effects (*Wirkungen*). Something is said, not in order that it shall correspond with something else, but in order to produce effects. This or that is said, in order to achieve this or that result.

This corresponds exactly to the situation with many scientific concepts. It matters not in the least whether they correspond to sense experience, or even whether they correspond to 'common sense'. The most important thing is that they *work*.

We can see here, too, how this kind of thinking has crept into social and political life – since Ahriman's conception of truth, as described by Steiner, amounts to 'the end justifies the means'. The whole world of power-politics, salesmanship and persuasion, is imbued with this element of untruths and half-truths used for a purpose.

One can detect here an element of tragedy in modern science, and in its inaugurator, Bacon. It was essential for humanity to rid itself of dependence on the past, on the authority of Aristotelian concepts which no longer had any living content and had become mere 'idols'. The last lecture in the series quoted above ends with a discussion of Bacon. His task, Steiner said, was to enable men to see through the old 'idols' handed down from the past, and turn their attention to the world revealed by the senses.

Both these aims have been achieved – but something else has happened as well. Through the growth of experiment, and the invasion of pure science by the techniques of applied science, the sense world has become obscured by a new set of idols, the remote concepts of contemporary science.

The experimental method, as soon as it ceases to be related to the world perceived by the senses, opens the way to concepts which have no roots in nature, but are infiltrated into men's minds from a kind of sub-nature by the Ahrimanic beings.

From other lectures of Steiner's, it is clear that these beings have long been seeking an opportunity of this kind. Historians of science have often commented on the peculiar part played by Arab culture in carrying over Aristotle's scientific teachings to the West. In the sixth century, when the Greek philosophers were exiled by Justinian, they founded the Academy of Gondi-Shapur in Persia. It was from this Academy that learned men were later invited to the court of the great Arab ruler, Jaroun al-Raschid, to impart Greek science and medicine to the Arabs.

When the revival of learning began in the West, the scientific writings of Aristotle and Ptolemy first became known in translations from Arabic. They had made their way through Egypt to Spain, and were taken over during the Christian invasions in the eleventh century.

In his lectures on reincarnation and karma, Rudolf Steiner describes how this impulse was then taken up in the West, and transformed by certain individuals who in previous lives had been intimately associated with the Arab culture.

One such individual was Bacon, and another was Darwin. Many other individuals who have profoundly influenced the development of science are no doubt closely connected in a similar way with what Steiner calls the 'Arabian stream' in history.

In another course of lectures, *Der Entwicklungsgang der Menscheit in seinen drei Kräfteströmungen*[2] (Dornach, 4-13 Oct., 1918), Steiner has more to say about the Academy of Gondi-Shapur.

There were at work there, Steiner said, strong spiritual influences which wished to interfere with human evolution by bringing a new and potent knowledge into the world. From this centre were to have come certain brilliantly inspired individuals who during the seventh century would have given a highly advanced medicine and science to mankind, and also certain knowledge concerning the nature of birth and death.

This knowledge, according to Steiner, is intended to grow only slowly in mankind, and will not be fully developed until the midpoint of the Consciousness Soul age, 2493 A.D. If the intentions of the spiritual influences which worked at Gondi-Shapur had been realised, knowledge appropriate to the matured Consciousness Soul would have poured over men still living entirely in the Intellectual Soul.

This impulse was, in fact, blunted. How this happened is described by Steiner in the same course of lectures, and it would lead too far to enter into this here. But Steiner describes how the same impulse which worked at Gondi-Shapur echoes on in Bacon, and into twentieth-century science.

Many people today feel that science is going too fast for man, that we are being presented with forces and problems which we are not yet mature enough to control. But imagine how far more helpless men would have been if equally potent knowledge had fallen into their hands more than a thousand years ago. Science today has a tremendous momentum, a kind of haste, a rushing forward into the future, which echoes the impulse that lived in Gondi-Shapur, and is characteristic of the Ahrimanic impulses behind it.

* * *

Steiner was born just as Baconianism was beginning to mature. He lived to see many of the early fruits of the scientific revolution – electricity, wireless, aircraft. And his life's work is related to Bacon's in a twofold way. He was concerned to turn men's attention once again to the world of spirit, but without losing the consciousness of self which would not have developed without Bacon's impulse.

In the realm of science – which is what this article is mainly about – Steiner pointed repeatedly to Goethe as the inaugurator of a new impulse, and he saw his own work as continuing Goethe's and taking it further.

In Goethe's approach to nature, there is the same interest in the world revealed by the senses as we find in Bacon, and the same emphasis on the importance of avoiding prejudice and preconceived ideas. But there is something more – Goethe emphasised that the scientist must never lose sight of the *phenomena that nature reveals to him*. He must not build mere *imitations* of nature in his mind, models which at best embody only part of the truth. Instead, he must form his thoughts in such a way that the spiritual realities which are behind the impressions of the senses can flow also into his mind. The outer expression of a plant, encountered through the senses, and the inner expression admitted through thinking, then meet in the soul and reveal the true being – the primary Phenomenon or Ur-phenomenon behind the plant.

The 'models' of modern science are a kind of caricature of the primary Phenomena with which the natural science of the future must be concerned. And as long as science is preoccupied almost entirely with producing effects and performing experiments, it will give men more power, but not the wisdom to use it properly.

What is needed is a reawakening of 'pure' science in a new sense, making full use of the powers of consciousness won since Greek times. In such a science, progress would depend more on acquiring new faculties than on performing new experiments. This does not mean that there should be no experiments. But the starting-point would need to be a clear apprehension of the real Ur-phenomenon with which the experiment was concerned. This cannot happen as long as concepts are treated merely as serviceable tools, constructed in the human mind for a strictly practical purpose.

Modern science has brought us to the point where the sheer

power of human thinking has been amply demonstrated. But because there is still no awareness that thinking has any connection with spiritual worlds or spiritual beings – either benign or malign – there is no feeling of *responsibility* towards thoughts; only towards deeds.

In *Die Geistige Hintergründe der menschlichen Geschichte*, quoted above, Steiner says: "In the years to come, for many millenia, it will be essential that we acquire a sense of responsibility for a thought we take hold of." He goes on to say that critical point comes when the thought is imparted to others, written down or spoken out. Then it has been let loose in the world, so to speak – and it is at this point that Ahriman can go to work, if the thought suits him.

Today there is a tremendous pressure in science to rush hastily into print in order to forestall rivals in the same field. New ideas, and new experiments, are not allowed to mature in the mind, but are thrust out immediately into the world. It may seem an offensive analogy, but it is really as though science were afflicted with a kind of spiritual diarrhoea.

The question of responsibility was raised in an acute form by one of the most extraordinary achievements of science – the atomic bomb – which turned an abstruse conception into a fearful weapon after a few years of hectic work. This gave many scientists a considerable shock. The apparently disinterested activities of the laboratory could suddenly uncover a tremendous new force – and once uncovered, there was a kind of helpless feeling among scientists that nothing could prevent it from being put into practice (although some attempts were made). For a time, there was much discussion about the responsibilities of science towards the world, and whether scientists should try to keep potentially dangerous discoveries secret.

It was concluded, quite rightly, that this couldn't and shouldn't be done. But scientists are continually aware that some apparently academic paper in *Nature* may have revolutionary implications for the whole world.

It was never suggested, however, that scientists should feel responsible for what they *think*. But once scientific thinking can come alive, can begin to reach to the spiritual realities behind the world of nature, the need for responsibility will become more apparent. And it is Steiner who pointed the way to such a new kind of thinking, dealing in living thoughts instead of ghost-like models.

When Bacon published the *Novum Organum*, he inaugurated a kind of thinking that has gradually and effectively eliminated the remnants of the past that clung to human consciousness. This method has reached maturity today, and threatens to fall gradually into decay unless it is given new life.

The Consciousness Soul must now take the next step: to re-establish a connection with the spiritual realities of the world. The 'Novum Organum' for this step was brought into the world by Rudolf Steiner, in works such as *Knowledge of Higher Worlds* and *The Philosophy of Spiritual Activity.*

It is thus highly appropriate that Steiner and Bacon should be remembered in the same year – and not surprising that Bacon should be easily comprehended while Steiner is still difficult. Since Bacon's day, his new way of thinking has become a common possession of a large part of mankind. Steiner's way has still to be acquired – and it will be a strenuous, arduous task.

1962

---

[1] Translations of all these seven lectures, partly in typescript, are in the Library at Rudolf Steiner House.

[2] A typescript translation of these six lectures (R LXVII) is in the Library at Rudolf Steiner House.

Science and Human Rights

Science is built on two ideals: To increase our understanding of the world; and to use this understanding for the benefit of all.

Today, neither of these ideals is being fulfilled. For most people, science is no longer a source of enlightenment but of mystification, while applied science is unleashing powerful and often frightening forces which we cannot confidently manage. How has this come about?

Science has become more remote from general understanding as it has become more abstract and mathematical. Yet increasing abstraction has brought increasing technological power. This reached a kind of culmination in the wartime Manhattan Project to develop the atomic bomb, which involved an intensive collaboration between academic scientists, working on the most mathematical and abstract frontiers of knowledge, with all the resources of industry and military power. It was a combination which has become familiar but was a novelty then. It is true that science had frequently contributed to industry and to military power before 1940. But academic physicists had never been so closely integrated with a major military and industrial effort. The association has left its mark. What one might call the industrialisation of science and its marriage with the State has gone ahead at a breathless pace. Almost three-quarters of American research and development is now Government-financed, a situation which recently prompted a leading business journal of free-enterprise America, *Fortune* magazine, to publish a long article entitled 'The nationalisation of U.S. Science'.[1] The main driving forces have been the demands of defence and space activities – but their influence has spread far beyond their immediate requirements.

One result is that many modern laboratories are now more like small factories than anything else. They have managing directors, full-time administrative and accounting staffs, huge power supplies, and the scientists work in ever larger teams. In one sense, this has made science enormously more 'productive'. Indeed, a senior official of the U.S. National Aeronautics and Space programme recently argued that a principal justification for the whole space programme was its 'forcing function' on the rest of science and technology. It acts like a greenhouse, dramatically speeding up growth.

This runaway development has produced some useful new inventions and products, and is sometimes exhilarating, like a ride in a very fast car. But for many people, the exhilaration is short lived, and is replaced by deepening alarm and confusion. Quite apart from the apocalyptic military powers now in the hands of nuclear armed states, there is a widespread sense of forces getting out of hand, of new developments pouring over us before we have learned to manage their predecessors. An American professor of physics recently wrote: "With all our mushrooming know-how and frenzied hurry to transform the world out of all recognition – if not indeed out of existence – we are increasingly helpless and confused in the face of the world we are creating."[2]

This process of industrialisation has taken hold, not only of applied science, but of pure science as well. It is not merely that the output of new 'knowledge' is accelerating, in a competitive atmosphere of 'publish or die'. But the actual character of knowledge itself has become, in subtle ways, industrialised. For the justification of modern physical theory is its predictive value, its power. It is essentially a collection of recipes for manipulating the world, a kind of intellectual tool-box from which the scientific artisan selects what he needs for his next experiment. These tools are now highly mathematical and their use a specialised skill. They are extremely powerful – but their effect has been to remove the conceptual side of science, scientific 'knowledge', into a realm remote from direct human experience.

As a result, the scientist has become for the layman a kind of sorcerer, in somewhat uncertain control of invisible forces which he has conjured up. His control depends on mathematical mysteries which are impenetrable except to a few. This is a far cry from science as part of the Enlightenment, as a bringer of light, of new and *public* understanding of the world. This experience of enlightenment may still come to individual scientists as they move in their mathematical worlds. They will speak of new 'insights', of the 'elegance' and 'beauty' of a mathematical procedure. But they have arrived in a situation curiously similar to that of many modern artists: their work is only accessible to a small group of initiates. Their remote concepts no longer function as 'knowledge' in the sense of something which brings new meaning into our experience of the world. Few people searching for meaning in their lives will find satisfaction in the equations of nuclear physics. And even to the physicist, these equations increasingly represent tools for guiding further experiments rather than descriptions of a 'real' world. For the nuclear world, like Kant's world of the 'things in themselves', is one which can never be 'known' directly, even if we acquire immense skill in manipulating it.

This present situation – a bombardment of society with unmanageable new forces, and a drying up of knowledge into conceptual abstractions – is the culmination of a process which began in the fifteenth century. At that time, men began to distinguish themselves in a quite new way from their environment. They ceased to feel embedded in a kind of womb-like universe, enclosed in concentric heavenly spheres. Instead, they began to see themselves alone on a sphere of dead rock, whirling through dark and empty space.

It was a deep change in what Butterfield calls 'men's feeling for things'.[3] It comes out strikingly in the struggle for a clear concept of motion. In real everyday experience, we seldom see a moving object without something or someone moving it, speeding it up or slowing it down: a horse pulling a cart, a wind blowing a leaf. The uniform motion in a straight line which is a foundation of Newtonian mechanics is something we never experience in our surroundings. In fact it is a motion which never actually occurs in the universe at all, since there can be no object which is not being acted on by forces of one kind or another.

Uniform motion is thus something which can be apprehended only in pure thinking – and the struggle to do so took a couple of centuries, until Newton crystallised out the new ability to treat abstractions as realities and manipulate them mathematically. It was an enormous achievement which we find difficult to appreciate in retrospect, as it is now almost second nature. But without it, we should have had no theoretical science as we know it today.

The other great influence was the gradual emergence of the experimental method (first clearly stated by Bacon) and an appreciation of its power. This, too, depended on changes in men's 'feelings for things'. To subject nature to experimental manipulation, to measure and weigh her, to 'torture her secrets from her' as Bacon put it, presupposes a detachment from nature, a feeling of separateness, which was quite foreign to medieval man. The attempt to gain power over nature – to develop technology in fact – depends on feeling detached from her. It was a consequence of the emergence of the new 'onlooker consciousness'.[4]

This abstraction of human experience from its earlier, much more intimate relation to the environment (a relation which Barfield calls 'original participation'[5]) gave birth to pure and applied science as we know them. But it also gave birth to something else. To the modern mind, the medieval world can easily seem claustrophobic, tightly shut both intellectually and socially.[6] The structure of society echoed the structure of the universe; both were hierarchical, fixed, God-given. Galileo and Kepler can seem a tremendous liberation, a breaking open of the spheres into a universe of infinite free space. At the same time, the intimidating authorities of the past – notably Aristotle – began to be questioned. The widening of intellectual horizons was   paralleled by a widening of geographical horizons. It was the time of the great navigators and explorers. And above all old hierarchical forms of society began to be broken down.

Out of these experiences, human beings could begin to feel their individuality in a quite new way. Thus, hand in hand with the development of science has emerged the concept of individual human rights. It is true that the citizen's rights before the law were recognised in ancient Rome. But the Roman citizen was a member of an elite, and he took slavery of the less privileged for granted.

The notion of a *universal* rule of law, attributing equal rights to all human beings, has emerged much more recently, and is still far from being recognised or practised in many parts of the world. Nevertheless, the social upheavals since the fifteenth century, the break-up of hierarchical societies, the removal of aristocratic privilege, are intimately related to men's new 'feeling for things'. There emerged a new freedom to think individual thoughts about the universe, to devise one's own experiments – and the right to such freedoms has become something most powerfully felt and fought for, particularly in those societies where pure and applied science have been pioneered.

In these societies, the 'rights of the individual', irrespective of class, race, wealth or intelligence, is now something deeply felt and shared by very many people, especially by the young. It is the basis of resistance to dictatorship and tyranny, of the rejection and horror of brainwashing techniques or other methods of manipulating the personality, and is the ultimate social assumption behind democratic institutions.

Yet this very fact underlines the dilemmas now being created by science and technology. What started five centuries ago as a liberation is today threatening to become a trap. For the abstractions of modern theoretical science provide no firm foundation for the concept of human rights; and many of the most modern scientific techniques, especially in biology and medicine, are beginning to pose the most urgent social questions in which human rights are central. Science has already brought far-reaching new powers of intervention in birth, life and death, but no help in judging how to use them. The churches, which once gave authoritative edicts on such matters, are losing not only their congregations but their doctrinal certainty. How do we manage contraception and abortion? Under what circumstances should medical technology be used to keep old people alive, perhaps leading a kind of vegetable existence? Should hallucinogenic drugs be banned? To what extent should drugs or brain surgery be used to treat criminals or the mentally disturbed?

These are already actual questions, but they are only a foretaste of what is to come. Quite soon it may become possible to determine the sex of a child. It is already possible in principle to extend to man the artificial insemination techniques used for cattle, so that one genius (or maniac) could father vast numbers of children, even (by freezing his sperm) long after his death.

Before long, too, the transplantation of whole organs – kidneys, livers, perhaps even hearts – may be achieved. The demand for organs may well exceed supply. How is the 'market' to be organised, and what are the rights of individuals, both donors and recipients, in respect of their organs? What shall we mean by an 'individual' when his heart comes from one body, his kidneys from another?

Somewhat further ahead, but perhaps not so very far off, lie the possibilities of 'genetic engineering' – direct chemical or manipulative intervention in the material of the chromosomes in order to remove genetic defects or insert desirable genetic features. It may soon be possible to remove a human ovum from the ovary, treat it chemically or surgically, fertilise it in the laboratory and then replant it in the womb to mature. Such procedures might produce monsters, freaks, or beings with all kinds of queer features; the whole concept of 'human being' would lose its present meaning.

Exactly what form these powers will take is speculative. But how they are used – if at all – will depend quite centrally on what we mean by 'the rights of the individual'. For to say that the human individual has rights is really another way of saying that his life has an individual meaning. But this is just where science fails us.

The nearest attempt at a scientific answer comes from biological humanists, who argue that an individual's value lies in the genes he carries for the species. But what are the 'rights' of a collection of genes? The individual surely cannot claim a right to genes potentially deleterious to the species? This line of thought leads inevitably to the conclusion that it is the species as a whole which is the true 'individuality'; its survival and further evolution must then be the basis of all decisions on rights.

This is an entirely valid and logical conclusion if the individual is regarded as simply the product of an interaction between his genetic inheritance and his environment. But this neo-Darwinist view, like so much of the conceptual content of modern science, bears very little relation to actual human experience. For the inner conviction that human individuals have 'rights' refers these not to the 'species', but to the person himself. Each individual is felt to be uniquely valuable *irrespective* of his race, sex, intelligence or genetic constitution.

The cruciual problem lies in the yawning gap which now exists between this inner conviction and our abstract intellectual life. Not long ago, the value of the individual was adequately explained in religious terms – with an assertion, for example, that God is equally interested in the salvation of each and every soul. The neo-Darwinists have produced a variation, when they say that the *species* is interested in the *genes* of each and every person; the more 'variability' and different gene combinations exist, the better the species' chance of adapting to future circumstances. In both cases, the value of the individual is referred to something outside himself. This can masquerade as a kind of 'unselfish' ideal. But the religious concept ('God') is losing its authority for increasing numbers of people today, while the scientific concept ('the species') is a remote abstraction. It hardly enriches the meaning of life to be told that the ultimate value of one's individual existence is to be sought in gene combinations which may come in useful for survival in unspecified future circumstances.

Thus, if we are to manage the new biological and medical technologies, we shall need a far more concrete *understanding* of the individual. Human rights need a foundation in *knowledge* – a knowledge which gives meaning to each individual life.

The biggest obstacle to such knowledge is a deep-rooted habit, nurtured by the scientific age, which may be called the 'atomic hypothesis'. It has become a basic procedure of science to seek explanations of phenomena in terms of simpler phenomena. The ultimate aim is to describe the complexities of the whole universe in terms of the interactions of a few elementary forces and particles. This has proved highly effective for studying and manipulating the inanimate world. But it is becoming increasingly apparent that it is quite inadequate in the realm of life.

An atomistic analysis of living phenomena can take us a certain way. It may have nearly reached its limits in the current molecular analysis of chromosomes, proteins, etc.. But it should be noted that the analysis depends on bringing the living substances into the dead world; they must be crystallised, x-rayed, chemically analysed, etc. The resulting molecular models may suggest powerful methods of intervening in and manipulating living processes. But there is one central characteristic of living phenomena which so far defies a clear scientific understanding, namely 'organisation'.

There are two particularly characteristic features of living organisms, one related to space, the other to time. In the living organism, the parts have a relation to the whole which is not found in the inorganic world. It makes no great difference to a rock if you cut it in half. It makes a very great difference to a mouse (or a man); they die, and start to decompose. This leads to the other characteristic: living organisms have a *life cycle*; they are born, grow old and die. They develop and change throughout their lives, yet every phase of development is part of the organism. The whole of a crystal is visible at every moment; an organism presents only a part of itself to the observer at any one time. To see it whole, it must be watched from birth to death.

These characteristics now form the central problems of modern biology, namely 'differentiation' and 'organisation'. Each 'atom' or cell of an organism contains in its nucleus a complete genetic specification for the *whole* organism. Yet in a liver cell, for example, only those genes relating to the liver are activated; in a brain cell, those relating to the brain. In the language of molecular biology, the problem is how appropriate genes are 'switched on and off' in different parts of the organisms and at different stages of its development. How is the genetic information organised into a meaningful whole in space and time?

A curiously similar problem is also at the forefront of another line of modern research: how are memories and sense impressions organised in the cells of the brain? Here, too, new impressions are organised and related meaningfully to concepts and memories in ways which are still almost wholly mysterious.

The basic problem is an old one, and many attempts have been made to grapple with it, ranging from various kinds of Gestalt theories, to 'explanations' which in effect deny that the problem exists. The latter are particularly popular nowadays, but when analysed they turn out in essence to be 'manipulative' theories of the type familiar in the physical sciences. They are 'models' whose validity resides in the fact that they work in certain experimental situations. They allow one to predict correctly the outcome of certain experiments. Such theories place one in the situation of a person who understands how to manage the controls of a car without necessarily knowing anything about its mechanism. One can become an extremely skilled driver and yet have virtually no insight into the principles of automobile engineering.[7]

The incomplete nature of molecular explanations may be illustrated by an analogy. It is possible to describe a house in terms of its bricks, mortar and other materials, their relative positions, load-bearing properties, etc. A descriptive 'embryology' of a house could describe how the various parts arrive on site and are assembled, and some general laws of house development could be deduced. These would enable one to predict how future houses would grow, and to devise experiments to interfere with the process in some precisely controlled ways.

But such an approach would never reveal the function of the house, nor the real cause of the parts adopting their particular ordered relationship. We would not easily recognise the completed house as a 'whole'. No explanation, in fact, can be complete without some comprehension of the needs of the human beings who live in it, and of the part played by the mind of the architect. The source and cause of the house's 'wholeness', of the unified relationship of its parts and the ordered procedures of its construction, is to be sought in the architect's mind.

This emerges still more vividly in a work of art, for example a painting. The meaning of a work of art must somehow reside in the special relation of the parts to the whole. To put it rather crudely, if a whole painting is worth £10,000, half a painting is not worth £5,000, it is worth nothing. Art obeys some similar laws to organisms.

One may study the parts of a painting in great detail, measure the areas of blue and red, weigh and analyse the pigments, make statistical comparisons with hundreds of other paintings – but no amount of such atomic analysis will reveal the meaning of a great work of art. Here again it is the artist's imagination which has organised the material parts to form a whole on the canvas – and no one part of the work can be removed without killing the entire organism.

It is not my intention to use this analogy as a simple-minded proof of the existence of a Divine Architect, or of Platonic archetypes informing living organisms. The 'argument from design' can carry no real conviction in the scientific age, and quite rightly. For an invisible Architect merely becomes another mental model or hypothetical construct, on much the same footing as mental models of atoms and molecules.

The real problem is to extend our knowledge, our actual experience, so that we may apprehend the 'wholeness' of organism more clearly, objectively and scientifically. We need insight into organism equivalent to the insight experienced by mathematicians in pure thinking. We need a method, a path of knowledge, which can lead us to new experience in relation to the living world, so that we go beyond the statement 'I can manipulate', and become able to exclaim 'I see!'

Most of all is this needed in relation to the nature of the human individual and the meaning of his life on earth. For it is already all too obvious that the atomic approach, the analysis in terms of parts and fragments, while giving many new powers, is obscuring or destroying the experience of *understanding*. It brings a kind of intellectual and emotional death to the human being.

The way forward is to be sought in the phenomena of organism and of art themselves. For they point to something within every person's experience which is, in its very nature, the antithesis of atomism. This is the faculty of imagination.

Recently, increasing numbers of scientists have begun to become interested in the imagination. One reason may be the very dust-and-ashes quality of the atomic view of the world, and a hunger for the life of the arts. But a more explicit reason is a growing recognition of the role imagination plays in science itself. Until quite recently, it was common to regard the imagination as the very opposite of science – subjective, untrustworthy, inaccessible to measurement. But it is increasingly realised that every scientific hypothesis is born out of the imagination, that every experiment must be imagined before it can be performed, and that the source of scientific progress is the imagination, which conceives new theories, mental models and experimental possibilities. There is growing awareness that crucial advances often spring from ideas which pop into the conscious mind unbidden, unexpected, and from unknown sources.

Both our conceptual and our material world have been shaped by the human imagination to an extraordinary degree. Although science set out, as it thought, to investigate 'nature' as something quite separate from the scientist, it has arrived at a position where 'nature' is increasingly obscured by man-made objects and man-made concepts, a mirror, in which what we see is mainly the results of our own activity. When we look at a motor car or a city, we fairly easily recognise it as the product of our own imaginations, realised in metals, plastic, bricks and mortar. We less easily recognise the formative role we have played in our own view of the universe. We learn, almost from birth, that the earth revolves on its axis, orbits the sun, and moves through infinite and largely empty space. It takes an effort to realise that this is not the universe we *perceive*, it is the result of a strenuous use of the imagination. We see the sun passing overhead. We have to *imagine* the earth revolving in its axis as an explanation of the sun's motion. No star – even through the largest telescope – is more than a point of light. There is no way of telling if a point is infinitely far or very near. We have first to *imagine* that the stars are 'really' large sun-like bodies, very far away, and then devise experiments to check our hypothesis.

But the imagination which has taken deepest root in the modern age, which is both very abstract and very powerful, is the concept of the 'atom'. The whole of science is based on it – on a search for simple building bricks out of which to construct more complex entities. It is taken for granted that a useful theory must analyse a phenomenon into simpler elements. Thus biology is reduced to chemistry, chemistry to atoms, atoms to 'fundamental particles'. This procedure is powerful, even essential, for effective manipulation of the physical world. Indeed it has proved so effective that we have become hypnotised by the atomic hypothesis, so that we seldom notice a curious fact about it: For neither in outer nature, nor in our inner conceptual life, are 'atoms' ever to be found as *primary* phenomena. They are always *the end of a process*.

'Particles' appear in nature as the result of disintegration: a rock is ground into sand; bones eventually fall apart into dust; radioactive elements throw off electrons as they decay into some other, more stable element. Something similar occurs inwardly when we *think* of an atom. It involves narrowing down the whole living, moving, changing life of imagination to a single point. Any further narrowing could only extinguish consciousness, producing darkness or death. It is thus very remarkable that we should have come to regard as the basis and beginning of all things something which *in actual experience* is, so to speak, the end of the line. The historical development of corpuscular theories of the universe, and of the impulse to account for the complex in terms of the simple, is well documented – but not thereby explained. But it is clearly connected, I suggest, with the emerging feeling of individuality, which has depended so strongly on the sharpening of independent critical faculties and the performance of precise experiments. If men had not practised, over and over again, a narrowing of their attention to the simplest phenomena, concentrating their consciousness to a tiny point, they would never, perhaps, have broken free of the all-embracing world organism in which medieval man felt himself to be embedded. Atomism was the basis for freedom.

Today, though, the process has gone far enough. It has separated man so far from nature, and led his intellect into such remote abstractions, that his life and self are in danger of becoming meaningless, while applied atomism is increasingly releasing destructive forces into society. If scientists are now showing a new interest in the faculty of imagination, therefore, it is a healthy instinct. For the nature of this faculty is the opposite of atomistic. Every imagination is born as a *whole*, as some kind of picture or concept; yet it is also an organic part of all the rest of our conscious life, intimately related to our memories and past experience. It has the same relation to our inner life as a part of an organism has to the whole. It can be studied as an independent entity – but if completely separated from its living context, it dies. Both in our consciousness and in living phenomena, organism and the whole are primary, parts and atoms are secondary. The living world, and our imaginations, point to an aspect of the universe which cannot be explained in atomic terms, in which 'causes' are *more* complex than their effects, and death has its origin in life.

It is this which led Rudolf Steiner to stress the importance of Goethe for the future development of science.[8] Goethe began to heal the breach between the poetic and the scientific apprehension of the world. He began to forge a new faculty, a marriage of the artistic imagination with precise observation of nature. He allowed nature to shape imagination, and imagination to recreate and enliven the observations. He moved towards what he called 'exact sensory imagination' *('exakte sinnliche Phantasie')* which could eventually grasp the realities expressed in the living world as precisely as the atomic imaginations can take hold of the dead world.

By holding strictly to the phenomena of nature themselves, and not allowing his imagination to project into them all kinds of concepts (like waves and atoms) foreign to what living processes actually displayed to his senses, Goethe began to apprehend and describe some of the laws of the organic world. But this practice began to extend his awareness of the living world so that his consciousness began to reach into a realm of which we are normally only indirectly aware. Most commentaries on Goethe's scientific work, when they come to his treatment of the *'Urpflanze'*, for example, take it for granted that Goethe was merely producing a botanical *theory*. He spoke of the *Urpflanze* as the archetypal reality lying behind all plant life; and we easily assume that he was speaking merely metaphorically. Schiller, on his first meeting with Goethe, thought so too. They walked to his study after a lecture, talking of plant development, and when they arrived, Goethe started making sketches to characterise his *Urpflanze*. 'But that', said Schiller, 'is not an experience, that is an idea.' Goethe replied: 'Then I am glad to have ideas without knowing it, and to see them with my very eyes.' The *Urpflanze* was for him not a hypothesis but a supersensible reality, which he had begun to perceive directly. Goethe had achieved an extension of consciousness.[9]

It fell to Rudolf Steiner to point out the full significance of Goethe's method and experiences, and to put them in a historical and evolutionary perspective. One of the oddities of the present age is that, since Darwin, evolutionary concepts should have been brought to bear on many branches of science, from sociology to the development of chemical elements in stars. But they have not been explicitly extended to human consciousness. Indeed it is still a deep-rooted assumption that men in the past had precisely the same basic consciousness as we have today, the same kind of awareness of nature, but that this consciousness was merely filled with different (and mostly mistaken) ideas about the world. One only has to begin to question such an assumption to see what a wealth of evidence exists to suggest that it is not, in fact, true. Some of the most vivid evidence can be delved out of the evolving meanings and uses of words – for language is the most intimate instrument of consciousness.[10] But it is also very apparent in the struggle, already mentioned, to acquire a new experience of, and relation to, motion. Butterfield's 'new feeling for things' was the result of an actual evolutionary change in human consciousness.

It was a change which was essential to come to a fuller experience of individuality. But it was also a kind of death, which closed the doors on an earlier, more direct awareness of a spiritual world, a world where that which we experience in the phenomena of organism and imagination, and which Goethe began to perceive more clearly with the *Urpflanze*, are manifest as active spiritual beings. The doors were already closing in Plato's time. When Socrates speaks, in the dialogue with Meno, of 'recollection' as the way to knowledge of what virtue is, he was referring to an experience which was very concrete at the time, but is abstract to us. For 'recollection' meant looking back to the experiences of the soul before birth, to the general experience of mankind of earlier times, and to the revelations still transmitted by inspired priests and seers who still commanded faculties which most had lost. Such 'recollection' revealed a spiritual world; 'virtue' was to live harmoniously as an organic member of this world; 'sin' was to be sundered from it.

This sundering has allowed us to grow into a strong experience of our individual selves, an experience in which the conviction of the value and rights of the individual is rooted. But if we are sundered for too long, or too completely, from the world of spiritual realities, we shall know only death.

The physical sciences have entered the unseen world of atoms with the help of physical instruments, artificial sense organs for moving around in it. But the scientific instrument for entering into the unseen realities which express themselves in the living world can only be man himself. The urgent, almost desperate demands which are being made of man by modern science and technology are really demands for an extension of human consciousness – an extension into realms where we shall find the forces and the understanding necessary to balance and manage those released by the atom-based sciences.

Such a step is needed, above all, to manage those aspects of medical and biological technology which are pressing hardest on what we call individual rights. If these rights are to acquire concrete meaning, they must be rooted in real knowledge of the meanings of human lives. An atomistic analysis of a life, of a biography, can only make it meaningless. No *single* event in any person's life can make sense except in relation to all the others. To see the meaning of a life, it must be seen as a whole, as a work of art. And when it is so seen, it begins to speak to the imagination of forces working into it which we cannot study scientifically either with physical instruments or with our ordinary everyday consciousness.

Light is thrown on the realities behind these forces in Steiner's account of reincarnation and the workings of destiny.[11] His descriptions spring, essentially, from an extension of the Goethean method to human beings and human lives; he was able to study precisely how a human life is both the fruit of a past incarnation and the seed for a future one. Much of what he says may be difficult for the modern mind to *believe*. But it is not particularly difficult to *understand*. For if one begins to see meaning in a human life, it is often apparent that the meaning is not complete. One is only seeing part of the work of art; it is a work which cannot have begun at birth, and will not end at death. One sees at most· one movement in an unfolding symphony, whose true form will only emerge as new movements are added.

There are a number of special difficulties in discussing the idea of reincarnation and destiny in the present age. But a central problem lies in the Hamlet-like experience of modern people whereby they feel separated and estranged from their environment. Just because this environment seems so separate, it is difficult to find a meaning in it which is related to the inner impulses and self-awareness of the individual. The scientist uncovers merely a series of impersonal and universal natural laws, which by their very nature cannot be related to what is experienced uniquely and personally within each human being.

Yet there seems to be at work in modern life a contrary, almost instinctive feeling, that the meaning of individual existence is only discoverable in relation to the lives of other individuals. A person may learn something about himself by introspection – but a deeper self knowledge can come only through his relationship during life with others. This theme preoccupies many modern novelists (for example Iris Murdoch).

Such writers sometimes seem to be saying that what happens to a person is as much a part of his individuality as what he consciously knows of himself and tries to achieve. The modern problem is to discover in such happenings – the events and people encountered without conscious decision – anything more than chance. But it is just to such events and encounters that Rudolf Steiner points as important phenomena in which quite different laws can be glimpsed – spiritual laws at work in personal human destinies and evolution. These laws are hidden because they work not in human thoughts but in human deeds, in that realm of the human being – the will – of which we are least conscious.

After some crucial personal encounter or event, one may look back and consider how many things could have happened to prevent it. Out of such a retrospect may be born some awareness that the individual's biography is far from being the result of chance – he has found his way, through countless other possibilities, to the encounters which are, in a sense, part of himself, the events which belong to him.

Just as a thought springs to full life only through the meeting of an inner concept with an outer percept, so the full meaning of an individual's biography unfolds in the interplay of inner impulse meeting outer event. But in both processes we are normally unconscious of the hidden wisdom in the will which orders these meetings. We do not know how we bring the proper concept to meet a particular percept (and sometimes we make mistakes and disorder results). Nor are we normally aware of how our feet have guided us to the encounters appropriate to ourselves.

A sense for the laws at work in this process may awaken in anyone who is alert and observant, although there are obviously the richest possibilities for illusion and self-deception. But to perceive spiritual laws clearly, we need a deeper but exact spiritual vision.

It can serve little purpose to debate whether reincarnation is a useful, or a convincing *theory*. The issue is whether it is a fact. If it is a fact, it is the central fact about the human individuality, and must place all the human problems now being generated by science and technology in a new light. And it is also obvious that such a fact can never be established by physical investigation or embraced by the atomic hypothesis. It cannot, in fact, be fully established without an extension of human consciousness into a realm where it can be perceived as a reality.

The problem is to see the way into this realm, and then to travel it. If it is to be a path to new knowledge, it must be travelled scientifically, carrying the objectivity and independence which the scientific age has brought. Steiner's life work was to indicate the way and offer help for the journey. This is why he spoke of a 'spiritual science' to help humanity find Anthroposophia, a wisdom of man.

1968

[1] *Fortune*, September, 1964.

[2] Paul R. Zilsel, *Bulletin of the Atomic Scientists*, April 1964, p. 28.

[3] Herbert Butterfield, *The Origins of Modern Science*, p. 118. (G. Bell and Sons, London, 1958.)

[4] See Ernst Lehrs, *Man or Matter*, pp.3off. (Faber and Faber, 1951.)

[5] O. Barfield, *Saving The Appearances*, pp. 4off. (Faber, 1957.)

[6] See A. Koestler, *The Sleepwalkers*, p. 94. (Hutchinson, 1959.)

[7] Barfield, op. cit., p. 55.

[8] Rudolf Steiner, *Introductions to Goethe's scientific works*: see Goethe's *naturwissenschaftliche Schriften (Sonderausgabe sämtlicher Einleitungen aus Kürschners 'Deutscher National-Litteratur', Goethes Werke)*. Rudolf Steiner Nachlassverwaltung, 1949.

Also: *Grundlinien einer Erkenntnistheorie der Goetheschen Weltanschauung*: Rudolf Steiner Nachlassverwaltung, 1960 and *Goethes Weltanschauung*: Rudolf Steiner Nachlassverwaltung, 1963.

[9] E. Lehrs, op. cit., pp. 65ff.

[10] O. Barfield, *History in English Words*. (Faber, 1952; and Wm. B. Eerdmans, 1966); and also: *Poetic Diction*. (Faber.)

[11] Rudolf Steiner, see for example, *Wiederverkörperung und Karma und ihre Bedeutung für die Kultur der Gegenwart*; Rudolf Steiner Nachlassverwaltung, 1959.

Scientific Progress and the Threshold

On a number of occasions when Rudolf Steiner spoke about the first world war, he emphasised that it was part of an evolutionary process – a process certainly not complete when the war ended.

Only by understanding the nature of this process, he said, could men hope to bring some order and harmony into human evolution. Otherwise, civilisation would stumble from one social catastrophe to another.

The second world war was a further such catastrophe, and since then, mankind seems to have been balancing precariously on the brink of still greater disasters. Thus Rudolf Steiner's demand that we should understand contemporary events is more urgent than ever.

Steiner sometimes summed up the essence of the situation by saying that humanity as a whole is beginning to 'cross the Threshold'. (See e.g., *Vergangenheits und Zukunftsimpulse im Sozialen Geschehen*, Dornach, 5-14 April, 1919).[1] It is a simple phrase for a very complex process.

How is this process related to the turbulent events of our time? In the last years of his life, Rudolf Steiner gave, not so much an answer to this question, as an indication of how to answer it. He created the vast carving now in the Goetheanum: the central Christ figure stands upright, holding Ahriman and Lucifer in a dynamic balance, as though to create a central space where the human individual can breathe the air of true freedom.

Steiner also called the central figure 'The Representative of Humanity'. The carving makes visible the spiritual ideal to which humanity must hold while crossing the Threshold. The essence of this ideal is the creation of a central realm where the human individual can stand upright and experience freedom, while the forces of Lucifer and Ahriman are held in balance. This realm can be sustained only with the help of the 'Sun of Christ' (in the words of the Foundation Stone verse). It is a realm within the human soul – but in the lectures cited above Steiner says that as humanity crosses the threshold, the soul will need the support of a corresponding balance in outer social forms.

Behind many of the tumultuous events of today, one can discern a kind of battle swirling round this central realm, both within individuals and in society. In these same lectures, Rudolf Steiner describes the first world war as a symptom of just such a struggle.

He traces the conflict back to the time of Goethe and Schiller, when the culture of central Europe achieved a certain flowering. But the Goethean impulses were not truly recognised and taken up by the world at large, and the culture began to decline. Behind this decline, and to an important extent responsible for it, was a kind of alliance between certain Ahrimanic and Luciferic influences.

Steiner describes how the Luciferic impulses were at work, in particular, in the great houses of the landed aristocracy of central Europe, typified by the house Hapsburg. In this aristocracy there still lived unchristianised forces from the old central Europe, before the forests were cleared. In contrast, powerful Ahrimanic impulses were active in the industrial revolution, with its emerging proletariat and expanding factory towns.

It is an alliance between these Ahrimanic and Luciferic streams which has gradually eroded the Goethean culture and destroyed the old central Europe. This destruction has reached a certain climax in our century. Steiner describes the first world war as part of this destructive process, and a direct outcome of an 'alliance' between the impulses at work in the old landed aristocracy and in the new industrial society.

Today, we can look back on the second world war as a further act in this drama. For the effect of this convulsion was to carry the destruction of central Europe to a certain conclusion. Hitler's declared intention was to create a kind of super-Central Europe. But the outcome of his actions was the establishment of the Iron Curtain. The war ended with the old Central Europe sliced in two, and the two halves have been drawn apart into the orbits of Moscow and Washington.

But, as the old Central Europe declined, a new impulse was born in it: Rudolf Steiner brought Spiritual Science into the world. The cultural impulses of Goethe and Schiller were reborn in a new form, not as part of a geographically limited culture, but as the starting-point of a new culture for mankind as a whole.

At the same time, there are signs that the Luciferic-Ahrimanic alliance which eroded Goethean culture is manifesting in new forms, which we must learn to recognise. In particular, I believe that the 'alliance' is coming to expression in the remarkable linking of science and industry which is so characteristic of the past few decades, and which is having such far-reaching effects on our society. The main purpose of this essay is to develop this suggestion.

*   *   *

Until recently, science was still a remote, largely academic activity, pursued by small numbers of scholarly men. Its ideal was pure knowledge, understanding of nature for its own sake.

In Britain, this tradition of academic science continues to be remarkably strong. The most brilliant scientists still tend to gather in universities and pursue 'pure' research, even though the facilities and the pay may be relatively poor. The pure scientists are widely regarded – and often regard themselves – as the aristocracy of the scientific community.

In contrast, applied scientists and engineers tend to be regarded as a kind of proletariat of science. Although engineering is now a highly scientific profession, the word 'engineer' still vaguely suggests a man with a spanner and dirty blue overalls, 'good with his hands' but not specially good with his head.

'Pure' science has created a vast conceptual edifice, a grandiose picture of the world which has a certain shining splendour. It conveys the impression that there are very few dark corners of ignorance left, and that these will soon be banished. But it is undoubtedly a Luciferic light that conveys this god-like sensation of understanding almost everything.

The technologist, by contrast, is interested in scientific concepts not for their elegance or beauty, but for their utility. He is less concerned to understand the world than to control it. He judges a theory by the ease with which it can be tested in practice and set to work. It matters little whether an idea is 'true' so long as it is useful. This habit of regarding ideas as a source of power rather than of understanding bears the unmistakeable signature of Ahriman.

During the last thirty years, however, science and technology have entered an increasingly intimate alliance. The modern engineer has become highly dependent on the findings of laboratory research, while the 'pure' scientists, in demanding ever more elaborate equipment, are increasingly dependent on first-class engineering.

Thus the scientific technology which is now gathering speed has emerged from a fusion between two originally very different streams: the 'disinterested' pure scientists, rooted in the universities, and the 'practical' engineers, descendants of the old craftsmen whose work has been transformed by the industrial revolution. It is a fusion of forces that start from the head with forces that originate in the will.

This fusion has been stimulated, almost created, by social and political events of the twentieth century. This becomes particularly clear if one examines two particular developments, the atomic bomb

– which emerged from 'pure' science – and the rocket missile, which emerged from advanced engineering.

During the first decades of this century, the major adventure of pure science was the dissection of matter into atoms and sub-atomic particles. This work was centred almost entirely in Europe, especially in Copenhagen, Cambridge, Göttingen, Berlin, Vienna, Rome and Paris.

When one reads of the life of atomic physicists at these centres during the 1920s, one is reminded a little of the cultural flowering in the time of Goethe. They formed an idealistic international community, burning with enthusiasm and richly endowed with remarkable individuals.

The rise of Hitler cast a shadow over their lives, for many – including Albert Einstein – were Jews, and were forced to flee. With Einstein's departure for America, it was widely felt that the centre of gravity of science had moved from Central Europe to the West.

The crucial discoveries which led to the release of atomic energy were made towards the end of 1938, just as Europe was heading into war. The wartime atmosphere of fear and distrust then provided precisely the right atmosphere for translating these academic discoveries into practice – even though many of the scientists involved had begun to realise what this would imply.

The war-time Manhattan Project for developing the bomb brought together, for the first time, some of the most outstanding physicists and some of the best engineers in the world. The 'aristocrats' of science found themselves allied with the driving energies of practical men of action, engineers and generals.

It is nevertheless true to say that in the release of atomic energy, the *conceptual* advances were primary; translating the concepts into practice was secondary. The atomic bomb is an 'aristocratic' achievement.

In contrast, the giant rockets, which were also pioneered in wartime, when German engineers developed the V-2, are primarily achievements of technology. They embody few new concepts but a great deal of 'know-how'. They call for a kind of industrialised craftsmanship, and individuals have emerged with a certain genius for making these complex machines work.

Since the war, these two products – the most refined products of 'pure' science and of engineering respectively – have themselves become allied. The linking of rocket and atomic bomb has created the weapon which dominates the military and political scene today.

It is just this combination which sustains the Iron Curtain, and produces a kind of paralysis across Central Europe. The alliance between science and technology stimulated in particular by the activities of Hitler, has rigidified the division of Central Europe.

But the alliance has also released a surge of new discovery and invention which is profoundly affecting society. In this connection, it is worth looking more closely at the effects of rockets and atomic energy, for they reveal a curious and instructive polarity.

When an atomic bomb explodes, it produces a fireball which shines with a kind of terrible glory. It is as though something of the Luciferic light which illumines the concepts behind it should shine forth directly for a brief moment. In its outward aspect, the atomic bomb can seem an inspiration of Lucifer.

Yet in the way it is used, and in its consequences, it is entirely the instrument of Ahriman. It is the most total instrument of power ever wielded by man. One may feel that its by-products, the radio-active debris, have an ageing effect on the earth, and that 'fall-out' is a kind of physical counterpart of the fear which these weapons inspire. It has given rise to new military strategies – the 'balance of terror', 'graduated deterrence', etc. – which have a kind of mechanical but totally inhuman logic. The end – 'defending freedom' – is held to justify the means – almost complete mutual destruction.

With the large rockets, the situation is reversed in a curious way. In their outward aspect, these devices appear as a wholly Ahrimanic inspiration. They combine a fantastic yet controlled power in their engines with a cold electronic 'brain' in their guidance systems. A rocket engine looks like a kind of mechanical digestive tract, which swallows fuel at a furious rate and produces great jets of flame, like a violent impulse of will, to drive the rocket upwards. In the nose, mechanical eyes and feelers peer into the sky, sense the movements of acceleration, and set the machine precisely on course.

Yet the use of rockets for space exploration is impelled by a child-like but burning enthusiasm. The rocket engineers see the exploration of space as a vast new step in the evolution of man, which will establish him as master beyond the limits of his planet. It is almost a religious impulse – to make man a kind of god – which fires the space enthusiasts.

This child-like enthusiasm is particularly apparent in the Russian approach to space exploration. Eminent Russian Academicians will indulge in flights of futuristic speculation which make western academic scientists squirm inwardly.

The machinery of the Soviet State, with its tendency to centralised authority and its emphasis on groups rather than on individuals, clearly derives from an Ahrimanic impulse. But this has been grafted, like a kind of mechanical armour, on to a people whose inward impulses are deeply religious – a religiosity which Lucifer can attempt to lead astray.

In America, there is in some respects an opposite situation. The outward ideals of American society are treated almost as religious principles. 'Freedom' and 'democracy' are ultimate virtues, 'Communism' is totally evil. Yet America has pioneered mass-production, developed mass-persuasion by advertising and propaganda to a fine art, and elevated mechanical efficiency into a major virtue. The most powerful Ahrimanic impulses are clearly at work within American society.

The aim of these remarks is not to criticise American or Russian society, but to underline what seems to be a fundamental characteristic of the Luciferic-Ahrimanic 'alliance'. Wherever the one impulse is more outward, the other is to be found working more inwardly, and *vice versa*. Let us now consider where this alliance, in so far as it is expressed in scientific technology, may be leading.

* * *

The triumph of pure science (the release of atomic energy) and the triumph of engineering (the exploration of space) have transformed the status of science in the eyes of politicians the world over. Science, both pure and applied, is now seen as the major source of power, both military and economic. The national purse strings are wide open, and scientists are allied with massive industrial resources as never before.

This is why the atomic physicists can plan and build vast machines such as the 'synchrotrons' near Geneva and at Brookhaven in America, for probing still further into the anatomy of matter.

Since the 1940s, atomic physics has become bewilderingly complex, and has raised more new problems than it has solved. But there are signs that the next five years will bring important new developments, in which the still vaster machines now being planned will play a part.

One of the most remarkable facts about atomic physics is that although it is now dealing with entities of almost unimaginable smallness, and intervals of time where a millionth of a second seems as long as a day in ordinary life, new facets of this 'universe within' are continually opening up. Atomic research is a kind of exploration into the 'infinities within'.

This exploration coincides with an opposite one – the immense effort to break out into space and explore the planetary system. But whereas atomic research must wait on new concepts to make progress, space research is dependent on new technology.

Yet here there is a remarkable paradox. For it is the effort which is apparently centred in the conceptual life which has released mighty physical forces; while the effort which is centred in technology is producing considerable conceptual upheavals.

Space research has begun to change our picture of the universe in quite far-reaching ways. The nineteenth century universe was dark, cold and silent. Hot balls of gas were scattered through this space, and some of them were circled by a few lumps of rock called planets.

Since then, but especially in the past five years, space research has been rapidly filling this 'void' with all kinds of surging, interweaving forces.

The focus of attention is now the 'magnetosphere' – a volume of space surrounding the earth where the earth's magnetic field predominates. It is found to be egg-shaped, and it interacts, especially at its outer surface, in a very sensitive way, to influences from the sun. The earth, with its magnetosphere, is now pictured as enfolded within the atmosphere of the sun, and as living in a complex community with it.

The understanding of this interrelationship is only in its beginnings – but it belongs to the approach to the Threshold. The time is passing when humanity needed the experience of total isolation in the universe.

Space research is today abolishing this isolation in purely physical terms, and it seems certain to cause similar upheavals in scientific ideas about the nature of the moon, the planets, and perhaps even the stars.

The efforts to send men into space and to the moon may produce the most far-reaching conceptual upheavals of all. There are already some small signs that men orbiting the earth experience changes in their perceptions. Two of the American astronauts have reported what seems to be a greatly enhanced acuity of vision, which is not so far explained in ordinary terms. Such experiences may be dismissed as hallucinations. But if ventures further into space have more far-reaching effects on consciousness, the scientific picture of the human mind could be profoundly changed. At present, ideas about consciousness have a nineteenth century character – static, mechanical, unchanging.

Meanwhile, one must ask what may emerge from the exploration into the 'infinities within'. This must be entirely speculative – but I think one should be prepared for the possibility that atomic energy is not the last of the forces to be released from this exploration into matter. There are indeed hints in some of Rudolf Steiner's writings of far-reaching discoveries still to come. (See, for instance, the lecture, *Was tut der Engel in unserem Astralleib?* (Zürich, 9 October, 1919).[2]

*   *   *

Rudolf Steiner sometimes spoke with great earnestness of the danger that mankind could cross the Threshold without becoming aware of the fact. Yet this is just what the scientific-technological alliance could help to achieve. For it is beginning to reveal spiritual realities in such a way that they are interpreted by men in purely material terms. Through space research, mankind is now becoming aware, for instance, that the earth is intimately interwoven with the rest of the universe. Through atomic research, he is becoming aware that thoughts – concepts – can release mighty forces. Yet the 'thoughts' which release atomic energy are held to be 'neutral,' no different from thoughts about the familiar world of nature we perceive with our senses; and the forces of the 'magnetosphere' are regarded as fundamentally the same as those found at ground level.

In *The Spiritual Guidance of Mankind*, Rudolf Steiner describes how humanity must cross the threshold in a two-fold way. During life, most people can survey only the waking hours between birth and death. Crossing the threshold means, in a certain way, beginning to survey the realms before birth and after death. It is striking that science and technology are bringing a kind of caricatured encounter with these two thresholds.

The great effort of applied science and technology to explore space is impelled by a Luciferic dream, which urges man to find his way into those shining realms from which he descended at birth. It is an effort to return to 'the heavens'.

The spacemen crouch in their curious womb-like capsules and undergo a kind of initiation. One can even suspect that these space flights include a physical caricature of spiritual ordeals. Is it far-fetched to see the experience of greatly enhanced gravity during the initial acceleration, so that each part of the body weighs four or five times more than normal, as a kind of ordeal by earth? Then, suddenly, the astronaut is floating weightless, as though in a vast ocean, undergoing an 'ordeal by water'. As he circles the earth, he must also keep control of his soul life, hold back fear, and calmly observe what is happening. He must survive a trial in the astral-soul element, an ordeal by 'air'. His 'initiation' is completed with an 'ordeal by fire', as he plunges back into the earth's atmosphere and survives the heat of re-entry.

In contrast, the emergence of atomic energy, the product of 'pure' science, has brought mankind as a whole face-to-face with death. Until now, each individual had to come to terms with his own forthcoming death. Today, atomic weapons force men to contemplate the possibility of the death of humanity. But this, too, is a caricature of what should be a spiritual process. In connection precisely with the destruction of Goethean culture in Central Europe, Rudolf Steiner said that in order to cross the Threshold, mankind must undergo a spiritual death, so that something new may be born.

It is the aim of the Luciferic-Ahrimanic 'alliance' to divert mankind's attention from a real spiritual evolution which he is embarking on, so that he crosses the Threshold unawares. Instead of penetrating spiritually beyond death and before birth, his attention is being diverted by spectres of physical death and dreams of a mechanical exploration of the heavens.

Why is it that pure science brings a kind of encounter with death, while applied science generates an urge to escape from the earth?

In a Christmas lecture, *Die Zwei Weihnachtsverkündigungen*[3] (1.1.21) Rudolf Steiner describes the origins of the faculties now used for pure and applied science. The mathematical thinking of today, he says, derives from the clairvoyant faculties used by the Three Kings to perceive the approaching birth of the Christ. They were faculties on which a true astrology was based, so that the sages from the East could look outwards at the stars and perceive the spiritual realities working behind them. Today, Rudolf Steiner says, these faculties manifest as a purely inward ability to think mathematically. Pure science, mathematical science, is thus a metamorphosed remnant of the mighty faculties of the Kings.

The Shepherds, unlike the Kings, received their summons to the Nativity while asleep. Rudolf Steiner tells us that they possessed clairvoyant faculties connected more with the metabolic pole of man, so that, looking inwards and downwards, they drew their visions from a deep connection with the earth.

These faculties manifest today in all materialistic experiment. Technology and applied science, with the outward-going urge to manipulate the earth, make use of a metamorphosed remnant of the faculties of the Shepherds.

In the Oberufer Christmas plays, the Kings are usually represented as two older men and one younger; the Shepherds, in contrast, include two younger and one older.

This indicates how the spiritual stream represented by the Kings, who draw their wisdom from the stars, is more connected with the forces of old age. While the Shepherds, who call on the earth-mother for their knowledge, are more linked with the forces of youth.

Today, the pure scientists, who have inherited a remnant of the faculties of the Kings, are leading mankind towards a materialistic encounter with death, towards the threshold which lies at the end of human life. While the technologists, using metamorphosed Shepherd faculties, are striving with child-like enthusiasm to carry mankind into the heavens, using a kind of mechanical womb. This caricatured initiation threatens to distract attention from a spiritual crossing of the Threshold into the worlds which lie before birth, and may bring great conceptual confusion about the nature of extraterrestrial realms, the moon, planets and stars.

This may help us to understand Rudolf Steiner's statement, in the Christmas lecture quoted above, that the pre-Christian Shepherds and Kings faculties work today in opposite directions. Before the Mystery of Golgotha, it was the Kings who were concerned with the stars. And they could use their faculties to perceive the forces working from the stars down on to the earth, the forces which lead souls from the heavens into earthly incarnation. Thus they could see the 'Star' of their previous spiritual teacher, Zarathustra, as it approached the earth for its most important incarnation.

Today the faculties of the Kings work inwards, carrying human thought deep into matter, where death-bringing forces are encountered.

The Shepherds' faculties were drawn from deep within the human being, and revealed something of the life of the etheric body of the earth. But today the remnants of these forces are urging mankind to escape the earth and explore the stars – although in a purely physical way.

It is clear enough that in this great metamorphosis of the King-faculties to mathematical thinking, and of Shepherd-faculties to the instincts of applied science, much has been lost. For the Kings were above all *wise*, while the Shepherds possessed great powers of reverence and devotion.

Pure science today is a structure of knowledge without wisdom. Indeed, the whole concept of wisdom has become very dim. But even now, the word still implies the *passage of time*, a certain period of ripening.

It is characteristic of modern science that there is no place for such ripening processes in its activities. A scientist who has an idea hastens to publish it, even in the most tentative form, so that it may be registered as 'his', and credited to his academic account.

The haste and pressure which dominate even the 'purest' science today ensure that new theories and ideas for experiments are poured into the world without considering their implications.

Applied science, on the other hand, often displays a certain brutality – the opposite of reverence and devotion. There is something
breathtaking about a huge machine like a jet engine. But in such a
machine, metals and other materials are placed under strains which
would have instantaneously shattered the gentler machines of earlier
times.

In the application of science to agriculture, pest-control and the
like, a similar brutality is often apparent. And in medical and surgical
experiments, it is now becoming possible to manipulate and interfere with living processes in unprecedented ways. Scientists often
feel instinctively that there are limits beyond which such interference
may not go. But lacking the soul-forces of devotion and reverence,
such qualms seldom advance to a clear perception of moral realities,
and are easily dissected by intellectual arguments.

It is a central characteristic of Rudolf Steiner's spiritual science
that it calls for both reverence and wisdom. It can come alive in the
soul only when supported by these two forces. Wisdom is the fruit
of meditation – and the essence of meditation is repetition over a
period of time. Concepts which are released too soon into the world
cannot further the evolution of humanity; but if they are allowed to
grow old in the right way, they can mature into a kingly wisdom.

In *Knowledge of the Higher Worlds*, however, Rudolf Steiner emphasises that every step in knowledge must be accompanied by three
steps in morality. The moral path begins, so to speak, with reverence
and devotion. Rudolf Steiner has emphasised their special importance in childhood for the development of the moral life later on.

If pure science and applied science are to help humanity to cross
the Threshold, they must summon these two qualities – wisdom
and reverence – to their aid. These are the forces which can dissolve
and redeem the Luciferic-Ahrimanic alliance which is now at work
in such subtle and complex ways within scientific thinking and scientific doing.

This fact is summed up by Rudolf Steiner in the final lines of the
Foundation Stone Meditation. The Light which enlightens the wise
heads of Kings can mature knowledge into wisdom. The Light
which brings warmth to simple Shepherds' hearts can purify the will-
forces of childhood, so that they become the basis of moral deeds.

The last lines of the Meditation are a prayer that this Light should
imbue our hearts and heads, so that our deeds on earth may bear
fruit, so that human evolution may follow the right path.

In his book on the Foundation Stone, Zeylmans van Emmichoven
has described how in this fourth section of the Meditation there is a
metamorphosis of the Christ statue which was mentioned at the
beginning of this essay.[4]

The statue shows the Representative of Humanity holding the Luciferic and Ahrimanic beings apart in a dynamic balance, so that they can no longer form an alliance. They can act only so that their forces can be transformed through the Light Divine, the Sun of Christ, into positive fruits for the evolution of humanity.

In the Meditation, Ahriman and Lucifer are not mentioned, for as Dr. Zeylmans says, they are here, in a sense, already overcome. But the process through which this victory is achieved is explicitly described.

There are thus to be found in the Christ statue and in the Foundation Stone Meditation a profound source of help for meeting the most central and pressing problems of our times. The Meditation can help us understand how the hasty concepts of pure science must be replaced by thoughts which are ripened meditatively into wisdom, so that humanity is not led by Ahriman to a premature and purely physical encounter with death. It shows, too, how warmth of heart is needed to generate reverence for the earth which is the only basis for a truly moral technology. This warmth can redeem the Luciferic dreams of using technology to escape from earth into the eternities of space, and transform them into ideals which can truly serve the spiritual realities of man's nature and his destiny on earth.

1964

---

[1] Six lectures, of which only the fifth has been translated, under the title of *Spiritual Emptiness and Social Life*, in the *Golden Blade*, 1954.

[2] *The Work of the Angels in Man's Astral Body* (Rudolf Steiner Press).

[3] Translated in the collection of eight lectures on *Christmas* (Rudolf Steiner Press).

[4] *Der Grundstein*, F.W. Zeylmans van Emmichoven, 2nd ed., Verlag Freies Geistesleben, Stuttgart, 1962. A translation has lately been published by the Rudolf Steiner Press.

Responsibility in Science
(Based on an original lecture given to a Wrekin Trust Conference on Mystics and Scientists)

Spiritual disciplines have always been coupled with moral disciplines. But the moral life of a scientist seems to exist in a separate compartment from the intellectual life which he uses for his science.

It will be a very far-reaching thing if science comes to see the pre-scientific descriptions of the universe embodied in various religious and spiritual traditions as in some way or other correct. But it will be of equal or greater importance if we thereby come to see the practice of science as a spiritual discipline, which cannot much longer be separated from questions of moral discipline.

There are three ways in which human beings function: cognitive, affective and motor. In other words, we think, we feel and we act. This trinity of functions has a relationship to three great traditional ideals of truth, beauty and goodness. As thinkers, we seek truth; beauty and ugliness engage our feelings; goodness and badness we look for in deeds.

In some way or other, science has to do with truth. But beauty and goodness do not seem to be its concern, in any fundamental sense. Increasingly, we have come to regard these qualities as 'subjective', the private concern of individuals. I find Bach beautiful. You go for Pink Floyd. We just have different tastes. It is all right for cannibals to eat one another, but not for stockbrokers. What is right for you is not necessarily right for me. On the other hand, the fact that twice two makes four is 'science' and therefore true for all of us.

Scientific activity is based on the conviction, seldom made explicit, that human beings can participate in truth, in a universal reality, through their common powers of cognition. We need to look at this conviction a little more carefully, because it leads into a curious state of affairs.

This conference may have an unorthodox theme, but its form is conventional. There is an audience, and a succession of speakers. There are questions and answers, and some discussion. Through these activities, we hope to achieve some 'meeting of minds'. Audi ences listen to speakers in the expectation that they will understand at least something of what is being said. The aim of speakers is to be understood, at least to some degree. What a speaker wants to say exists, to begin with, in his mind, and ends up living in the minds of his audience, who thereby come to participate in something that a few minutes before was part of the speaker's inner life.

I hope this sounds like a commonsense description of what happens at conferences. But we should notice that it begs a number of philosophical and scientific questions, and certain kinds of scientist could not possibly go along with me in what I have said. Some scientists will allow us to talk about 'minds' in a loose kind of way, but these are usually imagined as somehow firmly attached to brain processes. At conferences, there is no meeting of brains. These remain firmly isolated in the skulls of their owners. So at best, one can imagine that in some way, by speaking, a lecturer awakens copies of his own brain patterns in those of his listeners.

However, a more rigorous school of thought would not allow talk of minds at all. They are unobservable and therefore inadmissable into respectable scientific discourse. Alternatively they do not exist. I once had a long conversation with a very distinguished behaviourist. I was trying to find out whether he was merely arguing that we can't discuss minds because we don't know how to study them scientifically – a self-imposed limitation which I could respect – or whether he was convinced that minds don't exist at all. He ended the conversation with a sight and the plaintive remark: "Mr. Davy, you should not imagine we've been 'having a conversation', or 'exchanging ideas'. We've just been behaving."

This is an expression of a very odd situation. We no longer find, in our scientific culture, much confidence that there are universal realities to be found in beauty and goodness. These spheres of our experience seem to become more and more contingent and personal. But we base a great deal of our lives on the conviction that we can participate in one world of reality through our powers of cognition. At the same time, one line of scientific endeavour, rigorously pursued, would seem to undermine this conviction.

By the end of the nineteenth century, science had somehow worked its way into a view of the world in which there isn't really any place left for scientists (or for anybody). The ultimate constitution of the universe was conceived as material and impersonal. Atoms don't think (let alone appreciate Bach). They have no inner life. They are subject to impersonal laws. In other words, the laws have no 'inwardness' either.

Such a description is a consequence of the famous Cartesian

dichotomy. Descartes divided the world into *Res Cogitans*, and *Res Extensa*, or what we might now call mind and matter. This was the essential basis for the idea of the scientist as the 'detached observer'. The scientific mind is supposed to extract itself from the more 'subjective' aspects of the scientist's own existence, such as his feelings and his way of life, and to 'observe' the universe. As an onlooker, he observes the outsides of things, the 'primary' qualities of position and motion etc. Extended to real, everyday life, this would have bizarre consequences. When we see a friend smile, we take the gesture, in our loose and unscientific way, as indicating something of our friend's inner life, his feelings of pleasure, or his intention to be nice to us. But the truly detached observer would see a widening of the mouth aperture, accompanied by the appearance of a variety of dermal indentations (i.e. wrinkles). Extensive and detailed research could then be done on the contractions of facial musculature involved, and the accompanying activity in the nervous system. For the same truly detached observer, conferences like this one must consist of playing out conditioned behaviour patterns, such as opening and closing our mouths in certain ways.

Such ways of thinking lead, rather obviously, into a waste land. Described in this crude way, they seem a bit mad. I don't see how such a view can be consistently lived. The most rigorous behaviourists often love their children, and the one I mentioned earlier is known to exhibit piano playing behaviour of quite a high standard. It may even be that he actually enjoys it.

The 'detached observer' does indeed permeate our culture, like a damp fog. We may call the effects 'alienation' , or worry about the 'problem of communication'. Yet we deny this description of the universe in each moment that we attempt a 'meeting of minds' . The extraordinarily important thing that is now happening is that developments in science itself, and particularly at the frontiers of physics, are impelling us to abandon this concept of the 'detached observer'. What will replace it is still difficult to conceive or articulate. But some kind of dissolution of the 'mind-matter' dichotomy seems inevitable. For one thing, it has become rather obvious, in many fields of research, that what we see cannot be separated from what we think. The subatomic world manifests as particles when we think about it as particles and design our experiments accordingly. It manifests as waves when we think of it as waves.

It is worth noticing that in certain ways, this is rather more like real life than the world of the strict behaviourist. If I look for a needle on the floor, I am more likely to see it if I have a picture of a needle in my mind rather than of a cotton reel. How I look at my friend affects how he behaves, and *vice versa*. Our relationships to things are as real and significant as the 'things' themselves.

Many scientific explorations are leading towards ways of describing the universe and our situation in it which seem rather more like those of mystical and spiritual traditions of the past than the pioneers of quantum physics could possibly have foreseen.

Perhaps the simplest way of entering into these older descriptions is to realise that it was taken for granted that what we now call our 'inner' experience is not totally separate, private, bound up with a material brain or organism, but that it is – or can be – 'participatory' in universal realities.

It is less often pointed out that this sense of 'participation' – which we might very well call 'mystical', since we can give no 'objective' scientific account of what we really mean – persists in our life of cognition, whenever we are convinced that through meeting and talking we can achieve some 'meeting of minds', a participation in one truth that transcends our individually limited perspectives.

Now I want to come to a crucial point. Let us grant that in some still rather embryonic way, we are beginning to know that in cognition, we do not simply think about the world while floating in some detached and separate private space, but that we somehow participate in aspects of reality. We may go on to wonder whether we should not therefore begin to imagine the universe as more like mind rather than 'matter' (however we may now imagine this). However this may be, I suggest that we will then be confronted with some still more far-reaching issues. In the first place, if we participate in the universe in our thinking, our thoughts are not entirely our private affair. Do we not have to become, in some way, responsible for them? This is linked with what is probably a still less familiar kind of question in our culture: If in our inner life, as knowers, we participate in reality in a way which we had lost sight of until very recently – even if we still live as though it were so – must we not also recognise that we participate in reality in our affective and motor functions also, in our feelings and will?

It is easy to see that we have not completely lost sight of a sense of such participation, however dim and ill-defined. Indeed we often feel that a 'meeting of hearts', or a shared striving, brings a more fundamental togetherness than a meeting of minds. Yet we usually imagine such a unity as the concern of those individuals and groups concerned, whereas in the search for truth, we retain some conviction that what we find is, or should be, valid for all human beings.

The idea of a universal aesthetic or moral order makes us feel uneasy. Are we being asked to submit our personal lives to a spiritual or moral authority? If we find ourselves rediscovering the spiritual life of the past, we shall have to face this too. There was no question but that all human beings were expected to live according to laws not only of knowledge, but of feeling and moral impulse. Thse may have been dispensed by a guru, an institutionalised church, or by some kind of direct guidance or revelation. But there was no question of a 'private' life of feeling and will. All such attachment to self brought separation from God. If we are going to engage in a serious consideration of science in relation to the spiritual life of the past, we shall meet this fundamental issue of freedom and authority. It will begin to become visible for many modern people once they begin to follow up the possibility that in some sense or other our 'private' life of thought, feeling and will is not as separate and detached from the realities of the universe as we have had the habit of believing.

All the pure forms of spiritual teaching from the past have emphasised that progress in understanding, or in spiritual experience, must be accompanied by a moral discipline. According to Pathanjali, the essential prerequisite for real yoga, is *yama*: the pupil must strive to put aside violence, theft, covetousness, lying and incontinence. Why? Simply in order to add a little moral uplift? Just because we have come to feel that the moral life is a private affair, our sense of the significance of *yama* tends to be feeble. It is commonplace nowadays for people to embark on all kinds of spiritual practices, in search of self-improvements or unusual experiences of various kinds, with little or no systematic attention to *yama*.

Having said earlier that scientific progress and moral progress seem nowadays to be worlds apart, we should acknowledge nevertheless that science is guided by a definite moral code, assumed by most and therefore seldom spelled out. Interestingly, the code shares some of the traditional qualitites of *yama*. For example, scientists must not tell lies. Faking results leads in effect to expulsion from the scientific community. Theft is also frowned on, although harder to detect. It is understood that you do not borrow ideas or methods from others without acknowledgement and thanks. But the other virtues of *yama* might receive more attention: public covetousness – of a Nobel prize, a knighthood, or even priority of discovery – is frowned upon, but is recognised nevertheless as a powerful driving force. What about incontinence? The pressure to publish quantity rather than quality is recognised as prejudicial to good science, but is mainly regarded as something caused by other people – authorities who give grants, control appointments, etc. One quality remains unrecognised by most – violence. Yet it exists, as a kind of buried ruthlessness to achieve results at almost any cost. We may set limits on the violence done to animals, but see no reason to limit what is done to plants and minerals. They don't seem to be sentient. Had we retained any sense of nature as a whole, as a being, as a mother goddess (the origin of the word 'matter' is *mater* – mother), we might of course feel otherwise.

But right at the root of scientific practice is a claim to absolute freedom to think what one likes. One can thus make any hypothesis one likes. The limitations are simply whether 'nature' will dance to our tune when we set up an experiment.

Probing more deeply into nature has led to experimental apparatus of increasing violence, so that experimenters often have to work shielded from it. Think of 'atom-smashers'. We forget that to release this violence, we first had to think it, to plan it. Yet we still assume there is an absolute gulf between whatever propensities to violence we may discover in our own souls, should we care to look, and the forces we release in experiment and technology, which we assume to belong to a different universe, the world 'out there' among the *Res extensa*.

Let us look at the reasons for practising *yama*. It was necessary because spiritual paths lead across a threshold, beyond which the distinction between inner and outer experience no longer holds. A human being crosses such a threshold as a whole, and takes with him what he is. What in his normal waking consciousness has seemed to exist 'within', will become equally describable as his surroundings. Nor will it continue to have the shadowy character of our private thoughts, feelings, and intentions, which enables us to believe that what goes on inside us doesn't much matter as long as our behaviour is outwardly acceptable. The realities of the inner life begin to be experienced in full force as part of the universe.

It is no accident that a kind of threshold crossing is visible in many spheres of life today. We have spoken about the adventure of physics, to some extent. It no longer lives, as in the nineteenth century, in a safe world of impersonal moving objects in empty space. It has broken through into a world of dynamic interacting forces, still barely comprehensible.

But just as physics began to cross its threshold, so did certain schools of pyschology. Psychoanalysis came on the scene, and told us that the part of our inner life which is accessible to ordinary consciousness is itself an outwardness, a surface below which there is an immensely dynamic world, which Alan MacGlashan called 'the savage and beautiful country'. Into it we push a lot of things we don't want to see. It peeps out at us in dreams. And it, too, cannot be looked at, with detachment, as things can, for we experience as reality also what we put into it. It is well known that patients undergoing Freudian analysis start having Freudian dreams. Jungian imagery crops up under a Jungian analyst. For the 'detached observer', this means that psychoanalysis is a hopeless field for investigation. Yet it has long offered one version of the same dilemmas confronting physicists as they peer into the 'unconscious' of matter.

Finally, we should not forget what has happened in art. This has been beautifully explored by Waddington in his book *Behind Appearance* (Edinburgh 1969). We all know how, around the turn of the century, painters quite quickly lost interest in looking at the world and representing it. The impressionists tried to get 'behind' the surface of the outer world. The expressionists delved into the inner world. We live today amid a good deal of confusion, but also in a remarkable adventure.

If the quality of mind and matter is breaking down, it follows that the threshold which we may seek to cross 'inwardly', and that which physics is crossing 'outwardly' through experiment, are in some senses the same threshold, and lead into one world, not two. But what sort of world?

By practising a habit of abstraction and detachment in our cognition, and convincing ourselves that ill-feeling and ill-will are somehow private and contingent aberrations of private and personal life, we have almost lost the ability to consider evil as part of the world in any real or universal sense. We easily imagine that to escape evil, all we need to do is to get away from the more tiresome parts of our personal selves. We tend to expect spiritual or mystical experience to be heavenly, even if the literature makes it very clear that it may just as well be hellish. Psychoanalysis has pointed clearly enough to the demons we carry within. But its epistemology is hazy, so the idea of demons as real inhabitants of the universe does not emerge with any clarity. Not so in most of the great religious and spiritual traditions. There, evil is not just a private affair, but part of the drama of the universe. Mystics have known the miserific as well as the beatific vision. (So, more recently, have the drug trippers). The practice of *yama* was to equip the pupil to hold on to his true humanity as he awoke to a more vivid consciousness of this drama.

I think we should now ask, in all seriousness, what relevance this may have to modern science. It is being argued that physics is penetrating experimentally, and understanding mathematically, the same universe as that known in mystical and religious experience. But it seems to be assumed that physics is thereby finding its way into heaven. There is certainly beauty and harmony in mathematics. But does this really apply to the phenomena?

We have to judge by experience. It is, in the end, our only guide. Classical physics dealt with forces with which we feel at home. They are clearly related to our ordinary physical experience. But a kind of crossing of a threshold began with the discovery of electricity. We began to meet an 'occult' reality, which has very rapidly brought about enormous changes in our civilisation. The naïve and immediate experience of an electric shock is like an encounter with a foreign will. It shakes you and easily overwhelms. It is in no way an illuminating or uplifting experience, although it speaks immediately of strength and power.

In crossing the threshold of matter, we come to radiations undetectable to our senses, but poisonous to our organisms. Radiation sickness is like an attack of acute old age. When the first nuclear device was exploded at Los Alamos in 1944, that remarkable man Robert Oppenheimer was in a bunker, feeling the earth shake, and watching the brilliant light of the fireball illuminate the dark desert. There came into his mind, so it is reported, a phrase from the *Bhagavad Gita*: 'I am become Death, the shatterer of worlds'.

The form of the phrase is significant, coming as it does from a great spiritual text. The detached observer would say: "I have learned to think about and to release a force of nature, which when wrongly used, can kill people". But the *Bhagavad Gita* uses the language of participation: I am become Death. To release atomic energy, the human mind has had to participate, through cognition, in a certain aspect of reality. What determines which aspects of reality we meet?

Physics itself is now telling us that we meet what we seek. We cannot separate our forms of thought from what we discover. So if we meet a force which is death-bringing, we have invited this meeting through our own forms of thinking. I believe we should begin to attend to this very seriously indeed. For if there is one universal habit of mind that has been practised by science for several centuries now, it is the habit of analysis and reduction. Applied to the inanimate world, it may be appropriate enough. It does not fundamentally change the nature of a stone to be divided into two stones. But applied to life, it brings death. If you cut a mouse in half, you do not get two smaller mice, but the divided corpse of a dead mouse.

The whole concept of an 'inanimate object', on which so much of the science of the detached observer is built, will probably prove applicable to only a very limited aspect of reality. It is fairly clear that it will not lead to an adequate biology, let alone to an understanding of human beings but in the microscopic direction, it does not hold very far either. We may meet cells, then molecules, then atoms. But then we cross into a different world, which consists of forces, not things. We discover this world with the help of qualities of thinking deeply permeated by 'death', by reduction and destruction. The door is opened experimentally by radioactive decay, and then by the smashing of atoms. Perhaps we should not be surprised if we find ourselves entering a realm more like hell than heaven.

For this, in all sobriety, is the actual experience of the way a good deal of science seems to be leading. Even as theory, as abstract thought, science has been presenting us with a universe devoid of either beauty or goodness in any sense that can resound with our real human feelings. We are offered enormous vacuums of space, empty vistas of time, black holes, an empire where chance events rule supreme and which ends in a 'heat death'. There is some pattern and order; at some higher mathematical level, the initiated ear may wonder at rarified harmonies. But is there not then a gap between this level of experience, and the actual qualities of what we meet through the ensuing discoveries? Why are we increasingly terrified by our own findings? How is the future of science to be managed and guided? There is much concern and discussion, but we grope.

By comparing scientific work and spiritual traditions, certain questions which are in any case implicit in our scientific culture can begin to develop in important ways. A crucial step is the dissolution of the absolute separateness of subject and object. To see and live the consequences fully will be a very long task. We cannot continue to separate our moral and affective natures from our cognitive, in science or anything else, since what we are will live with increasingly dynamic reality in what we do and what we discover as we 'cross the threshold'. To the *yoga* of physics, we must add a *yama*.

1984

THE EVOLUTION OF EVOLUTION
Evolution: The Hidden Thread

Anyone who studies Rudolf Steiner's teachings will soon realise that
the descriptions he gives of the way man has evolved are not easy
to reconcile with the descriptions given by modern science. The
purpose of this article is to try and indicate how some of the difficulties may be resolved.

When Darwin was born, the *idea* of evolution was already perco-
lating, so to speak, into men's minds. Darwin's great achievement
was to put forward a theory to explain evolution, and to collect a
vast number of facts to back it up. He suggested that evolution
could be brought about by 'natural selection'. That is, any variations
from the 'normal' displayed by an animal would confer on it either
an advantage or a disadvantage in the 'struggle for existence'. Animals with advantageous variations would be more likely to survive
and to pass on their advantages to their offspring. They would, in
other words, be 'selected', and an accumulation of such advantageous characters, in the course of generations, would, Darwin supposed, eventually produce new species.

In Darwin's day, very little was known about the 'fossil record',
and Darwin thought that the present-day higher animals must have
descended from animals very like the present-day lower ones. As
palæontology developed, however, it became clear that in the past
many kinds of animals, now extinct, had flourished. Also, the fossil
record seemed to confirm Darwin's suggestion, which caused such a
furore at the time, that man is descended from the higher animals
– for if the fossil record is traced back a point is reached where human remains no longer appear, while further back still there are no
mammal, no reptile, no amphibian, and finally no fish remains.

Genetics

Towards the end of the nineteenth century the work of Mendel
was rediscovered, and the science of genetics began to develop. It
became clear that variations could arise from genetic mutations –
changes in the 'genes' which are regarded as the bearers of inherited

characteristics – and that these variations could be handed on intact to the descendants. For some years genetical theory proved not altogether easy to reconcile with the idea of gradual evolutionary change caused by natural selection. In 1930, however, R.A. Fisher published *The Genetical Theory of Natural Selection*. In its way, this book was almost as much of a milestone as Darwin's *Origin of Species*. Fisher showed how apparently insignificant mutations could confer a selective advantage if the 'selection pressure', even though very slight indeed, continued over long stretches of geological time. (Selection pressure is the term used to describe the 'pressure' of the environment on the animal which produces natural selection). Such apparently insignificant selective advantages, he showed, were sufficient to account for the formation of new species, for the development of new sub-groups, and even for the most improbable adaptations such as are described in every 'wonders of nature' book.

Fisher's work, which in recent years has been much supported and extended in great detail by such scientists as H.J. Mueller, J.B.S. Haldane and Sewall Wright, involves a lot of difficult statistical mathematics. Indeed, the whole of modern genetical theory is so complex that it cannot be discussed here. Three points will be enough.

First, Fisher describes natural selection as 'a mechanism for generating an exceedingly high degree if improbability'. His theory thus effectively undermines the empirical argument that the odds against evolution having occurred 'by chance' are almost inconceivably great.

Second, present-day ideas about the scale of geological time give ample scope for the slow speed of evolution demanded by Fisher's theory.

Finally, it is worth remembering that while the theory is extremely consistent and convincing – it has certainly convinced over 99% of the biologists who have studied it – it is, and must remain a theory. Like a newly invented kind of mathematics, it could correspond to a reality, but it need not if there seems to be sufficient reason to look for an alternative.

The modern theory of evolution is thus a formidable and coherent structure, which is being continually backed up by work in many branches of science. Nevertheless, some of the adaptations and patterns of behaviour found in the animal kingdom are so extraordinary that non-scientists often feel that to explain their evolution merely through the action of natural selection on chance variations is far-fetched – and that there must therefore be something wrong with the theory. However, it is important to understand the scientist's attitude to this kind of objection. Hardly any scientists now doubt that modern evolutionary theory is broadly correct, and it would not normally occur to them to regard for instance, the social organisation of the ants or the extraordinary nest-building behaviour of many birds as a challenge to the theory. Rather, such phenomena are regarded as a challenge to the ingenuity of the biologist in thinking of a way in which such phenomena could have evolved gradually, through variation and selection during stretches of geological time measured in millions of years. Indeed, in more cases than the layman often realises, very plausible evolutionary schemes for many 'wonders of nature' have been worked out, and there seems to be *a priori* reason why similar schemes should not be worked out for others. The basic idea that even the most extraordinary specialised adaptations develop from an interaction between the organism and the environment is, I think fundamentally sound – although, as some modern work in genetics and embryology is beginning to indicate, the interaction may not be quite as simple as the classical Darwinian picture has it.

*   *   *

At this stage, one might reasonably ask why, if the generally accepted theory of evolution appears so convincing and watertight, one should need to take account of Rudolf Steiner's differing views?

There are two reasons. The first is simply that there are, nevertheless, certain aspects of the modern theory which present some fundamental difficulties. But the second reason is more important. Evolutionary theory is, in the last analysis, nothing more than a certain interpretation of the facts. With the help of Rudolf Steiner's work, one can interpret the same facts quite otherwise. Such an interpretation leaves room for man to be understood as something more than simply a higher animal, and for the evolutionary process to be understood as something more than the operation of chance. Let us now take a closer look at some of the facts.

The hardest facts, so to speak, of evolution, are the fossils of the fossil record. How are these fossils distributed through the strata? In the Palæozoic strata, for instance, fish and plant remains of all kind abound. Reptile remains are particularly abundant in the Mesozoic. Mammals dominate the Tertiary strata. But what is especially characteristic is that well-defined groups of animals tend to appear comparatively suddenly in the record, to flourish for a while, developing in the process all kinds of variations and specialisations of their basic form, and then to die out.

For instance, the reptiles which begin to appear in the fossil record at the beginning of the Mesozoic, gradually become very abundant, and a process called 'adaptive radiation' begins. That is, the 'basic' reptile type splits up into more specialised types adapted to particular modes of life – crawling reptiles, running reptiles, swimming reptiles, flying reptiles, carnivorous reptiles. It is as though all kinds of complicated variations on a theme were being elaborated. At the end of the Mesozoic virtually the whole vast and varied group dies out, and mammal fossils begin to appear, gradually becoming in their turn the dominant group. This process repeats itself, on a larger or smaller scale, throughout the fossil record.

Here we meet a real difficulty in modern evolutionary theory. The later representatives of most groups of animals in the fossil record are extremely specialised. On the other hand, the early representatives of a new group are generally relatively unspecialised. It is very difficult to see how the specialised animals of one group could have given rise to the unspecialised animals of the next group up the evolutionary scale. What is more, even the unspecialised early representatives of a group often seem, on closer examination, to be already too specialised to be direct ancestors of a higher group.

Neoteny

This is a very real problem, and modern biology is well aware of it. It is not simply that real fossil 'links' between most of the main groups of animals are lacking. A major obstacle is the difficulty of imagining how animals could get out of their specialised ruts, in order to give rise to higher animals. In a recent essay entitled *The Evolutionary Process*[1], Dr. Julian Huxley writes: "Thus one result of specialised improvement is an eventual restriction of any further improvement. In addition, high specialisation for one mode of life restricts the possibilities of switching over to another . . . Specialisation thus almost invariably forces organisms into a deepening evolutionary groove out of which it is increasingly impossible for them to climb."

One interesting suggestion for avoiding this dilemma is elaborated in an essay in the same volume, called *Escape from Specialisation*, by A.C. Hardy. He summons to his aid a phenomenon called 'neoteny'. Neoteny is the process whereby a larval or embryonic form, which may itself undergo evolution and develop special features independent of the adult, becomes sexually mature and able to reproduce itself. The most often quoted example of neoteny is the Axolotl, which is found in Mexico, has external gills, and lives in the water. But it is also identical, except for its sexual maturity, with the larval stage of the North American Salamander, *Ambylostoma tigrinum*, which lives on dry land and breathes with its lungs. What is more, the Axolotl can be experimentally induced to postpone sexual maturity, develop further, and become a North American Salamander.

This phenomenon makes it possible to conceive of an animal escaping from a specialised groove by means of a pre-adult stage; during this it would develop certain evolutionary novelties and then, after becoming sexually mature through neoteny, it would give rise to a new race, less specialised, and with new opportunities for adaptive radiation.

Dr. Hardy ends his essay thus: "However specialised a race of animals may have become in its typical adult condition, provided it has a less or differently specialised young or larval form (which naturally will be well-adapted to its particular way of living), and has a gene-complex which may sooner or later produce neoteny, then, given sufficient time, it stands a chance of escape from its path to extinction. In the great majority of stocks the end must come before this rare opportunity can intervene, but in a very small minority, the chances come earlier, before it is too late, and such lines are switched to new pathways, with fresh possibilities of adaptive radiation . . . Rare as they may be, these escapes from specialisation seem likely to have provided some of the more fundamental innovations in the course of evolution."

This picture of evolution is in many respects considerably different from Darwin's. The idea of natural selection, originally invoked as a process to explain the progressive evolution of more and more higher types of animals, now seems to be playing the opposite role of a process which tends to lead animals to extinction when they become too specialised. Invoking neoteny as a means of escape from this impasse makes it necessary to picture the actual ancestors of the major groups of animals, and presumably also of man, as having certain larval or embryo-like qualities.

Neoteny is thus now considered by many biologists to be the means by which evolutionary progress has ultimately been possible. But what is actually meant by 'evolutionary progress'? For many years science has been groping for a clear answer to this question. Do the terms 'higher' and 'lower', as applied to animals, really mean anything? Mere complexity is no final criterion – is a man more or less complex than a leopard or a beetle? There is no real answer.

Huxley, in the essay quoted above, considers this question, but reaches only a rather nebulous conclusion. "Biological progress," he says, "consists in biological improvements which permit or facilitate further improvements . . . It is the process by which 'higher' types come into being, the process operating in the succession of dominant types, the process by which the upper level of improvement or biological achievement has been steadily raised during geological time."

Emancipation

But there is a particular characteristic of 'biological progress' which has not yet been granted any fundamental evolutionary significance. This is that if, broadly speaking, the panorama of animals from the 'lowest' to the 'highest' types is considered, animals can be seen to have become progressively less dependent on their environment.

To take only the vertebrate group, the fish, for example, is dependent on a watery environment to bear it up, but reptiles and mammals can support themselves with their limbs by their own efforts. Reptiles' bodies, however, remain at much the same temperature as that of their environment, whereas mammals can maintain an even body temperature, independent, within certain limits, of the temperature of their surroundings. Young mammals develop, to begin with, inside the bodies of their parents, thus becoming independent of the external environment during their early stages.

This process can be followed through the animal kingdom, even into anatomical details where it is reflected as a kind of individualisation and consolidation of organs. Here, again, this process is evident even within the vertebrate group where the basic structure is relatively similar in the various types.

Compare the circulatory system of the fish with its mammalian counterpart, where the heart is divided into four chambers, and the circulation to the lungs is independent of the circulation to the body. The fish's head is fused to its trunk, whereas in higher animals the head has much greater independence of movement, and the jaw is an independent grinding apparatus instead of simply a kind of door into the mouth. The eyes of the fish are more or less static 'windows' – in the higher animals they are much more active and mobile. The fish's sense of hearing is spread out over its body in the lateral line system, and is barely distinguishable from a sense of touch or pressure. The bones of some of the gill arches of the fish are metamorphosed, in higher animals, into the ossicles of the highly independent and specialised organ, the ear.

The final and most dramatic effect of this process is man's upright posture. In this way, head, arms and hands achieve a certain emancipation from the environment. They are not forced to function in such close connection with the earth as are the front legs and snouts of animals. The head can, as it were, sit back and think. The hands are freed from the limited function of helping to move the body from place to place.

A Counter-force

There is a clear connection between the ideas of emancipation from the environment and of neoteny, in that neoteny produces an animal which is less specialised, and hence able to live in a more generalised environment. Both a neotenous and an 'emancipated' animal would be less dependent on a specialised environment for survival. The distinction between the two concepts is that while neoteny is assumed to have occurred repeatedly for many groups of animals, emancipation seems to have been a process operating steadily all the time. What the relationship between the two actually is will emerge in due course.

Emancipation clearly provides a kind of counter-force to natural selection. The tendency of natural selection is to edge the organism into an ever narrower and more specialised environment, to make it increasingly dependent on a special combination of external circumstances, to bind it more strongly to the earth. Emancipation works in the opposite direction.

Why, then, do adaptive radiation and specialisation play so important a role in modern evolutionary theory, while the polar concept of emancipation from the environment does not? There are two reasons. First, adaptation and selection can be observed actually happening – Darwin collected many examples – whereas emancipation, having occurred gradually throughout the course of evolution, is harder to define and identify.[2] Secondly, whereas a 'natural' explanation for adaptive radiation is available in the idea of natural selection, there is no really satisfactory corresponding explanation for emancipation. The tendency therefore is to assume that it has not really occurred, at any rate in any consistent way. But one can find an explanation in Rudolf Steiner's teachings.

It is curious that while science postulates all kind of unobservable entities to explain, in particular, atomic and sub-atomic phenomena, it shies away in alarm if asked to postulate supersensible spiritual entities to explain other phenomena. Yet Rudolf Steiner asks, to begin with, little more than science asks of itself – namely that his descriptions of events and beings in a spiritual world, not immediately accessible to the senses, should at first be neither accepted nor rejected, but *tried out*, by considering them side by side with natural phenomena to see if they are mutually illuminating. Accordingly, if we are prepared to examine some of the things Rudolf Steiner says about the spiritual aspect of the evolution of the world and man, the phenomenon of emancipation begins to fall into place, and the fossil record, the concept of neoteny, and the relation of man to the animal kingdom appear in a new light.

Descent into Matter

What distinguishes man from animals, Dr. Steiner says, is his possession of Ego. This is a spiritual entity, man's ultimate spiritual individuality, which lives in each human being. What we dimly experience as the central 'personality' of a person is the reflection of his Ego. In order to live on earth, the Ego must have a suitable physical vehicle – the human body. This vehicle had to develop gradually, over a long period of time. Evolution is really the story of the gradual descent of the Ego into matter, and of the gradual development of a physical body capable of containing it. The only physical form in which the Ego can express itself freely, into which it can descend completely, is the human form.

What, therefore, is the connection between the animal forms preserved in the fossil record and the evolution of the human body? Modern science accepts that the majority of known fossils are already so specialised that they represent evolutionary dead-ends. At the origin of each major fossil group, therefore, an unspecialised neotenous form, which has left no fossil trace, has to be postulated.

This implies that neoteny must have occurred repeatedly – i.e., that each neotenous form is related to the next one up the scale only via a more specialised form which then at some stage undergoes neoteny. The problems involved in this rather unlikely sounding process disappear if we turn the whole concept the other way round. That is, we consider the series of unspecialised forms, (which science postulates but which do not appear in the fossil record), *not* as the outcome of repeated neoteny, but as a *continuous evolutionary line*, from which the specialised fossil groups have developed by *branching off at various stages*.

This raises a fresh difficulty – that in order to remain unspecialised, this 'embryonal' line must have somehow avoided being subject to 'selection pressure' from the environment. At the same time, it must have remained constantly subject to the emancipation process described above, since new specialised fossil groups appear at a higher stage of emancipation than their predecessors.

This difficulty is resolved if we recognise that this line of embryonal forms really represents the *stages through which the human body has evolved.* In the emancipation process, cosmic spiritual forces can be seen at work preparing a vehicle for the human Ego, the principle of independent individuality.

A more dynamic picture of evolution here begins to emerge, with the Ego principle gradually wresting a suitable physical vehicle from out of the grip of earthly forces. Neoteny is no longer required to account for the avoidance of specialisation, and indeed it is evident that science has introduced this concept largely in order to be able to explain the existence of an 'embryonal line' of evolution – which the fossil facts themselves demand – without having to admit into its picture of evolution any guiding process other than natural selection.

However, it is not easy to imagine this process of the gradual incarnation of the Ego clearly unless one associates with it a conception which modern science must inevitably find very hard to accept. All modern theories of evolution are based on the assumption that physical conditions in the past were essentially the same as they are now, and that physical laws known to be true now can be extrapolated backwards indefinitely. According to Rudolf Steiner, this is not so. Both physical substances and the laws which govern them, have themselves undergone evolution.

We must imagine, Dr. Steiner says, that before the beginning of the earth's evolution, substance itself existed in a purely spiritual condition. The first 'physical' manifestation was a kind of subtle interplay of states of warmth. Later, a gaseous, airy state was reached; then a vaporous, watery condition. Not until solid substance began to appear did geology begin, so to speak. But the particular characteristic of this process is that the earth must be imagined as a great *living organism*. All substance was more alive than it is today, and the 'dead' minerals we are now familiar with should be imagined as having been deposited gradually within the living earth, in the same sort of way that mineral bone is deposited in the developing embryo. When solid substance first appeared, says Dr. Steiner, it assumed horny, waxy, colloidal and jelly-like forms.

This makes it easier to imagine the sort of conditions under which the 'embryonal line', the human body-form, must have developed. They must have been in a certain way similar to the conditions under which embryos develop today; in the embryo; even bone, the most mineral part of the adult organism, is alive and cartilagenous.

One can therefore picture the animal kingdom as having arisen through a kind of series of premature births of the living form which eventually developed into the present human body. An Ego which did not resist the pull of the physical forces of the earth for long enough, so to speak, would find its half-formed physical vehicle becoming bound too tightly to the physical environment, developing specialised forms and becoming irretrievably mineralised and rigid. Such an Ego would have lost the chance of fashioning a physical vehicle into which it could descend completely. The result would be an animal form.

Thus, when fossil fish appear in the fossil record, this is indeed a sign that the human germ was at that time passing through a 'fish-like' stage. But an idea of what this germ was actually like can be formed only by imagining what the *embryo* of the fossil fish must have been like. The adult is already too specialised and hardened in a particular direction.

Haeckel's Law

Modern science has recognised this indirectly in the way it now interprets Haeckel's famous 'biogenetic law'. Haeckel suggested that 'ontogeny repeats phylogeny' – i.e. that in its embryological development an animal repeats, in a modified and condensed form, its evolutionary history. This used to be taken to mean that the fish-like stage in human embryology, for instance, when the embryo possesses gill-pouches, represents a 'repetition' of an *adult* fish ancestor. Modern embryology, however, has realised that this stage of the human embryo is really comparable only to an *embryonic stage* of a fish, not to the adult stage. In an excellent critique of the 'bio-genetic law', Professor G. de Beer writes in this connection: 'All that can be said is that the fish preserves and elaborates its gill-slits, while reptiles, birds and mammals do not preserve them as such, but convert them into other structures such as the eustachian tube, tonsils, and the thymus glands.'[3]

However, in the light of Dr. Steiner's teachings we can take Haeckel's law almost literally. For the embryonic development of man really does reveal his evolutionary history much more accurately than does the line of fossil animals, for in it is reflected the 'embryonal line' of evolution which *gave rise* to the animal fossils.

The Other Thread

Seen in the light of Rudolf Steiner's teachings, therefore, it becomes clear that modern biology has so far confined itself to studying only one of the two threads of evolution – that thread which is visible in the process of adaptive radiation, and in the development of specialisations. The forces of the environment which give rise to natural selection, and the forces of genetics which bind the organism to the earth and maintain a physical continuity from generation to generation, represent forces of the earth. But modern evolutionary theory is coming to need more and more an understanding of the cosmic, heavenly, forces which have worked down into substance to fashion a vehicle for the Ego of man.

As it stands at present, the theory is really half a theory, since it can explain man only as the highest of the animals. Rudolf Steiner's work makes it possible to make the theory whole, and to begin to understand man as a being who is, at the same time, the 'lowest of the Angels'. Darwin's book, *The Descent of Man*, although what it is really concerned with is the *ascent* of man's body, is well-named, since the story of the evolution of man is the story of the descent of a spiritual being on to the earth. The animals represent beings which have descended too soon and too far – and perhaps the most tragic of all animals are the apes and monkeys, which descended just too soon to become men.

Among the multitude of spiritual beings which comprise the spiritual worlds, Rudolf Steiner sometimes described the human Ego as a Spirit of Freedom. Man he also once said, is not *yet* free, but he is *on the way to freedom*. The first task of the human Ego was to evolve a body in which freedom could be achieved – and this is what lies behind the process of emancipation, which from the physical point of view culminates in the form of the human body, as described earlier in this article.

It is interesting to find that modern biologists have realised something of the same kind – that man is in a unique position on the earth. He has reached a position in which he is not the passive subject of external forces, but in which he can take his future in his own hands, and mould his own environment. In the essay already cited, Julian Huxley writes: ' The present situation represents a . . . highly remarkable point in the development of our planet – the critical point in which the evolutionary process, as now embodied in man, has for the first time become aware of itself . . . and has a dawning realisation of the possibilities of its future guidance or control. In other words, evolution is on the verge of becoming internalised, conscious, and self-directing.'

The 'highly remarkable point' mentioned by Huxley is surprisingly similar to that often described by Rudolf Steiner from many different points of view – namely, that the human Ego is now beginning to be able to exercise control over evolution, working in full consciousness within the body.

The future course of evolution will thus be directly affected by the ideas man holds about his own nature and about the evolutionary process. If he remains conscious only of one of the two threads of evolution, if he persists in seeing himself as primarily a higher animal, he will shape his life and his society accordingly. But if he allows his ideas to be fructified by Anthroposophy, so that he becomes conscious of the other, cosmic-spiritual aspect of evolution and of his own nature, he will understand that his task is to carry the spirit into matter and transform it.

1956

---

[1] Included in *Evolution as a Process*, a collection of essays by various authors (Allen & Unwin, 1954).

[2] Perhaps the best-known example of natural selection in action today is 'industrial melanism'. In the past hundred years, black or dark forms of several moths have spread and become increasingly common in manufacturing districts of England and Germany, while their 'normal' varieties have become increasingly rare. All these moths have a habit of settling on exposed places such as the trunks of trees, so that the dark varieties are almost invisible on the soot-blackened tree-trunks in industrial areas. Moreover, they appear also to be generally tougher and better able to survive the dirty air and vegetation of their environment. The detailed genetics of industrial melanism is still a subject of discussion and experiment by entomologists, but there is no doubt that its rapid spread is correlated with the blackening and pollution of the landscape. In country areas, the dark varieties are still fairly rare. See E.B. Ford, *Moths* (Collins, New Naturalist Series, 1955)

[3] *Embryos and Ancestors* (Oxford University Press, 1952)

Epochs of Evolution

The previous article was devoted mostly to a discussion of modern 'neo-darwinian' ideas about evolution and their relationship to the picture of evolution which emerges from the teachings of Rudolf Steiner. I tried to indicate how some of the apparent contradictions may be resolved, and to sketch briefly the kinds of evolutionary concepts which then emerge.

This article is intended as a sequel to the first, although it is written from a quite different point of view. Rudolf Steiner's account of the evolution of the earth and man includes many detailed descriptions of changing conditions of consciousness, of the activities of various spiritual beings, of the different relationships of the spiritual and physical members of man to each other during evolution, and so on. But he gives only the briefest indications of what the *physical* aspect of development was like, and only the sketchiest clues as to how the modern animals and the vast panorama of extinct fossil forms fit into the picture. To pursue this theme a little further is the purpose of the present article.

*   *   *

Geologists divide the fossil-bearing rocks into three broad divisions, according to the nature of the fossils contained in them. The divisions are: Palæozoic – the rocks containing ancient forms of life; Mesozoic – 'middle life'; and Cenozoic – or rocks containing recent forms of life. Broadly speaking, remains of invertebrate animals and of primitive fishes dominate the Palæozoic strata; reptile remains dominate the Mesozoic strata; and mammal remains dominate the first part of the Cenozoic (the Tertiary strata). Not until the later Quaternary strata, after the great Ice Age[1], are fossil remains found of man as he is today.

The following very simplified table (to be read upwards) will summarise this:

Cenozoic	Quaternary	Man appears / Ice Age
	Tertiary	'Age of Mammals'
Mesozoic	Cretaceous / Jurassic / Triassic	'Age of Reptiles'
Palæozoic	Permian / Carboniferous / Devonian / Silurian	'Age of Fishes' / Ordovician / Cambrian

Pre-Cambrian . . . . No fossil remains

Between these main groups of animals, various other groups mediated. For instance, towards the end of the Palæozoic, especially during Carboniferous times, remains of all kinds of amphibian creatures, half-way between fish and reptile, abound. During the second half of the Mesozoic, and at the beginning of the Cenozoic, various 'mammal-like' reptiles, and curious primitive mammals, are found.

These geological epochs are relatively simple compared with the complicated series of evolutionary stages described by Rudolf Steiner, but it will be helpful to try to see how the two sequences are connected. In the first place, Dr. Steiner refers to three 'planetary incarnations' which preceded the present earth; he calls them 'Old Saturn', 'Old Sun' and 'Old Moon'. Between each of these incarnations, creation returned to a purely spiritual existence for a while.

The present solar system can be regarded as the fourth incarnation of the cosmic bodies which have evolved through these stages. Man himself, and also the animals, plants and minerals, are not simply a product of evolution on this earth, but were involved in the earlier stages, too. Man's physical body, according to Rudolf Steiner, began its evolution on Old Saturn. His etheric body, which endows his physical substance with the capacity for growth and reproduction, began to evolve on Old Sun. His astral body, the bearer of feelings and passions, began its evolution on Old Moon. Man's individual spiritual core, his Ego, has only just begun its evolution, and the central significance of the present planetary incarnation – the Earth stage – is to allow the Ego to begin to transform the three older members of man so that it can come to full expression in them.

The minerals have only a physical body on earth, and are therefore at a stage comparable to the evolutionary stage of man on Old

Saturn. (Dr. Steiner says that if the minerals could talk, they would tell you about conditions on Old Saturn. They have, so to speak, an 'Old Saturn consciousness'.) Similarly, the plants have a physical and etheric body, and an 'Old Sun consciousness'. The animals have an astral, etheric and physical body, and a consciousness reminiscent of that possessed by man on the Old Moon. Only man himself has an individual Ego incarnated on the earth.

In another sense, however, the hard, solid, present-day minerals are very much a product of the present stage of evolution. On Old Saturn, Dr. Steiner says, matter did not become material at all in our sense; it condensed from out of a purely spiritual condition into a state he describes as one of finely differentiated warmth. On Old Sun, something like a gaseous state was reached; on the Old Moon, a liquid state; solid substance as we know it now is a product of the Earth evolution. But in speaking of 'gas' and 'liquid' it is important to realise that this is only an analogy. Nowadays, we mean by gas something just as solidly physical as stones and rocks, but very finely dispersed. We must picture the 'gas' of Old Sun, or the 'liquid' of Old Moon as permeated with tremendous spiritual forces, and the entire planet as a vast living being in its own right.

The present earth-evolution began with a kind of recapitulation of the previous stages, and substance itself passed through these earlier conditions. Just as the human being passes through embryonic stages and develops a really hard skeleton only gradually, some years after birth, so the present mineral body of the earth developed gradually through various 'embryo-like' stages, when its substantial condition was quite different from what it is now.

* * *

Rudolf Steiner describes five main evolutionary stages of the earth up to the present. He calls them Polarian, Hyperborean, Lemurian, Atlantean, and Post-Atlantean (our own).

The Polarian epoch began in a way reminiscent of Old Saturn with a kind of condensation from out of the cosmic periphery of a planetary body consisting of 'differentiated heat'. This body contained the present sun, moon, earth, and all the other planets within itself. During the Hyperborean epoch further condensation took place, and gave rise to a body consisting of warmth- and light-filled air. At the same time, the outer planets, Saturn, Jupiter and Mars were separated off from the parent body, which still contained the sun, earth, moon, Mercury and Venus. The Hyperborean epoch closed with the separation of the earth – still containing the moon – from the sun.[2]

The Lemurian earth was the scene of a great many events of the utmost significance for mankind. Dr. Steiner's descriptions of this epoch take some getting used to, for the whole aspect of the earth at that time was extremely strange. But, unlike the Polarian and Hyperborean epochs, the Lemurian age is the first which has left direct physical remains which we can study, and is therefore in some ways more accessible to our understanding.

We must imagine the earth at the dawn of the Lemurian age as a huge, egg-shaped, living body, much larger than it is now, consisting of liquid imbued with air and warmth. The densest matter was in a fine colloidal, or 'aerosol' condition. Gradually the centre of the earth began to differentiate from the periphery, and, in particular, heavy metals such as iron and nickel began to condense into the centre. The present heavy metallic core of the earth originates from this time.

On to this inner core a 'rain of silica', in Dr. Steiner's phrase, began to fall, condensing down out of the surrounding warmth- and air-permeated liquid to form the first beginning of the earth's crust. This kind of sedimentation from out of the fiery, misty, watery, living atmosphere, continued throughout the Lemurian epoch to a greater or lesser extent, and to this process a major part of the geological strata we know today are to be attributed. The pre-Cambrian, Cambrian, Ordovician and Silurian rocks were laid down in the first part of the Lemurian epoch, but it must be borne in mind that they had a quite different consistency – colloidal and 'foamy' at first, then jelly-like, and later more waxy and horny, but still 'alive' to some extent and 'dying' to become minerals as we now know them only at a much later stage.

To an orthodox geologist this whole picture will, of course, sound simply fantastic – but this is largely because scientists have got so used to the assumption that 'laws of nature', and the physical conditions to which they apply, are eternal and immutable. But there is no special evidence to support this metaphysical assumption, and it would clear the way for a much more subtle and dynamic view of evolution if orthodox science would consider the notion that not only plants and animals, but the whole earth, the matter of which it consists, and physical 'laws' themselves, have been subject to evolution. If one looks at a cliff face containing convoluted layers of rock which seem to have been twisted about like plasticine, it becomes almost impossible to believe, as orthodox geology would have it, that ordinary hard rock was slowly bent into such shapes simply by enormous pressures. It is much easier, for the naïve observer at least, to imagine a time when the rocks had a more toffee-like consistency, and the whole surface of the earth was far more active and flexible.[3]

*   *   *

The strata known as Carboniferous, Permian, and Triassic belong to the middle part of the Lemurian epoch. During this period, according to Rudolf Steiner, an extremely important event occurred – the separation of the moon from the earth. In the part of the earth where the Pacific Ocean now is, a kind of infolding of the earth's crust occurred, and a separate planetary body was formed, which was then ejected to become what is now the moon. Into this body were concentrated all those substances and forces which had tended to make the solidification and hardening processes of the earth go on too fast.

The departure of the moon left a huge 'wound' in the earth, and many of the geological revolutions of the period were caused by the whole earth's crust trying to 'grow' over from the western pole of the earth, in order to 'heal' this wound. The whole Pacific basin is today surrounded by mountain ridges which provide evidence of this process, and the constant volcanic activity and colossal chasms which still exist in the floor of the Pacific show that the wound is still not healed.

Through the steady precipitation from the thick colloidal atmosphere, a hot watery earth surface, with islands of denser material floating in it, gradually formed. The core of dense fiery material was constantly breaking through the very thin crust. The atmosphere itself was still extremely heavily laden with water, but was thinning slowly all the time.

The swampy regions of the tropics today are a kind of echo of conditions during the final part of the Lemurian epoch, after the departure of the moon. But one must imagine everything mineral in a more plastic state, temperatures higher, the air still much thicker, and volcanic activity, often on a tremendous scale, going on all the time. Above all, one must remember that all matter was still far more intimately woven through with spiritual forces. The Lemurian epoch ended when the Lemurian continent – roughly on the site of the present Indian Ocean – was destroyed by a fiery volcanic catastrophe, and the principal scene of evolution, as far as mankind was concerned, became Atlantis, where the Atlantic Ocean now is. The beginning of the Atlantean epoch coincides approximately with the beginning of the Tertiary. During this period the earth's crust gradually became much more solid; volcanic activity diminished, and the atmosphere, though still very watery by our standards, became gradually clearer. During the later phases of the Atlantean epoch parts of the earth began to get much cooler, and the Ice Age drew on. Atlantis itself was destroyed by a water catastrophe and now belongs to the bed of the Atlantic Ocean.

By this time the glaciers which had covered most of northern Europe were receding; the end of the Ice Age marks the transition from the Atlantean to the first post-Atlantean epoch. At last, conditions on the earth had become very like those of today.

This is a very simplified account of a very complicated series of events, but to go into more detail would make this article too long. The table below is an amplification of the table on page 94.

Cenozoic	Quaternary	Post-Atlantean epoch . .	Modern man
		Ice Age	
	Tertiary	Atlantean epoch	Mammals
Mesozoic	Cretaceous	. . . . . Late Lemurian epoch .	Reptiles
	Jurassic		
	Triassic		

Differentiation and departure of the moon.[4]

Palæozoic	Permian	. Middle Lemurian	
	Carboniferous		. . . Fishes
	Devonian		
	Silurian		
	Ordovician		
	Cambrian	. Early Lemurian	
	Pre-Cambrian		

Geology begins

———————————

Condensation as far as air- and warmth-filled liquid . . . . Hyberborean
Condensation as far as warmth-filled air . . . . Polarian

———————————

Purely spiritual existence.

*   *   *

When we look at the huge panorama of geological strata and fossil animals, together with the existing animals we know today, several important questions force themselves on our attention. Why, in the first place, is a distinctive group of vertebrate animals associated with each of these geological divisions (which match at the same time Rudolf Steiner's evolutionary stages)? What is the significance of the 'Age of Fishes', the 'Age of Reptiles', etc.? Why are mammals and birds the dominant vertebrate creatures now (excepting man himself), rather than reptiles or amphibians?

The physical remains of past evolution reflect spiritual and cosmic evolutionary processes which were going on at the same time. The series of fossil animals reflect – but only *reflect* – the evolutionary processes which prepared a physical body into which the Ego of man could incarnate. How, then, are the spiritual events which took place during the epochs described by Dr. Steiner reflected in the physical events we have been considering?

The succession, fish-reptile-mammal-man, is in itself suggestive. The fish lives suspended in water. It is dependent on the sea for everything – for moving about, eating and breathing; the sea looks after its eggs; its behaviour is closely interwoven with things happening around it in the water. The consciousness of fish seems to be spread out in a kind of deep watery dream through the ocean; it has little or no internal soul-life of its own. Fish are united with, given up and abandoned to, their environment.

The reptile breathes air. It has limbs on which it supports itself, and eyelids of a kind, so that it can shut out impressions from the environment. It is still bound up with the environment in many ways – if the weather gets cold, it gets cold too, and many reptiles depend on the sun's warmth to hatch their eggs. But the reptile seems to have an internal life which is more separate from the environment than that of the fish is; there is a new sort of action and reaction between the creature and its surroundings.

If one looks at the fossil skeletons of mesozoic reptiles, one can read something of the 'character' of the various forms: the fierce carnivores, with predatory jaws and powerful limbs; the huge, placid looking Diplodocus - a reptilian version of the cow; the delicate bird-like flying reptiles, and so on. It is true that primitive fossil fish also may look extremely fierce, or fantastic. But this impression is not derived from the *internal* skeleton of these animals, about which little is known in many cases, since it was cartilagenous, and has left few fossil traces. The fishes' 'expressions' derive largely from the elaborate external armour of plates of various kinds in which most of these early forms were clad. Here again, one feels that the fish's 'character' is somehow 'impressed' upon it from outside.

The mammal is warm-blooded. It can maintain its own internal world of warmth, which the reptile cannot. It can reproduce its own kind with negligible help from the environment, and, from its larynx, it can give birth to a wealth of new sounds, where the reptile can only produce, at best, mechanical hissings or drummings.

Thus the fish is a water creature; the reptile 'conquers' dry land with its limbs, and air with its lungs. The mammals 'conquer' the element of warmth, and can express their inner experiences to a limited extent in sounds.

*   *   *

What does this succession of 'water animal', 'air animal', and 'warmth animal' suggest in the light of Rudolf Steiner's teachings? The watery element may be regarded as a kind of gate through which *etheric* forces can enter the physical world. Seeds start to grow when they are wetted, and the physical bodies of all living things contain more water than anything else. Similarly, air is in a sense the gateway for *astral* forces. The air carries the cries of animals which express their pains and pleasures. Our breathing is particularly sensitive to our feelings and passions. The soul-life of the whole planet is expressed in the winds and weather which swirl over the earth's surface. The atmosphere is in a sense the physical expression of the earth's astral body.

The warmth element bears Ego forces into the world. We speak of the 'warmth' of someone's personality. We may also speak of a 'cold fish', where the Egohood of a person does not come out into the world properly to meet other people.

I think we should regard the 'Age of Fishes', the 'Age of Reptiles' and the 'Age of Mammals', therefore, as a reflection of the changing and evolving relationship between the physical, etheric, and astral bodies, and the Ego, of man himself. By the dawn of the Lemurian age, a tenuous etheric-physical vesture for man had already evolved, formed in the fiery misty living atmosphere out of which the more solid parts of the earth were gradually condensing. The astral and Ego principles of man were still hovering in a more purely spiritual condition round the earth's periphery. Where this tenuous vesture was taken hold of by beings who were over-eager, so to speak, to unite themselves with the solid earth-element which was beginning to emerge, primitive fish forms began to appear, swimming in the denser parts of the earth's watery, fiery atmosphere (a division between air and water had not yet taken place). In this way, the fish lost the chance of beginning to incorporate astral forces into itself in a more intimate way.

Gradually, something like solid land – but still very plastic and imbued with life-forces – arose, and in the atmosphere a less dense, hot, gaseous, steamy part began to divide from the denser, more watery part. Astral forces were beginning to work down into the body of the earth, and into the physical-etheric vesture of man. The human bodies of that time lived in the thick Lemurian atmosphere, half-floating, half-flying. They would have looked grotesque, as an embryo looks grotesque, and were distinctly reptilian in appearance. (Dr. Steiner describes the physical body of mid-Lemurian man as looking rather like a 'soft-bodied dragon'.) In the Mesozoic reptile fauna we can trace the expression of beings which seized on the human physical-etheric-astral substance in order to descend at once into material existence, thus creating forms in which they were, so to speak, imprisoned, with no opportunity of evolving further.[5]

There is, however, a further essential aspect of the evolutionary process which must be taken into account (however briefly and inadequately) at this stage. According to Dr. Steiner the departure of the moon in the middle of the Lemurian age had a definite connection with what we call the 'Fall of Man'. The Fall occurred when certain spiritual beings – the Luciferic beings – entered into man's astral nature and were able to endow it with a certain independence from the higher beings who had previously guided it. Through this, man became the possessor of a wild and fiery astrality which his Ego was too young to control. This astrality-run-wild is reflected right down into the Mesozoic reptiles, with their often terrifying and stormy aspects.[6]

The Luciferic influence had the effect also of drawing man into closer connection with the fiery, or astral, forces of the earth, and thus causing him to 'fall' from the cloud-regions to the earth's surface. The departure of the moon may be regarded as a necessary counter-influence to these events. By reducing the gravity and hardening forces of the earth, it enabled man to take an upright posture, thus freeing his hands for creative work, and also to postpone the hardening of his physical body until it was sufficiently developed to bear the Ego. While mankind was living in physical-etheric-astral form on the volcanic turmoil of Lemuria, where astral forces were running wild, the human Ego was able to hold back, so to speak, and not become involved in physical existence until the beginning of Atlantis. (The volcanic fiery catastrophe which destroyed Lemuria was caused, Dr. Steiner says, by a release of astral forces which man could not control.)

Man's adoption of an upright posture is reflected also in the reptiles. During the middle of the Mesozoic, many forms arose which walked or ran on two legs, and stood almost upright. But during the second half of this epoch something particularly interesting happened. On the one hand, the reptiles were gradually overcome again by gravity, and sank back on to four legs – some even took to the water, like the crocodiles. At the same time, some forms seem to have gained a certain freedom from gravity, and various flying, bird-like reptiles, together with the first primitive birds, appear in the fossil record.

By the end of the Mesozoic – which is also the end of the Lemurian – something like the present-day division into dry land, sea and air had taken place, although – compared with any conditions we know today – the land was much softer and wetter, the water much thicker, and the air much waterier. At this point the real task of earth evolution – the gradual descent of the Ego into the physical world – could begin. Gradually, the physical-etheric-astral vehicle for the Ego was made ready to receive it. In the wonderful panorama of fossil animals during the Tertiary period, from the so-called mammal-like reptiles, up to the apes, we see a remote reflection of this process. Remote, because the beings who expressed themselves in the Atlantean-Tertiary mammals had parted from the human evolutionary stream right back in the Mesozoic, and had then renounced the possibility of ever giving full expression to the Ego-principle in the physical world. Nevertheless, the warm-blooded animals represent an attempt to incorporate the Ego - but an attempt which had to stop half-way.

*   *   *

By the end of Atlantean times the human physical vehicle had reached a stage when it could begin to receive the Ego fully into it, and when also it was mineralised enough to leave fossil remains. (This is a rather simplified picture. In his book, *Der Mensch der Eiszeit und Atlantis*, Sigismund von Gleich traced the connection between some of the fossil forms of 'primitive man' and the later Atlantean races. But to go into this would need too much space.)

However, the picture can be developed a little further from another aspect. As we have seen, the physical, etheric and astral bodies of man began their evolution on Old Saturn, Old Sun, and Old Moon respectively. When the earth evolution began, these principles already existed, in a certain sense, as spiritual 'Ideas'. The first three evolutionary stages of the earth, the Polarian, Hyperborean, and Lemurian, were recapitulations of Old Saturn, Old Sun and Old Moon, necessary in order to adapt the physical, etheric and astral principles of man to earthly conditions, ready to receive the Ego. But a similar recapitulation can be discerned within the Lemurian age itself.

The 'Age of Fishes' is like a memory of Old Sun; the fish, with its consciousness spread out in its environment, given up to the watery element, is the nearest a vertebrate animal can get to the plant-like consciousness and condition which characterised the stage of evolution reached by man on Old Sun. Similarly, the Age of Reptiles is a recapitulation of Old Moon, in which astral forces come to expression with great force. The Atlantean (or Tertiary) sees the beginning of something new, which belongs to the earth alone.

In this connection it is interesting to observe how all the mammals seem, in a sense, much *younger* than fishes or reptiles. Reptiles, in particular, seem to bring an almost uncanny recollection of times long, long ago, before man was man at all. Most of them live secret lives in parts of the world, such as the tropical jungles, where man is not welcome or at home. Just as we may look at the plant kingdom as a legacy of Old Sun, so are the reptiles a legacy of Old Moon, as well as of the Lemurian Age.

The animals with which man has most to do on earth today are 'new' animals, so to speak. There are still some 'old' animals about – the reptiles, curious creatures such as the rhinoceros (which while a mammal has a prehistoric air), and various eccentric forms. But we are most familiar with the modern birds, and with herbivorous and carnivorous mammals such as the cows, the cats and dogs. These groups somehow 'belong' to the present age.

The special connection of these groups of animals with the present age, the 'Age of Man', is indicated in the figure of the Sphinx, which is at the same time a kind of composite figure of man himself. The Eagle, the Lion and the Bull are expressions of forces which work in the head, the heart, and the digestion and limbs of man respectively. Now looked at zoologically, so to speak, the Sphinx is curiously lop-sided – the Eagle is a bird, but the Lion and the Bull are both mammals. This implies that man's heart and limbs have something in common which is not shared by the head. I believe a key to this problem lies in the fossil record.

During the Mesozoic a division took place between 'mammal-like' and 'bird-like' reptiles. But while modern mammals, in their whole character, have 'broken' with the reptiles, so to speak, the birds, in an interesting way, have not. A bird is like a reptile in disguise: its feathers make it into a beautiful creature. As it swoops and circles in the air, it seems a creature of light, air and warmth, ignoring gravity completely. But look a bird closely in the face, and one becomes aware of the curious mask-like quality of the head, with its hard and often cruel beak, and unwinking eye. A plucked bird, or an unfledged nestling, has loose, wrinkled skin, reminding us of the skin of an extremely ancient man or woman. Removing the feathers from a bird unveils it as a reptile. A thrush running across a wet lawn betrays its reptile connections immediately: it runs a few twinkling steps, like an agile two-legged lizard, and then stops, with the same uncanny frozen immobility as the lizard – a peculiar immobility of which mammals are incapable. The bird fauna, represented in the Sphinx by the 'king of birds', the Eagle, seems to point back to a distant past, to the 'Age of Reptiles', in fact. Why should this be?

The Eagle represents the head forces in man. (Dr. Steiner described birds as animals which are 'all head'. The legs are insignificant twigs, while the digestive system – compared with that of a cow – is little more than an afterthought.) In another connection, Dr. Steiner has also described the special connection which man's head has with the past. When we return to earth for a new incarnation, we bring what we have experienced through our limbs, and what we have learned through our deeds, back into the world, but transformed and 'summed up' in our head. Every child bears its past life in a metamorphosed form in its head, while in its limbs lie the germs of its future life. Now the bird fauna seems to me a sort of reincarnation of the Mesozoic reptile fauna. It brings over into the earth-evolution proper – into Atlantean and post-Atlantean times – a transformed summary of the physical-astral-etheric nature which expressed itself on Lemuria, and was really a recapitulation of something which developed on Old Moon. The bird is a metamorphosis of an animal form whose great achievement was the development of limbs (the reptile) into an animal which is 'all head'.

In the same way, the Eagle in the Sphinx points us back to our past – to our past life, but also to our whole past evolution. The emergence of the birds reflects the transformation of man's Old Moon nature into its earthly form. In his head, man bears not only the imprint of his past life, but also the imprint of his past as a whole. In his head he is a metamorphosed denizen of the Old Moon. (In his rhythmic system, his blood and breathing, on the other hand, he is a citizen of the earth. Through his limbs, he already works towards a future planetary incarnation of the earth, called by Rudolf Steiner the Jupiter incarnation.)

The fact that the bird reproduces by means of an egg – that there is a kind of discontinuity in the physical world between mother-bird and offspring – is a hint that the head aspect of man is connected with his past through reincarnation. In the mammalian part of man's nature, that which bears the forces of his present and future life, he is connected with his past through the continuous stream of heredity, expressed in the milk which the young animal draws from its mother.

*   *   *

The fossil record is taken by orthodox scientists to express purely physical events. But with the help of Dr. Steiner's teachings, these old, stone bones can take on quite new life. They reflect, often in a quite startling way, the great cosmic and spiritual events which Dr. Steiner described in his account of the evolution of the earth and of mankind. There is nothing fortuitous about the huge fossil fauna, or about the animal forms which surround us today. They all have definite parts to play in the scheme of things; every animal 'makes sense'. Sometimes, to our eyes, the aesthetic quality of a creature – a tiny tropical fish, for example – may be more apparent than its usefulness. But it should be possible to 'read' in the forms of all existing and extinct animals an expression of specific spiritual forces, beings, and events. A future 'spiritual zoology' will have to try to do this.

Here I have tried only to trace, broadly and rather sketchily, the way spiritual and physical evolution have intertwined in the animal kingdom – or, rather, in the vertebrates – and the relationship of the animals to man, both in the past and today. It is as a very provisional sketch that this article should be read.

1957

---

[1] There is evidence of other ice-ages during earlier geological epochs, but in this essay I shall use the term to refer only to the most recent one, which – with warm intervals – occupied most of the Quaternary, and ended about 8,000 B.C.

[2] Dr. Steiner says that Mercury and Venus did not separate from the sun until after the latter had separated from the earth.

3   Similar considerations apply to time-scales. According to Dr. Steiner, the
     Atlantean Age ended, and the post-Atlantean began, about 7200 B.C. This
     corresponds very well with the end of the Ice Age, in about 8000 B.C. On the
     other hand, Dr. Steiner puts the middle of the Atlantean Age at something over
     15,000 years ago – but the geologists put the middle of the Tertiary at some 15
     million years ago. The geologists' calculatations, however, are based on the
     assumption that physical processes have always gone on at the same sort of
     speed as they do now. But Dr. Steiner says that even the idea of a year is no
     longer valid earlier than mid-Atlantean times, as it is only since then that the
     earth has been revolving round the sun at the same speed and in the same
     orbit as it does today. Thus when geologists put the beginning of the Cambria
     at some 500 million years ago, this represents an extrapolation of
     contemporary time-scales back into ages when they do not apply. Before
     Atlantean times, in fact, it is pointless to think in terms of numbers of years;
     one has to think purely qualitatively, instead.

4   The departure of the moon was a *gradual* process. I have not been able to find
     an exact indication by Dr. Steiner, but it seems likely that the differentiation of
     the moon-substance began towards the start of the Carboniferous, and that the
     whole process of separation was complete by the end of the Triassic. The
     Permian is a mid-point. It is noteworthy that geologists can never quite decide
     whether to include the Permian in the Palæozoic or the Mesozoic.

5   Dr. Steiner has spoken also of this process from another point of view. The
     premature descent of these beings into matter was at the same time a sacrifice
     which made it possible for man to continue his intended evolution. In taking
     form as the reptiles of Mesozoic age, these beings absorbed into themselves
     part of the powerful limb- and lung-building forces which were working on
     man at the time, amd might have drawn him down prematurely to walk on the
     earth and breathe physical air if they had not been partially diverted, as it
     were, into the reptiles. Similar considerations apply to other animal forms.

6   It is not without significance that the Devil comes to Eve in the Garden of
     Eden in the guise of a reptile. But I do not think we should picture this Devil
     as a snake – he did not crawl upon his belly until he was himself cast out of
     Paradise – but rather as a winged and fiery dragon (and in the Oberufer
     Paradise Play this is indeed how Lucifer appears). The whole of Mesozoic
     evolution bears this dragon-like imprint of Lucifer.

Darwinism and the Archetypes

Darwin's theory of evolution by natural selection is a hundred years old. This is perhaps an appropriate moment to consider what has happened to the theory since it was born, and what its effects have been.

Its main effect, one might think at first, has been on man's picture of man: the being created in God's image has been replaced by a sort of superior ape. To put it another way, most biologists, and very many ordinary people, now assume that man must look for the causes of his evolution in the material world. His ultimate origin is held to have been an obscure, fortuitous event in some primeval mud which gave rise to a self-reproducing chemical.

What is often forgotten is that this picture has nothing directly to do with the process of natural selection itself; it is simply a deduction from it. As we shall see, quite a different picture can be deduced.

The whole subject has got into a fine muddle because of the constant confusion between fact and theory which plagues it. The first thing to recognise is that natural selection is not a theory but a fact. It can be observed happening. Perhaps the best example is the case of the white moth, *Biston betularia*. It has a dark-coloured variant, *carbonaria*, which turns up among its offspring from time to time. This always used to be a rarity, but has lately become very common near industrial towns in this country. The reason is that on soot-blackened tree-trunks it is very inconspicuous, while the 'normal' white form quickly gets eaten by birds in this environment. In country districts the situation is reversed: the black form stands out more on tree-trunks, and so gets eaten more often. The dark form may eventually establish itself as a distinct species in industrial areas. Several other species of moths are showing the same effect. The whole process – known as 'industrial melanism' – has been studied in minute detail by biologists; and similar processes undoubtedly go on throughout the animal and plant kingdoms.

The essential effect of natural selection is to fit plants and animals more closely to their environment. It tends to diversification of habits and habitat, to increasing specialisation. A species of insect-eating bird might separate in the course of time into several specialised species, one living only on flying insects caught on the wing, one on ants, one on insects picked from crevices in the bark of trees, and so on. As each species finds a more exclusive 'niche' in the environment and becomes more closely adapted to its new way of life, there will be less competition with other species.

This process, which is an inherent consequence of natural selection, is well known to biologists under the name of 'adaptive radiation'. The melanic form of the white moth is an example of adaptive radiation of an insect into a new environment – the blackened trunks of trees. In this environment, it is better 'adapted' than its white relative.

Now what happens if we think this process backwards in time, so to speak? We must imagine the various species coalescing, becoming gradually less specialised, less various, and less intimately connected with their environments. We come eventually, in imagination, to a stage when all the bird species were contained, or fused, in one, original generalised bird. We come to a sort of 'Ur-bird'. The same applies to other animal types – we can arrive at an Ur-mammal, an Ur-reptile, an Ur-fish. Simply by thinking the process of natural selection backwards we arrive at a picture of animal archetypes.

The remarkable fact is that the fossils found in the earth present just the sort of picture we have been imagining, but a picture spread out in time. I mean that in the earliest fossil-bearing rocks we find, to begin with, some fairly generalised forms of fish. Gradually, as the geological strata succeed each other, we can see these fish radiating out in a wealth of various forms.

Later on, as the Mesozoic strata begin, we come across some remains of fairly unspecialised reptiles – but gradually these, too, radiate out into all kinds of specialised forms: crawling, flying, running, and swimming reptiles branch out.

The same story can be followed through the Tertiary strata with the mammals. In more recent times, it can be followed also to some extent with the monkeys and the apes. They too, display this process of adaptive radiation.

Only man himself shows no physical evidence of this process. He is not at all intimately adapted to his various environments – he has not undergone adaptive radiation. We do not find human species with webbed feet for swimming, or with green and brown skins for camouflage in the countryside. The only thing at all resembling animal specialisation is the variety of human races.

Now at certain points the fossil record is obscure. These points occur just at the transition between the main geological epochs – Palæozoic, Mesozoic, Tertiary, Quaternary – when one dominant type of higher animal begins to fade out from the record, and another begins to rise in its place. This is not to say that fish vanish from the record at the end of the Palæozoic, or the reptiles after the Mesozoic. They continue, but in reduced variety and numbers – and forms which are clearly aberrant or degenerate tend to appear.

*   *   *

All that I have described so far is accepted biology. The only difference is that modern biologists would not call the generalised forms of bird or fish, which we conceive by thinking back through the process of natural selection, 'Ur-forms' or 'archetypes', they are termed simply 'common ancestors', or 'ancestral forms'.

At this stage, biology faces the obvious question: Where do those common ancestors come from? The question arises both when we think the process of natural selection backwards and when we study the fossil record.

The answer given by biologists is that these ancestral forms, too, must be the product of natural selection. The ancestral mammal must have diverged by natural selection from some reptile; the ancestral reptile from the amphibian; the amphibian from a fish; and the fish from some invertebrate creature (thought nowadays to have had some relationship to the sea-urchin family).

This idea demands that unspecialised ancestral forms should have arisen repeatedly at times when 'adaptive radiation' was already well advanced in the dominant species. It means, for instance, that the ancestral, *unspecialised* mammal must have arisen from a *specialised* reptile.

How did these ancestral forms 'escape' from specialisation? This question has been faced by biologists, but no very satisfactory answer has been forthcoming. The best that can be done is to invoke a phenomenon occasionally observed in the animal kingdom, called 'neoteny'. This occurs when the young stage of a creature, before it has developed specialised adult characteristics, becomes capable of reproduction. A 'neotonous' creature then arises which, compared with its specialised adult parent, is unspecialised. Some process of this kind is supposed to have happened on several occasions during the course of evolution, to account for the appearance of new, unspecialised creatures in the fossil record.

I believe that anyone who studies the fossil record, and can think through the process of natural selection vividly and without prejudice, will feel that there is something false about this final step in the argument. No single, actual common ancestor of any species can be identified with certainty in the fossil record – and at these transition points the record is often complicated and difficult to interpret.

But biology is forced to take this step, since otherwise some other principle, besides natural selection, would have to be allowed into biological theory – some effect which makes itself manifest only at certain crucial points in the fossil record.

The concept of natural selection was first clearly grasped in Darwin's day. It was a time when men were looking for universal 'natural laws' to match the great system of physical laws set up by Newton. Natural selection has trailed its nineteenth-century atmosphere into the twentieth century. It has become, in biologists' minds, a universal principle, sacrosanct, to which all biological phenomena must conform. Some way must therefore be found to make it bridge these curious gaps which confront us both in fact (among the fossils), and in imagination, when we try to conceive the starting points of natural selection in the physical world.

If we contemplate these obscure transition points for a while, they begin to hint at something different. *It is at these points that higher levels of organisation emerge*. Water-living fish are succeeded by land-living reptiles. Warm-blooded mammals succeed cold-blooded reptiles. Finally, succeeding the four-legged creatures, with their backbones parallel to the earth, man apppears, with upright posture and free hands.

Whatever is responsible for this process, its effects are almost the opposite of those brought about by natural selection. At each higher level of organisation, the animal kingdom displays a new degree of *emancipation* from the earth. The reptile no longer depends on the water for its support – it supports itself with legs. Its eggs are hatched by the warmth of the sun. The mammal no longer depends on external warmth for its life and reproduction – it can maintain its own body temperature at a steady level, and bring forth its young alive.

Natural selection is not adequate to account for this process. By its very nature, it tends in the opposite direction. Indeed, it is impressive to observe in the fossil record how, when the new type of animal appears, natural selection immediately goes to work on it, drawing it into diversification, specialisation, into a more and more intimate relationship with its environment.

*   *   *

The facts of biology thus seem to lead to a question for which no answer is easily found in the world of physical nature. The answers normally advanced by biologists are rather forced efforts to bridge awkward gaps in what both the fossil record and imagination suggest to us. At this point, I want to leave biological theory, for the moment, with this riddle suspended, unresolved, and go on to consider current biological *practice*.

*   *   *

In Darwin's day the study of animals was very largely anatomical. Animals were examined and dissected in laboratories and museums, and classified in ever finer detail according to minute physical differences.

The effect of Darwin's theory has been revolutionary. Gradually, biologists realised that every aspect of an animal must have been subject to natural selection, and must have conferred some advantage on the creature. It began to dawn on anatomists that every feature of a creature's body and behaviour must have some *functional* significance; it must bear some definite relationship to the animal's natural environment and way of life.

The result was that biologists had to emerge from their dusty museums and begin to study animals intensively in the field. This is a trend which is still gaining momentum – and it is completely transforming biology.

Two new branches of science have emerged in this century as a result: ecology, or the study of communities of plants and animals in their natural environments, and their interaction with each other; and, more recently, ethology, the new school of animal behaviour studies originated in its present form by the Austrian scientist, Konrad Lorenz (author of *King Solomon's Ring*).

These studies are revealing the fruits of the process of natural selection. They are showing the extraordinarily intimate inter-relationships which have evolved between the earth, plants, and animals. It is as though a sort of river of wisdom which flows half hidden through nature were gradually being discovered and understood.

This is the curious paradox. On the one hand, Darwin's theory seems to have led to almost universal acceptance of a materialistic view of the nature of man. On the other hand, it has, in a literal sense, brought biology to life. Biologists are being confronted with the river of living wisdom which flows through nature. They may persist in trying to *interpret* their observations materialistically –

although, in fact, many of the concepts of ecology and ethology seem to be asking to be linked to some of the concepts of Anthroposophy.

Hand-in-hand with the development of field biology has gone the growth of genetics, the study of the laws of heredity. Here again there is a paradox. In Darwin's day, nothing was known of these laws, but they have since become the core of modern evolutionary theory. The raw material for natural selection, according to the theory, is genetic mutation. Each mutation is essentially a chance event. Therefore, it would seem, evolution is based on a series of fortuitous events.

But out of this rather sterile ground a quite different picture seems to be sprouting. It is becoming clear that the actual raw material for natural selection is something much more complicated than single, simple mutations arising now and again in single animals. Instead, geneticists are beginning to think of the 'genetic apparatus' of an animal, and even of a whole population of animals, as a kind of whole. This apparatus seems almost like a delicate musical instrument, on which nature – the environment – plays different chords.

The genetic constitution of a species determines how it can respond to the environment, to the pressures of natural selection. There are species with great inherent 'genetic variability', which can respond in a very flexible way to a change in the environment. Creatures whose genetic apparatus is too set, so to speak, cannot respond so easily, and may suffer gradual extinction. Here, too, the subject is coming alive, because of the need to understand animals not in isolation but as whole species, related to the earth in particular ways.

*   *   *

Modern biology, therefore, is gradually moving towards a much deeper and subtler understanding of nature. The problem is to find a proper place in this picture for man.

Some modern biologists, among whom Sir Julian Huxley is perhaps the most famous, know this. They are coming to realise that man is in a different category from the plant and animal kingdoms. He is not subject to natural selection in the same way as animals, because he can insulate himself from its effects. Man is acquiring a large measure of control over his material environment; he is becoming less subject to its demands, more detached from it than animals who are constantly urged by natural selection into a closer union with nature.

Man differs obviously and profoundly from animals in his power of speech, and in his ability to accumulate tradition and pass it on from generation to generation. Having mastered the material environment, he begins to create his own environment – a *cultural* environment. Cultural competition, competition between ideas, traditions and ways of life, replace biological competition. Above all, man has begun to become self-conscious. He is waking up to an understanding of the evolutionary processes in nature around him, and to the fact that he can shape, and must take responsibility for, his own evolution.

Thus far, Sir Julian Huxley and some other biologists have come, simply by pursuing the consequences of Darwin's ideas, and observing the world around them.

Students of Rudolf Steiner's work will recognise, by now, the way in which modern biology is groping towards some of the familiar concepts of Anthroposophy. Considering the nineteenth-century origins of Darwin's ideas, the rigid materialistic interpretations of nature which still imbue science, these trends are remarkable.

Rudolf Steiner often described how, in the present century, knowledge of the spiritual nature of man, and of his spiritual history and destiny, are struggling to break through into men's consciousness. In biology, the symptoms of this struggle are becoming vividly apparent.

Nevertheless, great obstacles still stand in the way of a reconciliation between biology and spiritual science. The study of evolution is beginning to show that man is in a quite different evolutionary situation from the animals. The question of the origins of the 'common ancestors' of the major animal groups is not satisfactorily solved. But the stride of thought and imagination demanded by Rudolf Steiner, when he begins to describe the spiritual history of the earth and man, is still a very formidable one for modern science.

He asks us to picture earlier times, for instance, when the whole physical condition of the earth was different. The actual *substance* of the earth has evolved, along with the earth's creatures. Moreover, Steiner says, man himself has been involved in this evolution from the beginning. Indeed, the evolution of the earth is to be properly understood only in connection with the evolution of man.

The fossil record is, in fact, a reflection of *spiritual* events – events which centred round the evolution of man. When a 'higher' form of creature emerges into the fossil record, it means that *man's* evolution has accomplished another step.

This evolution consisted in the gradual development of a suitable physical body into which the spiritual individuality of man could incarnate fully. There was a constant tension at work in this process.

On the one hand, there was the evolving living body of the earth itself, its substance gradually developing from a hot, airy condition, towards more liquid, colloidal, horny and finally mineralised states. The forces at work constantly tended to draw down the spiritual beings in the earth's environment towards incarnation in the earth's substance.

Opposing these forces were those spiritual beings concerned to create a physical body for man on earth in which his spiritual individuality could develop in freedom. The animals are the expression of spiritual beings which could not resist the pull of earthly incarnation for long enough. They descended prematurely to earth, and thus appear in the fossil record long before there are human remains.

At the time of the appearance of the first fossil fish, the first beginnings of the human body must be pictured as airy, watery rudiments, existing in the fluid atmosphere surrounding the earth. In so far as they could have been observed, however, these human bodies would have had a resemblance to fish forms. In other words, at the time when fish forms were dominating the fossil record, the human body was developing through a fish-like stage.

During the Mesozoic (corresponding to the late Lemurian age in Rudolf Steiner's terminology), when reptiles were dominating the animal world, the bodies of human beings resembled, in Rudolf Steiner's words, 'soft-bodied dragons'. There is a strange description in a lecture given to the workers at the Goetheanum of these Lemurian men half flying, half skipping, half hopping through the thick Lemurian atmosphere. The form of their bodies was not even fixed, but changed constantly under the influence of their experiences and feelings.

These are difficult things to imagine. I think that we begin to get some idea of the physical aspect of the human being in these past ages if we study, not the forms of animals, but rather the forms of *embryos*. It is true that man was passing through a fish-like stage during the Palæozoic (or early Lemurian). But the fossil fish of that era were heavily armoured, bowed down with thick plates and scales, mineralised creatures looking, somehow, incredibly *senile*. It is an instructive exercise to try to give these creatures back their youth, so to speak – to imagine them growing younger, shedding their scales, becoming softer-bodied, more mobile. This leads towards a more accurate picture of the condition of the human being at the time – much more like a fish embryo than a fish. The forms of embryos seem still to reflect something of the strange conditions and appearances of those earlier times.

If this thought is pursued, through the reptiles and the mammal forms, it becomes clear that each species of animal, as it appears in the fossil record – and, indeed, as it is today – is to some extent afflicted with excessive physical *age* – sclerotic, inflexible, deeply committed to one, specialised, intimate relationship with the earth. When this is understood, it becomes obvious that man can never have passed through a monkey or ape-like form. These creatures are withered and ancient at birth, sad caricatures of men. Only their embryos resemble the embryos of men more closely.

To imagine what man looked like shortly before he emerged in his present form in the fossil record (during the Quaternary, or after the Atlantean epoch), we should contemplate children, babies, and even fœtuses. This is not to say that Atlantean man looked like a child or human fœtus – but it will lead our imagination in the right direction.

The great contrast between man and animal, then, is this: the spirit of man can live wholly on earth, because he now has a body which is divorced from the earth's forces to the maximum extent. The bodies of the animals, on the other hand, were woven into the earth's forces and substance much earlier and more deeply than man's. Therefore, the spiritual individualities of the animal species, the animal Egos or archetypes, cannot descend so deeply into these bodies. Animals cannot be individuals; they can experience only a group-soul life, focussed in the spiritual animal archetypes which remain outside the physical world.

Now we can understand what 'natural selection' and 'adaptive radiation' really are. They are the expression of the pull of the earth's forces on the animal archetypes. These forces entangle the animal kingdom ever more closely with the forces of nature.

The process of 'emancipation', on the other hand, which is reflected in the step-wise emergence of higher levels of animal organisation into the fossil record, really represents the gradual wresting of a physical body for man from out of the earth forces, fashioning it so that the human individuality inhabiting it will be free of the world of nature, largely independent of 'natural selection'.

This picture is already there, in modern biology, as a kind of open secret. But to hope that modern science, as it is today, will unravel this secret, is unrealistic. For this involves understanding the evolution of *substance*, as well as the evolution of plants and animals; accepting the existence of man as a spiritual being long before he appears as a physical one; reversing the whole direction of evolution in the sense that animals must be seen as having descended from man, incarnating prematurely in physical bodies, and being drawn into the process of 'adaptive radiation' .

It is from a different direction, I think, that evolutionary ideas will have to be transformed. Instead of starting from animals, natural selection, the fossil record and genetics, it will be more fruitful to start from man.

*   *   *

The study of the animal kingdom shows clearly only one thread of evolution – the descent into matter, the gradual involvement of both man and animal in the forces of the earth. It is not so easy to discern there the struggle to establish the conditions for the human Ego to develop in freedom here on earth – although, as I have tried to show, the phenomenon of successive 'emancipation' of higher animals points to this.

But in human history, and in the study of human language, thinking and consciousness, this other side of the story is more accessible. And then the links with biology begin to emerge.

In this connection, Owen Barfield's recent book, *Saving the Appearances*, a study of the evolution of human consciousness, seems to me highly suggestive. He describes this evolution as marked by a change from what he calls 'original participation' towards our present-day consciousness. The essence of 'original participation' is that man did not experience himself as *separate* from the world around him. He lived *in* his experiences. Modern man, on the other hand, feels separated from the world around him; he is an onlooker, watching both the sense impressions which reach him and his own thoughts and feelings. Rudolf Steiner described this 'onlooker' condition as that of the 'Consciousness Soul'.

The evolution of human consciousness, Barfield goes on, points towards 'final participation' . Man will again establish a more intimate connection with the world around him, but imbued with that freedom and independence developed during the onlooker stage – a stage which Barfield calls 'idolatry'.

Now behind the progression from original participation to onlooker consciousness there is clearly the same process which is reflected in the phenomenon of 'emancipation' which appears in the fossil record. Natural selection, on the other hand, is, in biological terms, a process which leads to *enhanced* participation. The animals are, in a sense, the ultimate expression of original participation; their whole life and behaviour is intimately bound up with their natural environment.

The sciences of ecology and ethology, referred to earlier in this article, are leading to a much deeper understanding of the wisdom-filled interdependence between the earth, plants and animals. Original participation is here being studied from the outside, so to speak – in terms of anatomy, physiology and behaviour. But these studies are also opening the way to some understanding of the soul-life of animals, to a comprehension of what original participation means in terms of consciousness.

At the same time, some biologists are realising that within this pattern of participation there is no place for man as he is today. Within the total interdependence of nature there is no room for the free individual. In Julian Huxley's writings about the nature of man there are unmistakeable signs of an approach towards the idea of the onlooker consciousness which characterises man at present; which separates him from nature and sets him apart from the animal kingdom.

Now I do not think that ecology and ethology would have developed as they have done, nor would Huxley have written as he has, if mankind as a whole were not already beginning to experience the first beginnings of 'final participation'. In the growth of field biology, the impulse to get outside the laboratory and observe plants and animals in their natural environment, there is a clear desire to carry man's skull-bound consciousness out into nature again. Huxley, too, wants to find new meaning in the being of man.

It is one of the strange quirks of history that these impulses have grown directly out of Darwin's theories a hundred years ago. It makes it easier to understand a paragraph in an early essay by Rudolf Steiner on *Haeckel and Karma*. He was concerned, there, to show how the materialism of the nineteenth century did not arise directly out of the discoveries of natural science. Rather, it was the other way round. "Materialism," he wrote, "was imported into natural science, and naturalists such as Ernst Haeckel accepted it unconsciously. Darwin's discovery *per se* need not have tended to materialism."

Today, most people accept materialism consciously, but unconsciously, perhaps, they are ready for something new. This is why Darwin's ideas, in their present form, are not leading towards materialism. In a very real sense, I think, certain parts of biology are getting ready for Anthroposophy.

1959

The Evolution of Evolution

Most people ask themselves, at one time or another, what is the meaning of life. A great many presumably conclude that they don't know for certain – but they manage to live with their uncertainty. It seems, though, that this uncertainty may be contributing to a spreading modern illness.

A psychiatrist from the University of Vienna, Professor Victor Frankl, says there is a 'world-wide phenomenon' which represents a 'major challenge to psychiatry'. He calls it the 'existential vacuum', and claims that growing numbers of patients are crowding clinics and consulting rooms complaining, not of classical neuroses, but of a 'sense of total meaninglessness in their lives'. Other psychiatrists have encountered the same phenomenon and it seems that one fifth of all neuroses may now be of this kind. A doctor in Gulfport, Mississippi, has even devised a PIL-test (purpose-in-life test) as a diagnostic aid.

Professor Frankl blames a modern form of nihilism, which he calls 'nothing-but-ness' – the practice of reducing everything to something less. Various schools of psychology 'reduce' features of our behaviour to instinct, conditioning, or the traumas of toilet-training in infancy. Physiology reduces our thoughts to electrical signals in nerve cells, and our emotions to glandular secretions in the blood stream. Chemistry reduces our organism to molecules, while physics reduces chemistry to a few fundamental particles and forces. And a good deal that happens in this reduced universe appears to happen by chance.

Perhaps the most crucial reductionist thesis for ordinary human life is Darwinism. For, while Darwin himself appears to have died believing that evolution was at least set in motion by a Creator (presumably for some definite if inscrutable purpose), in its modern form the only *deus* in the *machina* is chance. We are, according to neo-Darwinist doctrine, the outcome of a string of accidents; our ultimate ancestor was some fortuitous conjunction of molecules in a primeval oceanic soup. A long chain of accidents, guided only by 'natural selection' of favourable combinations, has produced all the ascending variety and complexity of life from amoeba to man.

So, at least, the conventional orthodoxy would have it. There are many scientists who believe that the essential secrets of life and evolution are now known, that they reveal 'nothing but' elaborations of physics and chemistry, that little remains to be done but to fill in the details.

It may be that this situation has contributed to the existential neurosis of Dr. Frankl's patients – but if so, the situation should be easily remedied. There is undoubtedly an unfortunate tendency for the public to believe that the science of their day is final, absolutely proven, completely true, and must be compulsorily accepted by every right-thinking man or woman (a belief that some scientists foster energetically). However, a rudimentary acquaintance with history will reveal that man's general view of things has evolved radically over the past centuries, and there is no reason to suppose that this evolution is at an end.

Physics itself, the most fundamental of the sciences, underwent a major revolution in the 1920s, the philosophical and metaphysical implications of which are still obscure but certainly far-reaching. And while science cannot be expected to develop new theories simply to comfort distraught citizens afflicted with a sense of meaninglessness, these citizens should recognise that 'reductionism' is essentially a *useful procedure* rather than an ultimate statement of truth. If some scientists have adopted it as a faith, it is because it has proved exceedingly successful: science can make things happen in the laboratories and in nature, and the ideas it uses to make them happen are obviously true in an operational sense. But the success has arisen through adopting a definite attitude to nature which is ultimately metaphysical. And there is no reason why other attitudes – a different way of imagining the universe – should not, in the future, prove equally rewarding.

There is now a good deal of evidence of a need for some such shift in mental position, because biology has been facing, for a long time, an absolutely fundamental and very obstinate problem – the problem of biological *organisation*. A living organism can function because a coherent pattern is imposed on the parts of which it consists – the organs are subservient to the organism, the tissues serve the organs, the cells serve the tissues, proteins and other substances serve the cells. It is a fairly feudal society, and if the lower orders assert their independence, they are either quelled (the cells round a wound stop growing when it is healed) or they bring illness, anarchy and death (cells which won't stop multiplying are cancerous). The problem is that no one knows how this ordered functioning is created and maintained as the organism develops from fertilised egg, to adult, to corpse.

A number of attempts have been made to invoke some mysterious 'vital force' (in Darwin's day, the most powerful incentive was to preserve some scope in the scheme of things for God). Today, traditional 'vitalism' attracts little interest since it only removes the problem to some still more mysterious sphere. Postulating life forces is not much help without suggesting their nature or some means of getting at them. On the other hand, the progress of research itself is highlighting the nature of the problem ever more clearly. Without a deeper understanding of how living things become 'organised' both in time and in space, there can be no adequate theories of embryology, evolution, or the origin of life itself.

A growing body of scientists are coming to recognise that the problem is somehow involved with the hierarchic characteristics of living organisms: the reductionists' approach would explain every 'whole' in terms of its parts. But in reality, the whole at each level (for example an organ like the liver) has properties which transcend the properties of its parts (the liver cells). This recalls a very old argument which was used to demonstrate the need for a Divine Designer: You can investigate the cogwheels of a watch in exhaustive detail, and produce learned theses on the metallurgy of mainsprings, without explaining the most important feature of a watch, which is that its parts are assembled in a coherent pattern which allows the wearer to tell the time. Thus there is a sense in which the *watch as a whole* is the 'explanation' of its parts rather than the other way round. In the same way, no explanation of the nature of liver cells is complete without reference to the coordinated functioning of the liver as a whole.

The ultimate source of a watch's organisation is the mind of its designer. The biologists' problem, to put it rather crudely, is to find a 'designer', or a hierarchy of 'designers' *in* the cell, the liver, the organism (there is no desire to introduce a supernatural Designer, which would solve the problem only by making it inaccessible to science).

These problems have been the focus for several recent conferences. In the summer of 1968, the writer Arthur Koestler assembled an eminent group of scientists in the Austrian mountain village of Alpbach, to discuss the theme 'Beyond Reductionism'. And over the past four years there has been an important series of international symposia at the Villa Serbelloni on Lake Como, where the aim has been to explore the possibility of a 'theoretical biology' as fundamental as theoretical physics. At these meetings, there has emerged a great deal of dissatisfaction with the current orthodoxies of molecular biology and neo-Darwinism – and there have been the beginnings of debate on some very new ideas. It looks, in fact, as though some profound changes in biological thinking are in the making, and the outcome could be very surprising.

To appreciate these discussions, some background is needed. Last week, Gerald Leach reported the development of research and theory on the origin of life. But ideas about evolution have been evolving too. This process had its beginnings well before Darwin himself, and involved a deep change in human outlook. We have got so used to this change that we have ceased to feel its import – it has been called 'the discovery of time' .

The theory of evolution is just part of this story. We have acquired, as part of our general outlook on life, a sense of living in a particular 'period' of 'history'. It is not only that phrases like 'You are living in the twentieth century' convey a distinctive flavour. But there is a lot of evidence that within the past two or three hundred years we have developed a new feeling for time altogether. Partly this is because previously there was much less information about the historical, biological and geological past. But it also seems clear that people simply did not pay the same attention to what evidence there was. Thus fourteenth-century painters clothed biblical characters in fourteenth-century costume, and Shakespeare's plays were at first produced in contemporary (i.e. Elizabethan) dress. The idea of dressing Caesar in a historically accurate toga was a revolutionary innovation of the eighteenth-century *avant-garde*.

Perhaps most crucial was a growing readiness to question authority, which began to make itself felt in the fifteenth century. Authority itself, whether political, intellectual, or spiritual, was inherited from the past, as part of a divine order constructed by the Creator. But once you begin to challenge authority, you begin to inquire into its antecedents.

During the next 300 years, men began to explore the remnants of the past in a quite new and more critical frame of mind. History and archaeology began to reveal a huge panorama of past civilisation and culture. Geologists and miners began to see a pattern in the rock formations of the earth which showed that landscapes had undergone major changes in the past, finding that some areas had been beneath the sea, then desert, then exposed to volcanic action, during the course of time. William Smith, a canal engineer at the turn of the eighteenth century, found similar beds of fossils throughout Britain, and published one of the first geological maps which laid the foundation for a *history* of the British strata.

By the time Darwin set sail from Plymouth in the Beagle, on 27th December 1831, it was beginning to become accepted that the world had changed vastly in the past. Both the earth and mankind were much older than had previously been assumed, and the biblical story of creation could not be *literally* true (even if many Bibles still reproduced the confident calculation of Archbishop Usher and Dr. John Lightfoot that the Creation began at 9.00 a.m. on Sunday, 23th October 4004 BC).

The debate was no longer about the *fact* of evolution, but about its *cause*. One school, the Catastrophists, fastened on evidence of interruptions and jumps in the geological and fossil record, and took these to be evidence of a periodic divine intervention in nature. The Uniformitarians, including the great geologist Charles Lyell, believed that nature had been managing its own affairs ever since it was first set up by the Creator, and was simply following unchanging and eternal laws. (The debate is echoed curiously in this century by the arguments about the Big Bang and the Steady State theories of the universe.)

Darwin, who was a conventionally devout man, and had been expecting to take holy orders and become a country parson, set sail as a catastrophist, but returned five years later as a uniformitarian. He had read Lyell's classic work on geology during the voyage. But he had also been deeply impressed by the gradual changes in flora and fauna as the ship sailed down the South American coast, and by the spectacle of many distinct, but clearly related, species on the Galapagos Islands. He arrived back in England in the autumn of 1836, convinced that each species could not have been separately created, but that what he had seen were the most recent twigs on a developing family tree.

He soon retired from London, a 'vile and smoky place', to Downe in Kent (where he was to spend the rest of his life). There be began to collect information on domestic animal breeding, as a possible clue to the evolution of species in the wild.

Then in October 1838 he read Malthus's *Essay on the Principle of Population*, which had been published over forty years earlier as an ecological warning. In the doom-laden vein that has become fashionable again today, Malthus emphasised that populations always multiply to outstrip resources, and except in the unlikely event of a sudden outbreak of 'moral restraint', they face inevitable catastrophes. Darwin, surrounded by an entrepreneurial industrial society, in which the poor were widely thought to be inferior human beings, deserving their lot and working only for later reward in some other world, immediately seized on Malthus's thesis to interpret the facts of natural history. Given some variation in offspring, a competitive environment, and sufficient time, the weaker would go to the wall, and the more favoured would survive, gradually giving rise to distinct new species.

He had the outline of his theory by 1839, and wrote a brief sketch of it in 1842 which came to light only after his death.

For the next fourteen years, he worked on, marshalling a massive array of detail to support his argument, and was only prompted finally to publish when he received a letter from another roving naturalist, Alfred Russell Wallace, outlining the same theory. Their famous joint paper was read to the Linnaean Society in London in 1858, and in 1859 the first edition of *The Origin of Species* was published. There was no single thread in the argument which had not been put forward by others before. It was the synthesis which counted, and the meticulous backing of facts.

The book, which quickly became a bestseller, meant that the issue could no longer be ducked: if Darwin was right, the Bible was discredited as a literal history book – and the emergence of man appeared to be a natural, not a supernatural, event. This was not yet out-and-out 'reductionism'. Darwin does not seem to have doubted that man was in some way also related to a divine order. But he no longer looked for God in nature. Science had parted company with religion.

The story up to this point is fairly familiar. But the fact that the theory of evolution has itself evolved, and is still evolving, is less appreciated except by specialists. Yet within forty years of its publication Darwin's theory was in deep trouble – not from theologians but from scientists. The trouble centred on the problem of variation, the essential raw material for natural selection. There prevailed at the time a theory of 'blending inheritance'. This implies that all variations would rapidly merge into a common denominator, all individuals would soon be alike, and there would be nothing for selection to work on. There seemed no way out of this *impasse* until 1900, when three scientists, a Dutchman, a German and an Austrian, independently discovered the work of an obscure monk, Gregor Mendel, who had died unrecognised in 1884.

Mendel was born in Heinzendorf, then in Austria, now in Czechoslovakia, and as a bright lad with no private means (his parents were peasants) he entered the Augustininan monastery at Brünn (Brno) and spent all his life there. In the monastery garden he carried through his meticulous plant-breeding experiments, which he first reported to the Brünn Society for the Study of Natural Science in February 1865. No one took much notice.

The following year, Mendel sent his monograph to the famous biologist, Karl von Naegeli in Munich, who replied rather patronisingly several months later. It is not clear if Naegeli even read it properly. He certainly did not appreciate its significance. Three years later, Mendel was elected abbot of the monastery, and as is often the fate of good scientists, adminstrative duties soon put an end to further research.

The importance of Mendel's work was not merely in the experiments he had made. It was in the leap of imagination with which he interpreted the results. He was looking, quite consciously, for laws governing inheritance of simple characteristics in plants (for example, wrinkled or smooth skins of peas). He observed these characteristics manifesting in certain definite numerical ratios through the generations (Darwin had noticed and recorded similar ratios, but drawn no conclusions). Mendel was the first to realise what may now seem obvious, namely that the ratios can be explained if inherited characteristics are transmitted through the generations as *distinct and permanent units* (of which some may be 'dominant' and some 'recessive').

The revolutionary nature of this concept can be appreciated by remembering that throughout recorded history, until that moment, heredity had been universally associated with the *blood* (a view which is preserved in many common turns of speech – 'bad blood', 'blue blood', 'bloodstock', etc.). The image was of a *river* flowing through the generations. Mendel substituted 'atoms' (which we call 'genes'), fundamental particles of heredity, an idea as revolutionary for biology as protons and electrons were for physics.

From the turn of the century, therefore, Darwinism took on a new lease of life as evolutionary theory began to be worked out in terms of a rapidly developing science of genetics. This phase started with a major and largely irrelevant controversy, hinging on the fact that many inherited characteristics are not of the 'either/or' kind studied by Mendel (smooth or wrinkled peas), but involve a range of variation between two extremes (such as height or weight). A paper had in fact been published in 1902 by a Cambridge statistician, Udny Yule, which showed that such effects could be accounted for by assuming that a breeding population contains a large number of genes affecting the character in question.

Yule's paper was more or less ignored, and the controversy went on for some years. A special journal was even published, called *Questions of the Day and of the Fray*. But the argument finally led several people, notably J.B.S. Haldane and R.A. Fisher in Britain, and Sewall Wright in the United States, to develop more rigorous mathematical treatments of evolutionary genetics, which form the foundation of true neo-Darwinism.

The outcome was a considerable change in emphasis. There is still abroad a popular version of Darwinism which pictures nature red in tooth and claw, each individual battling for its life, the survivors owing their greater 'fitness' to some genetic mutation. But neo-Darwinism is less rugged and bloody, and a great deal more subtle. The evolutionary unit, so to speak, is no longer the individual animal, but a *breeding population*. The issue is not so much 'survival' as the degree of adaptation to a particular environment.

But above all, the genetic picture has become very elaborate. It has become clear that most mutations are harmful, and that spectacular mutations of any kind are more likely to upset a creature's relations with its environment than to improve them (the same thing happens in science fiction stories, where mutants with X-ray eyes or telepathic capacities usually experience nothing but trouble from their peculiar gifts and come to a sticky end).

The important source of variation in a population (at least in all creatures that reproduce sexually) is not mutation, but the shuffling and recombination of genetic material when male fertilises female (rather as bridge remains an infinitely interesting game because different hands are dealt each time from the same pack of cards. It would be a very boring one if the hands only varied at rare intervals when a Jack mutated at random into some new kind of card).

In a breeding population, little of the variation in each generation will have a decisive effect on the survival of any particular individual. But over many generations, genes and combinations of genes which confer *slight* advantages will become more frequent in the 'gene pool' of the population. At the same time, a small, refreshing stream of new mutations will be flowing into this gene pool, which may not show itself immediately, but which provides a precious reserve of 'variability' which will allow the population to evolve and adapt to any change in the environment.

This is a considerable contrast to the private enterprise aura of original Darwinism. To neo-Darwinists, a species is more like a modern corporation, producing a variety of goods for which it has found a market. If it has a lively genetic management, it will diversify successfully into any new environmental niche that opens up.

Some more specialised species, in a static environment, will have grown set in their ways and be staffed by old genes with little flexibility. They are vulnerable to extinction when the market changes.

Other species keep taking in bright young men ('mutations'), assembling teams to try out new possibilities, and sacking executives whose notions fail to sell. Thus the contrast between nineteenth and twentieth century Darwinism is curiously parallel in flavour to that between the individualistic, patriarchal family firm battling for individual survival, and the anonymous, diversified corporation filling a complex niche in a national economy.

The subtle interactions between gene pools of populations and the environment have been studied in great detail, and a number of actual examples of natural selection in progress have been identified and analysed in genetic terms. One of the best known examples is the Peppered Moth, *Biston betularia*, which is normally whitish and perches on pale birch bark where it is difficult to see. When the industrial revolution turned a lot of Midlands tree trunks black, the moth became rather conspicuous and was increasingly eaten by alert birds. However, a rare dark-coloured variant (which looked conspicuous on clean trees) was harder to spot on the grime, and its numbers increased. Seventy species of British moths were showing similar effects – at least until the Clean Air Act began to work.

Neo-Darwinism has become established in the textbooks, and in the minds of many, as firmly established truth. So it can come as a surprise to discover that it is under severe fire from two directions: a number of surprising new discoveries, notably in genetics, are bringing the basis of the theory into question. Secondly, and more fundamentally, the theory is being accused of an essential 'triviality': It does not and cannot, the critics say, explain the really important events of evolution.

This situation prompted Professor C.H. Waddington of Edinburgh University, who has organised the Serbelloni symposia, to remark at the Alpbach meeting: 'I think we are going to see extraordinary changes on our ideas about evolution quite soon'.

1970

Do We or Don't We Understand
the Secret of Life

Perhaps the most important controversy in biology today hinges on whether a particular problem *exists*: Do we, or don't we, understand the secret of life and its origins – at least in general outline?

There are scientists who claim that to all intents and purposes we do: molecular biology, which now knows the chemical constituents of living cells, has explained in principle how life works. And neo-Darwinism has shown how natural selection, acting on chance variations, can adequately explain the evolution of the present panorama of living organisms from some primeval and fortuitous collection of molecules.

But quite a lot of other scientists – apparently equally intelligent and eminent – claim that these 'answers' are not answers at all, and that the 'real' problem still exists. We do not understand, they say, either how life works, or how it evolved. If they are right, it is obviously a matter of considerable importance. For it is out of the recognition of problems that new discoveries arise – and new discoveries, as we are now rather uncomfortably aware, have a habit of changing the world we live in.

This is why the discussions at the Villa Serbelloni, on Lake Como, which I mentioned last week, are of more than academic significance. With the support of the Rockefeller Foundation, Professor C.H. Waddington of Edinburgh University has gathered together during the past few summers groups of leading biologists, mathematicians and physicists, to explore the possibilities of a firmly founded 'theoretical biology'. And it is quite clear from the reports of the conferences that most of those present were agreed that a very major problem exists.

At the heart of this problem is one central phenomenon: the *organisation* of living things – their capacity to arrange and maintain their cells and their organs as coherent wholes or 'organisms'. And again and again, in discussing this problem, the suggestion was made that the answer will have to do with the peculiar relationship of living things to *time*. This is the most important contrast between living and non-living things. Stones and crystals do not have life-cycles, and they do not evolve in any significant sense. Understanding life means understanding processes in time – conception, birth, maturation, death, evolution.

At the Serbelloni meetings three things have happened: new evidence has been reported which reinforces dissatisfaction with orthodox theory; the 'real' problem has been defined more precisely; and some remarkable new ideas have been discussed which promise to lead further. I will deal with some of the new evidence first.

Neo-Darwinism assumes that we now have a thorough understanding of the principles governing heredity (principles which have been given a further dimension in the past ten years, now that molecular biology can define a gene in molecular terms). However, in certain laboratories – notably in Professor Waddington's Department of Animal Genetics at Edinburgh – some very odd things are being discovered. For example, two very closely related species of fruit fly have been found, which are almost identical outwardly, but whose genetic material turns out to be, in parts, extraordinarily different.

It has long been realised that genetically identical individuals may grow up to look very different if they inhabit distinct environments. But it is astonishing to find two almost identical individuals with big differences in genetic constitution. The whole of genetics is based on the assumption that heredity works because the genetic material contains an exact blueprint for the development of each organism. Now the question is how two substantially different blueprints should give rise to almost identical organisms.

Another phenomenon to which Waddington drew attention at Serbelloni involves cultures of cells grown outside their parent organisms (for example, skin cells from mice). Very often, such cultures will grow only for a limited number of generations. But every now and again a curious 'crisis' may occur, involving a major upheaval in the genetic system (including changes in the number and shape of the chromosomes which carry the genes). After such a crisis, the culture becomes an 'established strain' which keeps going indefinitely (and can be advertised and sold by laboratory suppliers). What is happening here is quite unknown, but reveals the possibility of large-scale genetic events quite different from those contemplated in neo-Darwinism, and conceivably of major relevance to evolution.

Conventional neo-Darwinism also assumes that natural selection works on large numbers of individual genes. But R.C. Lewontin from the University of Chicago presented a paper at Serbelloni with the challenging title: *On the irrelevance of genes.* He pointed out that, in real genetics, hereditary factors seldom manifest singly, but normally occur in linked groups associated by their positions on a particular chromosome. He has now worked out the implications of this for evolutionary genetics, and the result is, he says, that 'genes have disappeared entirely from the theory, leaving only the chromosome units to be considered'. This demands a theory which treats the chromosomes as wholes, and means, Lewontin says, that 'we must completely re-orientate our theoretical framework'.

Findings like these suggest that present evolutionary theory, built on conventional genetics, cannot survive without substantial modification. But another and even more fundamental question was raised by Howard Pattee, a physicist from Stanford University in California. How, he asked, has life preserved its orderly properties over such huge spans of time?

The conventional answer is that the source of this orderliness is the inherited genetic 'blueprint', which is handed down through the generations recorded as a code in the molecules of DNA which make up the chromosomes. Each growing organism, and each cell, then refers to the blueprint for 'instructions' on what to do next. Molecular biology is largely concerned at present to trace how these instructions are issued by the DNA to the rest of the cell.

But Pattee points out that the instructions have to be copied each time the cell divides, and the copies must be made accurately through countless generations if life is not to dissolve into chaos. Elaborate explanations of this copying process are given by molecular biology in terms of interactions between complex molecules. But, according to Pattee, the interactions at present known to physics and chemistry could not possibly be *reliable enough.* A great number of copying mistakes would arise in quite a short time (just as they do when manuscripts are copied by hand). So some further 'constraints', whose nature is still wholly obscure, must be sustaining this long-term orderliness. At this level, too, there is a fundamental problem of *organisation.*

Neo-Darwinism came under fire at Serbelloni, not only because it may be based on faulty genetics or inadequate chemistry, but also because it may not explain anything important. What then is the 'real' problem? All that neo-Darwinism does at present, the critics say, is to pronounce that 'what survives, survives'. It is obvious that if a species *has* survived, it must be fit to survive, and its organism must be 'adapted' to its environment. It is also obvious that organisms which are *not* adapted will cease to exist.

No one doubts that forms of life can be modified through natural selection, and that there is some kind of interplay between the genetic system and the environment (even if, as the findings on Edinburgh indicate, the interplay may be more complex and surprising than is now realised). But Professor Waddington thinks that neo-Darwinism 'may only explain how species *keep going* and maintain themselves in a changing environment'. It gives no real explanation of the origin of the types of animals that actually exist.

There are two aspects to this problem. The first is to understand why animal life has *progressed*, from simpler to more complex organisms: an amoeba is extremely fit to survive (possibly more so than men, who are now busily inventing things with which they could make themselves extinct). But why did evolution go on from amoebae? One scientist who is in general satisfied with neo-Darwinism said at Serbelloni that there may have been 'nowhere to go but up' – starting from simplicity, any major changes would presumably have been in the direction of greater complexity. On the other hand, he said, 'it is equally easy to imagine that the first living organism promptly consumed all the available food and then became extinct'.

The second question is why, in progressing, evolution has given rise to certain distinct groups of animals. As Professor Waddington remarked, evolution is pictured as a slow and gradual process, proceeding by very small steps – yet it has produced a restricted number of basic 'archetypes' – single-celled animals, worms, insects, vertebrates, etc. Why are these basic 'designs' especially favoured by natural selection, and not others? And if the test is mere survival – the leaving of large numbers of offspring – why should animals have evolved extraordinary ways of life (think of ant-eaters) instead of being reduced, in Waddington's phrase 'to bags of eggs and sperm like parasitic worms'? No theory of evolution can be complete without some explanation of why evolution produced 'higher' forms of life from lower, and why these forms can be grouped into 'archetypes'.

It seems likely that this problem is closely connected with that already mentioned, namely the development of complex organisms from a single fertilised egg cell, and the maintenance of the form through a lifespan. The essence of an organism is that although it is involved with, and depends on, the environment, at the same time it establishes and maintains a certain independent 'individuality'. This is achieved despite physical and chemical forces all round it which could destroy it (and do destroy it, by turning it into compost, when it dies). As one scientist at Serbelloni put it, organisms have their own 'goals' which are distinct from those of the physical environment.

Molecular biology assumes that the instructions for coordinating an animal's various parts, for directing it to its 'goals', are coded into the inherited blueprint. But copies of the blueprint sit inside each cell of an organism: how does one blueprint know what instructions all the others are issuing? How does one cell keep in step with another? How does each part 'know its place' in the organism as a whole?

A number of scientists at Serbelloni emphasised that, however this control is achieved, it must be involved with the *hierarchical* nature of living organisms: each organism consists of organs, which consist of tissues, which consist of cells, which consist of a variety of molecules, which consist of atoms, which consist of fundamental particles (what the fundamental particles consist of is now the central problem of nuclear physics – for it has become clear that they are probably not 'fundamental' at all). At each level, the parts serve a whole on the next higher level, which somehow organises the parts of which it consists.

The 'reductionist' tradition of science assumes as a matter of course that a complex phenomenon must be explicable in terms of something simpler. The cells must explain the organ, the molecules must explain the cells, the atoms must explain the molecules, etc. Perhaps the most surprising event at Serbelloni was that this assumption was explicitly challenged by a physicist. To understand the nature of this challenge requires a slight digression.

Earlier in this century, physics faced a problem reminiscent of the 'organisation' problem in biology. Atoms, consisting of electrons and protons, have definite complex structures (consisting of successive 'shells' round the atomic nucleus containing particular numbers of electrons). The problem was 'solved' by quantum theory in the 1920s which showed that these structures made a coherent mathematical pattern. But a penalty was paid, for the theory meant that 'fundamental particles' could no longer be treated as separate, individual objects, but only as *statistical* effects. All one can say about an electron is that there are definite odds that it will be in a particular place at a particular time. It was turned from a thing into a kind of blur, which behaved as a 'particle' when observed in one way, and as a 'wave' when observed in another. And it became accepted that it was impossible to search further into the 'causes' of the patterns of atomic shell structure.

However, quantum theory has long been a focus of vague unease, and recently Professor David Bohm, of Birkbeck College,

London, has reopened the whole question. In effect he is arguing that the apparently *chance* behaviour of particles at one level in fact reflects an *orderly* pattern at a higher level. (Some experiments are being planned at University College to test these ideas.) At Serbelloni, Bohm suggested that there is an analogous situation in biology, and that rather than the parts of a living structure determining the whole, the whole may be determining the parts. Perhaps 'hierarchies of order' are as fundamental a feature of the universe as 'particles'.

Bohm admitted that such an idea runs contrary to all usual scientific habits, and is therefore difficult to digest. But he claimed that the 'reductionist' view is 'merely a rather poorly tested assumption' and alternatives should not be rejected because they 'don't fit into current mechanical hypothesis'.

Bohm's paper was not rejected at Serbelloni, but was taken up by several others, who asked whether something analogous to quantum theory is not needed for biology – some form of mathematical analysis which accounts for the hierarchical order of living systems. In particular, an outstanding French mathematician, René Thom (who was recently awarded the Lieper Prize – the mathematician's equivalent of the Nobel Prize), described how he is drawing on 'topology' to describe the development of living forms. Topology is one of the most recent and rapidly advancing branches of mathematmatics, and is a kind of universal geometry of surfaces. According to Thom, 'in biology there exist formal structures, in fact geometric entities, which determine what forms living matter can take up. These forms "aspire towards existence", although only a minority of possible forms succeed in "coming through to existence"' .

A particularly interesting aspect of Thom's work is that it apparently allows a mathematical description of organisms, not as fixed structures in space, but as changing structures in time. And it was repeatedly emphasised at Serbelloni that any 'theoretical biology' must take account of the fact that living organisms are highly organised in time – all the multifarious processes of growth and metabolism keep in step through a lifetime.

Professor Waddington has been exploring this aspect of life throughout his scientific career. He emphasises how, when a fertilised egg develops into an adult, a number of parallel processes flow along well-defined channels of development, which he calls 'chreodes'. He points out that biological theory must account for the evolution and control of these chreodes.

This approach led him to discover a quite new effect called 'genetic assimilation'. When fruit flies, for example, are reared in higher temperatures, the adults show certain changes in wing form and other features. If those flies which respond most strongly are selected for further breeding, after a few generations the modified form appears and is inherited at *normal* temperatures. This looks like the kind of thing Mendelian genetics says is impossible – a direct modification of heredity by environment. In fact, Professor Waddington says, it is a perfectly orthodox effect: there has simply been selection of a capacity to respond in a particular way during development – a capacity which is under normal genetic control.

The idea that an organism should be regarded as a co-ordinated pattern of processes in time is being followed up by several scientists, notably B.C. Goodwin at the University of Sussex. Living processes at various levels all have characteristic 'time constants' – rhythms of cell division, secretion of hormones, turnover of nutrients, and so on. Goodwin suggests that an important feature of the hierarchical nature of living organisms is the characteristic time span at different levels (a lifespan for the whole organism, a shorter time for the renewal of tissues in an organ, a very short time for protein synthesis within cells, etc.). And the forms of living organisms may be an expression of these interacting rhythms or oscillations.

The 'form-producing' capacities of oscillations are well known in the simple phenomena of the 'Chladni figures' – patterns which appear when a metal plate strewn with sand is stroked with a violin bow. Much more complex effects have been demonstrated recently by Dr. Hans Jenny, a Swiss doctor, and Waddington comments on the 'biological look' of the forms produced.

Thus whatever ideas and experiments emerge out of this rich and complex endeavour, they are likely to centre on rhythmic processes in time. We may come to see, Waddington suggests, that organisms develop like a kind of musical composition. There is an early stage of development when a particular group of cells in the embryo is 'determined' as a future limb. Perhaps this means that those cells have gone into a particular pattern of oscillation, like the statement of a musical theme. Then, as development proceeds, the cells differentiate into bone and muscle as the 'theme' is worked out as an extended composition. But if the music breaks down cacophony results – and there is a cancerous growth. (Cancer is essentially a disease of disorganisation. When we understand how living cells are ordered, we shall understand how the order breaks down to produce cancer.)

Thus the total impression of the discussions at Serbelloni is certainly not of a science which is largely complete and is only filling in details. On the contrary, there is an unmistakable sense of an exploration only just begun. Whatever is found will in no way diminish the triumphs of Darwin and Mendel in the last century, or of neo-Darwinism and molecular biology in this. But it may well alter the way they are interpreted, and show them as just a part of a larger, rapidly evolving picture.

1970

A SENSE FOR LANGUAGE

Inner Language and Outer Language

Red Indians used to teach their children never to speak out their own names – for if someone uttered his own name, a devil could steal it, leaving the poor person nameless. A nameless human being had lost his identity, and became, literally, a nonentity.

Today we have a somewhat firmer grip on our identity, and speak our own names without hestitation when introducing ourselves to a stranger. But we are gradually acquiring a different anxiety, that our names could be annihilated by numbers. Soldiers have long been accustomed to being numbers, but civilians are now numbers to their insurance companies, their bank managers, the Ministry of Health, and to many other large organisations with which they deal. You can do what you like with your name – the trouble comes when an organisation loses your number. Then, for the computer behind the scenes, you cease to exist.

This contrast has to do with our changing relationship to language. For the Red Indian, language could still be magical, because words were part of the things and people they denoted. To know the true name of something was to have power over it. But we have come to regard words as mere labels of convenience which we attach to things. As labels, they are often inefficient and inaccurate, and are better replaced with numbers. There are a great many Charles Browns in the telephone books of the world, but the number 03407621 is unique, and if attached to a man, labels him unmistakeably.

Magical language and label-language imply quite different relationships between a speaker and the world around him. Magical language entails not only that a word is part of the inner nature of the thing it denotes, but that the speaker who forms this word inwardly and then utters it is also part of the world around him: his inner life must participate in the inner life of nature, or else he could not hope to be a magician.

Label language implies the opposite, namely that the things of nature exist quite separate from, and indifferent to, the inner life of human beings and the sounds which they generate to label them. The latter are mere conventions, which take different forms around the world and might be replaced more conveniently by a universal code. Human beings also modulate these noises with others which indicate private emotions – language may be used for 'expression' as well as 'communication'.[1] But what is expressed has to do with the private internal state of the individual, and has no objective significance for the surrounding world.

This view of language reflects faithfully not only the beliefs, but the actual experience of many – perhaps most – adults in the modern Western world. For nature does seem to be quite separate from the private inner world of thoughts and emotions; and while language is used for referring to the surrounding world, it does not seem to be in any way part of it. This experience was enshrined philosophically by Kant (for whom the 'things-in-themselves' which constitute outer nature were separated from human thinking by an uncrossable gulf), and more recently, in terms of language, by linguistic philosophy.

In the study of language itself, until very recently, the label theory of language has dominated the field in various forms. It has therefore been assumed that when a child learns a language, it simply 'picks up' the sounds it hears, gradually assembling a kit of linguistic labels and tools for its own use. This view, while denying any objective relation between language and nature (by reducing it to human convention) still allows it some real connection with the inner life of human thought and feeling. Most people, however 'alienated', still assume that language allows one human being to enter into the real inner world of thought and feeling of another. It may be felt increasingly that this entry is problematic – there would not otherwise be so much discussion of the 'problem' of communication. Nevertheless, as long as we recognise that the problem exists, we imply that there is a possibility of resolving it – human beings still recognise each other's existence, even if a gulf separates man from man, and language provides only a rather shaky bridge across it.

The really chilling situation would be if this bridge were to vanish, and human beings came to regard each other as Kant came to view the things-in-themselves of nature, as fundamentally inaccessible and unknowable. Other people would then become for us, not beings, but things, objects among other objects with which we find ourselves surrounded.

During this century, the behaviourist school of psychology has been developing a view, not only of human nature, but of language itself, which implies just this (not surprisingly, for this psychology explicitly bans all consideration of any 'inwardness', not only for nature, but for man himself, on the grounds that what we call man's 'inner life' is not scientifically observable or measureable, so that even its existence is at best speculative).

In 1957, Professor B.F. Skinner, of Harvard, the leading exponent of this approach, published his book *Verbal Behaviour*.[2] There he argued that language is learned through selective 'reinforcement' of random items of behaviour – movements of larynx, lips, lungs, etc. – which are the basis of speech. Thus one day, by chance, a baby may say 'ma-ma' when its mother is nearby. She thereupon smothers it with kisses, for she believes that the child has begun to talk to her. The behaviourist, though, sees merely coincidence; but the kisses 'reward' the child and thus 'reinforce' the actions entailed in uttering 'ma-ma'. The result is that when the mother-stimulus is again near the child, it is more likely to emit the response 'ma-ma' again, and this behaviour will be further reinforced by kisses.

On this principle, which I have only slightly caricatured in this description, the whole of human speech is supposed to be built up. All adult conversation then represents behavioural responses – complex motions of tongue, larynx and lungs – which have been selectively reinforced by reward in the past. But to ask the 'meaning' of this behaviour would be to put into it some 'inner' content inaccessible to scientific observation and measurement, and would therefor be a waste of time.

When Skinner's book appeared, it was reviewed by Noam Chomsky, now Professor of Linguistics at the Massachusetts Institute of Technology, in an article[3] which became famous not only for the way it demolished Skinner's book, but for its formidable attack on the whole behaviourist position. But equally important, a wider public began to become aware of a new movement in the study of language in which Chomsky has played a formative part.

It is too soon to know where this movement will lead, but it has had already one important effect: it has re-awakened a sense of wonder for human language. People have begun to recognise afresh how extraordinary it is that we can speak and understand, and to be deeply astonished at the way in which little children all over the world acquire, without much apparent effort, such a very complex skill.

This work is showing unmistakably that it is insufficient to study merely the 'surface' of language, the sounds and forms of speech regarded merely as labels or conventional signals, for language is deeply bound up with the whole function of the human mind: it leads us through a speaker's speech into his meaning, and thus into his inner world of thought and feeling. We cannot therefore account for language unless we recognise it as the end product of a complex and still rather mysterious *process*, by which the speaker's inner world is shaped, transformed and uttered as spoken sentences. In understanding speech, this process is reversed: when listening, we are barely aware of the sounds and structure of the speech itself, unless we give it special attention. But as we listen, we become inwardly aware of the thoughts and feelings which live in the speaker.

All this may seem commonsense. But it has new force in contrast to half a century of linguistic studies which have concentrated almost entirely on the end product – on the surface structure and forms of the world's languages. These have been dissected and catalogued in great detail, rather as Linnaeus and later generations of naturalists dissected and classified plants and animals. But the process which gives rise to speech – the translation of thought into words – has been too easily forgotten.

The naturalists easily fell into the same trap. Botany books usually illustrate plants in full bloom, without roots, perhaps with drawings of fruit and seed as an extra. They do not, and cannot show directly the very obvious fact that every living plant is not a finished object in space, but a *process in time*, only part of which is visible at any one moment. To know the plant itself, therefore, we must discover how this process is ordered, and look for both the archetypal and specific capacities of each plant.

Modern science is now hunting for this 'time-form' of the plant in its inherited genes, which are regarded as a kind of blue-print to guide growth and development. This exploration is encountering fundamental difficulties, to which I will return. But linguistics is now following a remarkable parallel course. Chomsky and others have recognised that as well as its surface structure, language also has a 'deep structure'. The surface structure embodies those rules for building orderly sentences which are recorded in conventional grammar books and give us such trouble at school. Yet every child, in speaking its native language, is unconsciously observing these rules. This grammar gives us an adequate account of the structure of the finished product, rather as a botanical flora depicts the anatomy of a plant. But to understand the *process* of speaking, we must discover how what a speaker means is translated into speech.

Here we come upon Chomsky's 'deep structure'. This is revealed, for example, by the fact that sentences with different surface structures can have the same meaning: 'The tiger ate the lady' and 'the lady was eaten by the tiger'. To the grammarian, the surface structure of the two sentences is quite different. But both have a common 'deep structure' which has to do with their meaning, for both embody the speaker's intention to express a particular relation between the tiger and the lady.

A converse example is the ambiguous sentence, where one surface structure may point to two quite different deep structures: 'These men may not shoot tigers' could mean, for example that they are likely to miss because they are bad shots, or alternatively that they are not permitted to shoot tigers because they do not possess licences. Two entirely different relationships between the men and the tigers, hingeing on the ambiguity of the words 'may not' are contained in one surface structure. The appropriate deep structure can only be discovered from a wider context.

These are small, simple examples of what are developing into very elaborate studies. But they may help to illustrate the contrast between deep and surface structures of language which Chomsky emphasises. The 'rules' of surface structure – conventional grammar – define how orderly sentences are constructed in a given language. The 'rules' of deep structure, in contrast, describe how we organise thoughts in an orderly way so that they can be translated into sentences. The attempt to understand deep structure is thus more like the task of understanding the organising principles of a living plant. The speaker must first organise his thoughts of ladies and tigers into a particular form and then know how to transform this relationship into an utterance. This deep ordering according to Chomsky, brings ladies and tigers into an archetypal relationship which is expressed in all languages, and which embodies one of the fundamental ways in which we think about the world, namely the relationship of a subject acting on an object. The speaker may then have a choice of how to translate this relationship into surface structure (in this case he may choose the active or the passive mood). But he cannot organise the surface structure except in relation to the particular deep structure he has chosen.

This outlook has some remarkable consequences, which have begun to link linguistics with child development and human psychology in general. The 'rules'[4] of surface language are given: we find them already built into the language which surrounds us from birth. But what about the 'rules' of deep structure? These are not the rules of orderly utterance, but are more like the rules of orderly thought.

This question acquires quite new dimensions when we begin to look at how children actually learn to speak. Such studies have been gradually reinforced by the invention of the tape recorder, which has made it easy to gather large samples of what young children actually say, and what they actually hear from adults, during normal life at home. From such surveys it quickly becomes obvious that children do not and could not learn to speak simply by 'picking up' what they hear around them. First, the surface structure of adult speech – even of educated adults – is commonly fragmented, incomplete and often ungrammatical. Secondly, the majority of the sentences we utter each day are *new* – they are modified in some way, even if only in small details, from anything we have said before. This may seem surprising, but the tape recorder shows clearly that we repeat ourselves exactly less often than we think. How, then, in this fairly unpredictable language environment does the child discover the principles on which his mother tongue is organised at all?

But there is a further problem: If children learned by simple imitation, why should they at first speak such characteristic 'baby talk'? It is much more common to hear mothers imitating their child's language than the other way round. One little boy called Adam, whose language development was recorded over a long period by two American workers, was in the habit of saying ' Allgone lettuce', 'Allgone shoe', etc. The *meaning* of these phrases was perfectly clear to Adam and his parents. It is fairly clear to you and me. But it can hardly be argued that Adam picked up this construction from his parents. It is much more likely that his parents will have adopted it from Adam. (Most families have private words and phrases originally coined by one of its members in infancy. We have a collapsible bed familiar to all of us as the 'Oh-what-happened?' Readers will easily deduce the genesis of this phrase).

Young children, in fact, select words and phrases from the language they hear around them, but often use these in a highly idiosyncratic, yet systematic, fashion. The surface structure of such infant language is often ungrammatical – *but not because it resembles the slipshod construction of much adult speech*. It is in fact very orderly. There are unmistakeable 'rules'. As one investigator put it, we are beginning to realise that the child is not so much an incompetent speaker of adult language as a competent speaker of an exotic language. His utterances, however fragmentary, are full of organised meaning if we can learn to recognise it (mothers achieve this long before anyone else: The child says 'car bang Daddy'. Mother can instantly interpret: 'Oh she means that she heard the car door bang in the garage, so Daddy is back from work and will be here in a minute').

The remarkable consequence of these studies is a growing body of evidence that children embody in their speech many of Chomsky's 'deep structures' long before they have mastered the full surface structure of adult language. The two-word phrases of early child language, or even the earlier one word 'holophrases' (single utterances like 'allgone' which attentive parents often recognise as embodying a whole sentence which the child has not yet the skill to form), contain just those fundamental structures of orderly thinking, such as relations of subject and object, which lie behind all speaking.

This raises a difficult question: Children hear around them only the surface structure of language – and a fragmentary and ill-organised sample of the language at that. How could they possibly extract from this evidence the knowledge of deep structure they reveal in very early speech, the rules they evidently embody in baby-talk? There is only one possible answer: in every human baby, an unconscious 'knowledge' of deep structure must be *inborn*. This conclusion, now upheld by the modern school of psycholinguistics with fair unanimity, is in stark contrast to many decades of psychology and sociology which have held that we are born as *tabula rasa*, and are shaped from birth wholly by our environment.

If we are born with 'innate ideas' of language, then learning a language is not a matter of imitation in the simple sense, but means learning to relate the inborn deep structure to the surface structure of the particular language which surrounds a child. The child then stands, as it were, between two 'givens': the structure of the language in its environment, and the inborn deep structure. His 'competence' then develops as he learns to relate the one to the other, to practice what Chomsky calls 'generative grammar' so that thoughts are related in an orderly way to what is spoken.

The parallel to the problems concerning biologists is clear: The surface structures of adult speech are very different all over the world; but all human beings speak. In the diversity there is a deeper unity. This unity is manifest in the very fact that languages can be translated, although often imperfectly, one into another. The unity is at the level of meaning, and Chomsky's 'deep structure' appears to be connected with an inborn capacity in every human being to transmute thought into speech and *vice versa*.

In plants, the surface structure is diversely shaped by the environment – weather, soil, other plants. But a rose also retains its rose-ness wherever it grows. The 'deep structure' of a plant is its 'time-form' which guides its orderly development. Yet the nature of this body of organising forces still eludes biology. The issues are complex and there is not space to describe them here in any detail.[5] But the attempt to locate the 'deep structure' of organisms in their genes is in effect to ignore the very nature of the problem. For genes are conceived as parts, while the problem is to comprehend an organised whole; and the genes are sought as things in three-dimensional space, whereas the aim is to find organising *processes* working in time. If one sees the problem at all, it is not very difficult to realise that progress will demand not merely new ideas, but *a new way of thinking*. I suspect something similar will apply to Chomsky's deep structure. It is obviously tempting to try to locate this structure in brain structure, but the difficulties are then similar to those of locating life-structure in genes. Chomsky himself has recognised this, and remarks that we are facing problems which are *qualitatively* different from those which have interested science hitherto.[6]

*   *   *

Those familiar with the work of Rudolf Steiner will by now have recognised how these problems need some understanding of what he called the 'formative' or 'etheric' forces in nature and man. Steiner sometimes called the sum of these forces in living organisms the 'etheric body', and sometimes the 'time' body, and he was emphatic that science would not make real progress in understanding life without learning to know these forces.

Now it seems to me that in Chomsky's 'deep structure', and in the 'inborn knowledge' of this aspect of language which children seem to have, modern linguistics is beginning to recognise something like a time-body of language itself, a kind of organic vehicle for language which must clearly be deeply involved in the time-bodies of human beings.

We find Steiner describing how the living formative forces of our organism are used in two ways: They are in part bound to the organism itself, and enable the spiritual form or idea of man to be 'translated' into a living physical form which develops, grows, and is maintained in an orderly way. But there is a part of our organism – the head and the associated nervous system – where growth is completed quite soon, and living processes almost cease. Here, Steiner says, a part of our life-body is freed from the physical organism, and its forces become available to the human soul for the activity of thinking.

When we say 'I must get my thoughts organised', or 'that is a well-formed argument', we are recognising our own experience of the living, formative activity which we use to shape thoughts into a form in which they can be born into the world through speech and shared with others. In practising 'generative grammar', therefore, we are drawing on our own life forces to build a time-body for the speech which will bear our meaning into the world. The wisdom which we can then find in the earliest speech of a child thus points to the organising wisdom in his whole etheric body a part of which is beginning to be free for his own thinking activity. Childish speech conveys meaning long before the surface structure of his language is complete. This means that we must locate 'deep structure', not in the physical brain, but in the life body .

How does this bear on the problem, not of speaking one's own thoughts but of understanding another's? It is very remarkable that children should begin to understand the meaning of quite complex adult speech when their own speech is still rudimentary. Here Steiner says that we must learn to know a still unrecognised mode of *sense perception*: as well as senses of smell, colour, sound, etc., we have, he says, *a sense of thought*. With this sense, we actually *perceive the thoughts of others*. Then Steiner goes on to describe, in a surprising way, the *organ* for this sense: ' . . . If you reflect that you have life in your whole organism, and that this life is a unity, then this life, which you carry within you, to the extent that it is expressed in the physical, is the organ for the thoughts which come to you from without . . . If we were not endowed with life, we could not perceive the thoughts of others . . .'[7]

To understand this fully will be a task for research for a long time to come.[8] But it provides a clue to the capacity for the communication and reception of meaning which awakens in a certain way very early in childhood. We owe this capacity to the wisdom in our life bodies which enables us to organise our own meanings into speech, and to apprehend, through the often ill-organised surface of their speech, the living meaning of others.

*   *   *

It might seem that this is to treat language as primarily to do with thought and meaning, and to neglect 'surface structure', the actual forms and sounds of spoken languages. What is it, then, which a child meets in the language which surrounds him where he is born?

He meets, inevitably, a kind of tragedy, for he finds himself drawn into an aspect of language which does not unite, but divides him from others born into a different language. He becomes, as it were, a specialist in his speaking. Furthermore, the forms and structure of each language to some extent limit the meanings it is possible to convey: 'I know what I want to say but I can't say it'. Or 'you can say it in Japanese, but it is impossible to express in English'. Why should communication be crippled in this way? And why not resolve the problem by adopting a clear, precise, universal language, like mathematics?

Yet as we listen to the world's languages, we become aware that they bring us something else, a gift as well as a limitation: We hear in their sounds and forms a kind of music, a music connected not so much with our thoughts as with our *feelings*. There could be no poetry without the music of words, and this music can 'mean' a great deal to us. Yet it is part of the tragedy that this meaning is not universal, like that of thoughts, but appears subjective, private, personal.

We are returning here to the tension between label-language and magical-language with which I began this essay. Poetry is a kind of descendant of magical language: in magical spells and incantations, the forms, rhythms and sounds of the words are as important as their meanings. Perhaps fortunately, we can no longer shape words of such rhythm and power that they work on the life of surrounding nature. But the poet can stir and change with words the inner life of other human beings. That is his magic.

We are stirred by these sounds – as the word 'emotion' implies – to inner movement. (We may, especially if we are born into a Latin language, be stirred to a good deal of outer movement as well.) In the sounds, rhythms and shape of spoken language, therefore, we meet a 'surface structure' which is very far from superficial: We meet, in fact, not the 'life-body' of language, but its 'body of feeling', which is also its 'body of movement'.

Steiner spoke of the human being's 'body of feeling' as his 'sentient body', and also as his 'astral body'. Here again, he described a kind of body of forces, bound at first to the living and growing organism. Where the life-body manifests at first in organised physical growth and development, the astral body manifests in the *wisdom of movement*. It is miraculous to watch small babies gradually develop movements wisely related to the world around them. Each act of drinking, grasping, and later of standing and walking, demands the finest co-ordination of tens of thousands of muscles, fibres, joints, ligaments etc. But the most astounding co-ordination of all takes place in the fine control of breath, lips, tongue and larynx, which enables the child to take hold and and utter the organised sounds of the language around him. In his speech organs, the child becomes a master-conductor of a symphony of movements long before he has fully mastered his limbs and hands.[8]

He learns this speech symphony from the sounds and rhythms of the language around him. But to do so, according to Steiner, he makes use of a further 'sense', the *sense of word* (or perhaps, more

precisely, the *sense of speech sounds).*[9] Here again, he describes the
'sense organ' which mediates these perceptions. He refers to 'the
physical organisation for the faculty of movement' and continues:
'This [organism of the faculty of movement] is at the same time the
organ for the perception of language, for the words which are ad-
dressed to us by others. We could not understand words if we did
not have in us this physical apparatus for movement . . .'[10]

In learning his 'mother tongue', therefore, the child is truly imitating; he is learning the movements of a kind of local dance – his
'native' language – a dance performed only with tiny gestures of the
speech organs.

He is learning to move in speech with the language of his surroundings, as his own body of feeling and movement draws in the
movement-body of his mother tongue with the help of his sense of
speech sounds.

In the development of the child, the movement – or sentient –
body is at first involved in the development of the physical body,
and particularly in laying the basis both for wise movement, and
for sentience (the nerves and brain). But at puberty, part of the sentient forces are freed and become available for shaping an independent life of feeling and emotion. As we know, though, our life of
feeling is strongly coloured by the movement and music, by the
'emotion' inherent in the sounds, gestures and forms, in the 'dance' of
the mother tongue absorbed in infancy. Through learning to talk
like Englishmen, we are also taught by our language to *feel* like
Englishmen!

And now we must come again to the tragic element in these events.
Why, nowadays, should 'deeper structure' and 'surface structure' be
distinct? Why are meaning and speech sounds separate, with a corresponding gulf between thought and emotion? Why do we separate
poetry and prose, expression and communication, magical language
and label language? We are contemplating here some consequences
of those events we know as the Fall of Man, which Steiner illuminated from so many aspects. Through eating of the Tree of Knowledge – by succumbing to self-seeking – man was expelled from
Paradise. In his soul life he began to feel separated from the world
of creative spiritual reality in which he had lived. Every child as he
grows up re–lives this process of separation, and with particular
force during puberty.

Steiner describes how the fall affected first our sentient or astral
being, drawing some of our desires and appetites into egotism which
ties us to the earth. Yet there are 'two souls' in each one of us, for
with part of our sentient being we are idealists: our 'appetites' are

selfless, and lead us to strive to find our un-fallen natures. In our own bodies, we find one expression of the Tree of Knowledge in the great tree of our nervous system, which however, is always on the verge of death. It gives us sentience, but also tends to lead us to think, not in living ideals, but in dead logical structures. So we have developed, especially in modern science, a death-bringing intellect.

In language, the drama of the fall is being played out in a special form. We have almost lost the sense for the heavenly music, the unfallen 'astral body' of language, which still sounds, though distorted and out of tune, through the rhythms and forms of the fallen languages of the earth today. These languages carry an egotistic impulse, isolating their users behind 'language barriers'. We know, too, how to exploit language to play on emotions, rouse crowds, inflame nationalistic feelings. Yet through each language, especially in its poetry, there can still sound a characteristic feeling which is one facet of the archetypal Word which shines into it. It will be the task of poets, or of the poet in each one of us, into a far-distant future, to rediscover the heavenly dance in the sounds of speech, to redeem language and make it selfless once again.[11]

Perhaps I should add that this is a task for parents as well as poets. Part of every child's soul life, his movement of feeling and the life of his ideals, is shaped by what he hears of his mother tongue. It is a fortunate child who is surrounded by musical, well-formed speech filled with warmth and idealism, whose mother sings to him in infancy and who meets at school some of the great poetry and literature both of his own and of other languages (irrespective of whether he fully understands what he hears).

*   *   *

The book of Genesis says, rather mysteriously, that man had to leave Paradise in order to protect another Tree, the Tree of Life (Genesis 4, verses 22-24). In our life-bodies, which guide the life processes of our organism, there is still an almost untouched harmony and wisdom, a wisdom which is kept inaccessible to our waking consciousness with its tendencies to death-bringing thoughts and destructive feelings. At the same time, those life forces which serve our thinking activity lead us into a selfless relation to truth – for this is what the world of meaning is: we may possess, or be possessed by, an emotion; but a meaning, a concept, in its living reality, does not belong to any one person: the creative idea which organises the plant belongs to the plant, not to us. And when we share a concept, we do not each fondle a separate copy of it; we stand in the presence of the same concept, we participate in a creative meaning of the universe.[12]

Yet just in this century we must realise that the Tree of Life, both in our bodies and in our souls, has begun to be vulnerable. In biology, we are beginning to recognise the possibility that we could learn to control and manipulate the organising forces of life itself. When we think of 'genetic engineering' we are aiming to take hold of and manipulate the formative forces themselves.

We face something similar in language: Label-language is leading us to treat speech as mere 'behaviour', and to regard the acquisition of language as mere shaping of behaviour from without. We are beginning to discover possibilities of shaping behaviour by conditioning, of shaping not only language but thought itself: In propaganda, and in brain-washing, the aim is to reach right into the 'deep-structure' of a person's thinking, to give him not merely new feelings, but new reactions, habits, instincts. One part of such techniques is to instil by repetition certain words, phrases and slogans until they become part of his habits of thought. George Orwell in *1984* and *Animal Farm* foresaw with terrible clarity the direction in which such an attack on meaning itself could lead.

So here, too, we have a protective and redemptive task. All routine, machine-like use of language, fixation in cliché, 'empty phrases', all 'dead' language (except insofar as we need precise communication for dealing legitimately with dead things, the machines and technology of our civilisation) weaken and harden the Tree of Life in our language and thinking. But it is strengthened and vitalised when we fill our speech with the fresh life of *imagination*.

When human consciousness was united with the life of nature, language lived in man as an echo of the creative utterances of the gods which shaped the plants, the animals, the earth, and man himself as a microcosm of the macrocosm. And human utterance was therefore magical – an event in nature as well as in the human soul. But language has separated from nature, as the human soul has awakened to independent self-consciousness. In achieving self-consciousness, language has been brought close to death. And indeed it will surely die unless human beings now learn to pour their own creative life into it.

We lay a basis for this in childhood, and especially in the first school years, when nature frees life forces for the first independent imaginative life. Here Steiner schools nourish this life with the great imaginative truths embodied in fairy tales, myths and legends. Without such nourishment, we grow up starved and ill-equipped for a great spiritual and social task of our time – to find a path to true imagination, to a living thinking in which we form from our own life forces a life-body to receive the truths of the spiritual world.

The new linguistics is a long way from seeing the full dimensions of this task, as it emerges from the work of Rudolf Steiner. But I hope in this essay to have shown that it is not unrelated. Chomsky and his associates have awakened a new wonder for language, and wonder is the essential starting point for the search for imaginative truth. Chomsky has also held back the advance of behaviourism into language, and sees that this is not only an academic matter, but a struggle to rescue the creative intelligence of man. In this, followers of Steiner's work can recognise a true service to our times.

1973

[1] See O. Barfield, *Speaker's Meaning* (Rudolf Steiner Press).

[2] Appleton-Century-Crofts Inc., New York.

[3] *Language*, Vol. 35, No. 1, 1959.

[4] Strictly speaking, the word 'rules' is misleading – but only in the same sense that it is misleading to call certain findings of science 'laws'. What is meant at this stage, are simply the empirically-determined regularities discovered in the forms and order of the parts of language as used by its native speakers.

[5] For much fuller discussions of the problem of 'organisation' in biology, see *Beyond Reductionism*, edited Arthur Koestler (Hutchinson 1969). Also *Towards a Theoretical Biology*, edited Waddington (Edinburgh University Press).

[6] Noam Chomsky, *Language and Mind* (Harcourt, Brace and World, 1968).

[7] *Das Rätsel des Menschen*, lecture 14, given at Dornach on September 2, 1916 (Rudolf Steiner *Nachlassverwaltung*).

[8] The late Dr. Karl König made an important contribution to this problem in *The First Three Years of the Child*, chapter 4 (Anthroposophic Press, New York, 1969).

[9] In German, Steiner uses both *'Wort-Sinn'* (sense of word) and *'Laut-Sinn'* (sense of speech sounds). In so far as a complete word already embodies a thought (which is perceived by the sense of thought), *'Laut-Sinn'* or 'sense of speech sound' distinguishes more precisely the perception of the way speech itself is organised.

[10] Rudolf Steiner, *op. cit.*

[11] See also *Eurythmy and the Word* by A.C. Harwood, p. 67.

[12] I realise that this is a scandalously brief assertion of the position which Steiner developed in great detail in his *Philosophy of Freedom* and elsewhere. Readers are referred to this, and also to O. Barfield *op. cit.*

On Coming to Our Senses

Every morning, I wake up. This simple phrase describes a mysterious – and in my case rather gradual – process. I wake up first to sounds – birdsong, the newspaper being shoved through the letter-box, a small boy playing trains in the next room. Next comes awareness of warmth (or cold if the blankets have fallen off), and of position and weight; cramp if I have been lying awkwardly, the pleasures of moving and stretching. Sometimes smells come next – especially if bacon is being fried downstairs – and perhaps a dawning awareness of hunger. Only then may I open my eyes, a bit dazzled at first, gradually beginning to 'see'. Getting out of bed, washing, shaving, dressing, breakfast, and the first conversations of the day continue the process.

On some mornings, I may feel 'all there' within a few minutes of waking; on other, more reluctant days, it may be well after breakfast before I feel fully able to cope with the world. But however this extraordinary metamorphosis of consciousness occurs, as it has done regularly and without fail since the day I was born, it marks a daily gateway to life on earth, to all conscious relations with nature and with other people.

Waking up is deeply involved with a sphere of human nature which is easily taken for granted – the senses, and the perceptions they offer. If we want to wake someone up, we switch on a light, call out, touch him, shake him by the shoulder, or as a last resort dribble cold water on his face from a sponge. In other words, we stimulate his senses of sight, hearing, touch and movement, warmth and cold. We bring him – sometimes a bit roughly – 'to his senses'. Wherever we may be during sleep, the senses bring us down to earth, to an awareness of ourselves, inhabiting bodies and surveying a surrounding world.

Once awake, and if we begin to attend more carefully to the role of the senses in everyday life, we find that they are essential to thought, feeling and action. Most of our thoughts have a content derived from past sense-experiences – memories and the like. Our desires demand satisfaction through the senses (normal people are not content to imagine a steak or a symphony; they insist on tasting the one and hearing the other, in reality). Our actions and physical skills depend on healthy senses of balance, movement and touch (as the drunk whose senses are disordered by alcohol may discover rather painfully). A damaged or destroyed sense can be far more crippling than loss of a limb.

If we reflect on these experiences, leaving aside all theories about sense-organs and sense-perception that we may have learnt, we can become aware that throughout our waking hours the senses are providing a kind of *nourishment* – a content for our thoughts, sensations for our feelings, an essential support for our actions. The most physically massive kind of nourishment that we need to live properly in our bodies and on earth is the food we supply to our stomachs and digestive system. A second, and finer kind of nourishment is the air we breathe into our lungs, so that the blood is supplied with oxygen. Without adequate supplies of either of these, we grow faint and may die. But through our senses, which are linked through the central nervous system to our brain, we are nourished in a still finer way. We are supplied, so to speak, with 'light' – the light of day. Without this nourishment we cannot wake up properly.

In preparation for manned space flights, experiments were made in the United States with volunteers who underwent almost complete 'sensory deprivation'. They floated in water at blood heat, immobile, surrounded by silence, wearing goggles which admitted only a dim diffuse light or no light at all, and soft gloves to damp out touch. Most volunteers quickly fell asleep at first. But later they would wake up, and in some cases be gradually overcome by uncontrolled fantasies, hallucinations, or disordered perceptions of their own bodies (feeling, for example, that a foot or a leg had grown to an enormous size and was floating away from the rest of the body). These experiments showed vividly how essential a free flow of normal sense-experience is for a healthy day-time consciousness.

Further exploration of our own sense-experience shows that this 'nourishment' reaches us as a variety of distinct sensations, which before we begin to weave thoughts around them, have the nature of pure *'activities'*: warmth, colour, sound, movement, etc. Each of these qualities of activity is differentiated within itself (we experience a whole range of colours, of tones, etc.), but offers a distinct realm or mode of experience (defined physiologically, of course, by the functioning of a particular sense-organ or set of organs). If we contemplate the senses in this way, we may begin to understand what Rudolf Steiner meant when he once described the senses as 'well-springs'.¹ These wells are filled with what I have called the 'light of day' from sources lying outside our direct daytime experience.² The human being, Steiner remarks, dips into these springs to meet the needs of his soul, his inner life.

Steiner goes on, both here and in other books and lectures to describe how there are really twelve of these 'well-springs' flowing into our waking lives, twelve distinct modes of sense-experience, or, more simply, that we have twelve senses. Of some of these, such as sound, sight, warmth, etc., we are vividly aware. Of others we are barely aware unless they go wrong, notably balance and movement (which textbooks usually call the proprioceptive and kinaesthetic senses). A few are not at present clearly recognised at all.

The twelve are: touch, life, movement, balance, smell, taste, sight, warmth, hearing, thought, word and 'I'. Of these, eight are clearly recognised in modern textbooks. A ninth, the sense of 'life', is less clearly defined, but in Steiner's terms is responsible for our sensations of general bodily 'well-being' (or ill-being), as well as the physical component of the sense of pain.³ The final three: 'word' , 'thought' and 'I' (by which Steiner means the direct perception of the 'I' of another human being), are not to be found in any textbooks. I shall have more to say about them below.

So far, I have described these twelve well-springs as bringers of a kind of nourishment for our healthy day-consciousness. But now we must recognise that the senses also bring problems which have had profound effects on human life throughout history. These problems are of two main kinds: problems of morality and problems of knowledge.

In the East, and in the past, men were much concerned with the role of the senses in moral behaviour. They can tempt to indulgence, egotism, excessive 'attachment' to the pleasures of this world. Again and again, ascetic and puritan teachings have arisen, urging men to 'purify' or even as far as possible to deny their senses – or rather, to deny satisfaction to those desires which can only be stilled temporarily with the help of the senses. The pleasures of this world, men have repeatedly been told, are vain, illusory, and divert the soul from its true path, which should be to seek a Divine and unfallen world by withdrawing from our daytime world.

Nowadays, there are only faint echoes of such moral debates in scientific cultures, although many people probably feel vaguely guilty after excessive bouts of indulgence in food, drink, sex or generally luxurious living. But the issue is still with us, in a new, unexpected and still barely recognised guise. It lives, in fact, in the problem of economic growth, and the struggle for 'higher standards of living'.

Of course there are millions of people struggling for a higher standard for simple reasons of health, strength and minimum human dignity. But in the 'advanced' countries, vast numbers of people consume quantities of food, goods and services far greater than they need for sufficiency. The essential product offered by many consumer industries consists of sense-experiences; and the true consumers are the insatiable human appetites attached to them magnified by advertising and elaborate forms of stimulation. When salesmen are taught 'don't sell the steak, sell the sizzle', they are acknowledging that their real customers are our senses of hearing (plus sight, taste and smell), and not our stomachs (where we are more or less unconscious, except when we have indigestion).

What an Eastern teacher in the past might have called excessive attachment to self and to earthly illusion, we might call addiction: enslavement to appetites and sensations which have got out of hand, so that we are no longer nourished and supported, but made dependent and ill. The very phrase 'a slave to such and such' expresses our direct experience that our true selves are not identical with these sensations and desires, but subject to and entangled in them. Monsters can lurk in our well-springs, and drag us in to drown.

The second problem in which the senses are deeply involved is that of knowledge. I have assumed that the senses enable us to 'know the world', that they bring us the true light of day. 'Seeing is believing', we say. If I am not sure whether I can 'believe my eyes', I may pinch myself to make sure that I am awake and not dreaming. If I *am* properly awake, the implication is, then I can and must believe my eyes.

Nevertheless, Eastern teachers and religions have frequently held that what the senses reveal is Maya – illusion, a veil over a different reality. In a new guise, this issue has re-emerged in modern times in science and philosophy, as we have come to believe that ultimate reality is something other than what our senses reveal to our normal consciousness. We do not see the atoms, particles, or waves of which the universe is supposed to consist. The experiences conveyed by the senses are held to be 'subjective' and therefore not to be naïvely trusted. In very recent times, the notion that our senses hide rather than reveal a more profound reality has also been revived in connection with drug experiences. Under the influence of mescalin, Aldous Huxley believed that 'doors of perception', which are normally closed, began to open.

At the same time there is a wider social problem, a kind of companion to the problem of growth and excessive consumption, which goes by the name of 'alienation'. This word has come to be used very broadly to describe a kind of inner loneliness and isolation, a sense of being 'out of touch' with the world, a stranger among strangers who can never really meet each other properly, and who are not perhaps to be wholly trusted. In political life, the problem of trust has loomed very large in recent years, and there is often a growing sense of a discrepancy between the public 'image' of a person and the private 'reality', hidden but perhaps fundamentally inaccessible, behind a mask.

Such problems point to a kind of illness or disorder in the sphere of sense-perception, whose true function, as we have seen, is to lead us into a healthy waking consciousness in which we 'come to our senses', and can thereby live properly in the world. 'Alienation' points to a kind of dream state persisting into waking life, an inadequate 'coming down to earth', whereas greed and addiction point to an opposite extreme, in which we become frantic consumers of sense-experiences to feed insatiable drives and desires.

These social disorders point to the need for a kind of therapy for the senses, a therapy which will depend on a deeper understanding of the twelve realms of sense-experience that Rudolf Steiner describes. 'The I', he once remarked, 'moves among the circle of the twelve senses as the sun moves among the signs of the Zodiac'. We have some direct awareness of this in the simple capacity to 'attend' to one mode of sense-experience or another – to be particularly awake in our hearing, for example, or in the sense of smell. When we are deeply absorbed in one mode of sense-experience, the others retire into the background. But if we attend in turn to the various senses Steiner describes, we shall discover that the circle is differentiated in many ways – it has a complex anatomy and structure.

One kind of distinction to which Rudolf Steiner drew attention[4] is between six more 'inward' senses – touch, life, movement, balance, taste, smell – and the remaining six which tend to take us more out of ourselves, so to speak – sight, warmth, hearing, word, thought, 'I'. In the first four of the first set, we are clearly concerned in perceptions of our own bodies. *Touch* defines for us the bodily boundary of the skin; *life* the harmony or disharmony of our body's contents; *movement* allows us to be aware of the motions of muscles and joints; *balance* allows us to perceive how our weight is disposed in space. When we attend to the sensations conveyed by these senses, we are turned inwards to our own bodies. Here we are seldom troubled by distrust of our perceptions. We use touch as a kind of ultimate test of reality; one does not argue about a sense of bodily discomfort – if we don't feel well, there is no room for doubt. Nor do we ever question the trustworthiness of our senses of movement and balance. Here, quite particularly, we find a sureness and security in our relation to our own bodies.

Taste and smell begin to relate us to aspects of nature outside our own organism. Nevertheless, these senses function only when we draw fine vapours deep into our nose, or dissolve something on the tongue. We also react in a particularly personal way to tastes and smells, the latter conjuring up personal memories and associations, the former often being involved with strong personal preferences. A person's 'taste' in food, drink, clothes, literature, etc., is a very individual matter.

Through these six senses we are strongly attached to our own bodies, and in taste and smell are 'consumers' of products of nature. It is through these senses, more particularly, that we are prone to indulgence in 'sensuality' and greed. On the other hand, the healthy function of these senses is the basis for secure, 'down-to-earth' waking consciousness, and it is through these senses that we know most directly and intimately, through knowing them in our own body, the 'primary qualities' of the earth – weight, movement, solidity, and so on. In early childhood, as we learn to manage our bodies and move around in the physical world, it is these senses in particular which serve us as we learn to become earth citizens.

Our whole orientation begins to change with the senses of sight (which in this context should be understood more specifically as the sense of colour), and warmth. Here we experience a kind of 'breathing' with the surrounding world, and the certainties of the more body-oriented senses begin to dissolve. Colour and warmth are most often quoted in popular text books as proof that all sense-perception is 'subjective'. If we emerge into a mild day from a cold room or from a hot room, the same outside air feels warm or cool. So we cannot trust our senses, we are told. This is revealed as complete nonsense as soon as we realise that these senses show us *relationships* – and show them with great precision. Our sense of warmth in effect tells us whether we are losing or gaining warmth from our surroundings, or from an object we are touching. Colour perception also brings us an experience of colour as a relationship between the hue of an object and the ambient illumination (This is why, when we buy clothes, we try to inspect them both by daylight and by artificial light).

These two senses are a kind of bridge to a world *other than* ourselves (in so far as we identify our 'self' with percepts of our own organism). With hearing, as Rudolf Steiner often described, we begin to enter into a kind of 'inwardness' of what is around us.

You see a vase in a room. It may not be clear to the eye whether it is made of metal, clay or stone – but tap it with a finger and you will know at once. The sound allows you to hear right into the matter of which it is made (this fact is widely exploited in engineering, where ultrasonic vibrations are used to detect flaws in metal structures, on the same principle as a crack in a bell is instantly audible as a flawed tone). The eye shows us a bird or a cow from outside; but the sounds uttered by these animals convey something of their inner joys and sufferings. Most far-reaching of all, of course, is the entry into the 'inwardness' of another human being which begins when he opens his mouth and speaks.

Hearing, as Steiner describes it, is the first of four senses which play the most crucial role in human relationships. The others are the sense of word, thought and 'I'. Steiner sometimes described these four senses as a kind of turning inside out of the four 'body' senses of balance, movement, life and touch. This is a theme on which much research will be needed in the future, and all I can do here is to point to a few phenomena which seem to me suggestive for further study.

The sense of hearing, as we all know, is anatomically closely associated with the sense of balance in the ear. But I am here concerned not so much with the anatomy and physiology of these senses as with exploring and comparing the sense-experiences themselves. Here it is worth noting that the sense of balance leads us into security of stance in physical space, while hearing leads us most strongly 'out of ourselves' into a totally different kind of 'space' which is essentially 'weightless': we can observe this most strongly when listening to music. If we could trust our senses, we would realise that a symphony is not *in* the air waves of the concert hall, but that we perceive the music *through* these waves, and with the help of our ears can reach directly into a reality of which the air waves are merely a bearer, not the cause.

The sense of word – or more precisely the sense of speech-sounds – reveals to us the 'sculpture', the gestures, made by a speaker's larynx, tongue and lips, which shape a stream of sound into the forms of vowels and consonants. These forms are composed by the speaker into a kind of 'dance' – something between gesture and music – a sequence of sounds which is characteristic of the particular language he is using. In perceiving this aspect of language, with the sense of speech sounds, we are concerned with feeling rather than thought, and indeed we can enjoy the speech sounds of languages of which we don't understand a word. Into the speech sounds there also flow the individual's own intonation and feelings, which 'move' us in various ways. With the help of our sense of speech sounds, we dance a little inwardly with the words we hear, using a metamorphosed sense of movement turned away from our own movements to apprehend the movement, as also the colour, mood and 'emotion', in the speech of another.

It is important to realise that the sense of speech sounds is not particularly concerned with the conceptual meaning these sounds may bear (except in so far as some words bear something of their meanings within the sounds themselves – 'thud', 'snake', 'rush', 'sting' etc.). To discern the thoughts borne by the words we need the sense of thought. How can we try to understand this sense as a kind of turning inside out of the sense of life? The latter is concerned with perception of the harmony or disharmony of our organic processes. These processes are essentially organised rhythms. With our sense of life we perceive how the stream of rhythmic time-processes is well-organised or ill-organised.

The physical medium by which thoughts are borne to us is also a pattern of organised movement. This may be the pattern or organisation – the *sequence* of movement – in a stream of speech sounds. Or it may be the sequence of gesture-movements made by a skilled mime (who may be able to convey remarkably complex thoughts in this way. Here, again, it is important to recognise that the *sense* of thought does not give us the thought *content*, but only the physical vehicle, the stream of organised living movement in speech or gesture, into which a content can flow. We ourselves search inwardly for the content – for the concepts which belong to the perceived speech sounds and organised pattern of speech flow. (This distinction applies to all the senses; they give us percepts which are themselves without 'meaning' until we find the corresponding concepts.)

Thus we may begin to understand the sense of thought as a perception of the 'life form' of the thoughts themselves which someone is trying to convey to us, apprehended by a sense of life turned outward from immersion in the organised flow of our bodily life processes, in order to apprehend the 'thought life' of another.

Finally, and perhaps most difficult of all, is the search for a clear awareness of the sense of the 'I' of another person. When we use the word 'tact', we indicate that in the meeting of two people there is a kind of delicate, non-physical touching. But it is not easy to become more aware of what the perception actually is. It can be helpful to recollect, soon afterwards, a first meeting with someone. There will be memories of what was said, of a physical appearance, emotional reactions, etc. But if all these are put aside, and one asks what is left, there may remain an impression which is best described as a kind of 'force-form', as though one had 'touched', very dimly, the essential *will* of the person one has met.

It is particularly with these three senses that the problems of truth and illusion become most acute (the more so because their very existence is not generally recognised). They already arise clearly with sight and hearing: we never normally say 'I could not believe my balance'; but we often say that we could not believe our eyes or ears.

Much more serious, though, is the 'alienation' which leads to doubt and distrust in every human encounter. Many people will remember vividly sudden moments of such doubt, probably in their ninth year, when children begin for the first time to feel separate, alone and perhaps surrounded by strangers. Such moments pass, but often return strongly with adolescence. The healthy side of this is an acute sense for the integrity or otherwise of those around, and a sharp nose for what is 'phoney' (except that it is not the nose, but the senses of 'I', thought and word which are particularly involved). But if this awakening to separateness becomes extreme, it may bring cynicism, chronic distrust and an inability as an adult to 'make contact' with other human beings – a contact which depends on a proper functioning of the senses of word, thought and 'I'.

It is probable that some elements of indulgence or illusion can touch every one of the twelve senses. Nevertheless, it seems clear that the problematic aspect of the senses which most concerned the East – attachment and entanglement in 'self' and in earthly existence – arises mainly in connection with the six bodily or 'self-centred' senses. The problem of knowledge, on the other hand, has arisen more strongly in science in connection with the six 'world-centred' senses. In the West, we have gained great confidence in the science of bodies, in grasping mass, motion, position, etc., with mathematical certainty. It is a certainty born out of the establishment of an inner security in our own bodies, in early childhood, as we learn to stand, walk and manipulate the objects around us. (Certain lines of research in child development are beginning to reveal what Steiner pointed to over fifty years ago, namely that the apparently abstract mathematical thinking of later life is deeply at work, although unconsciously, in small children learning to know the world of bodies.) At the same time, we are deeply uncertain about any realities outside our capacity to touch, weigh, measure and manipulate – so much so, that they may be banished to an inaccessible realm of 'things in themselves' (as with Kant), or in the case of spiritual realities to a realm accessible only to faith. The division in the sphere of the twelve senses is reflected in the split between 'science and religion', and the emergence of a kind of empirical and manipulative knowledge working with 'laws of nature', but empty of *moral* laws.

It is therefore not surprising that it is the West, particularly, which has produced a body-centred, consumer society, plundering the earth to assuage disordered appetites, while at the same time experiencing an increasing emptiness of moral life and human relationships, and a deep uncertainty about the meaning of existence.

I mentioned earlier the need for a 'therapy' of the senses. I believe that we can begin to see our way if we take a new look at the whole sphere of the senses, not dualistically, but as a threefold structure. Rudolf Steiner often classified the twelve senses in this way also, speaking of four 'will' senses (touch, life, movement, balance), four 'feeling' senses (smell, taste, sight, warmth), and four 'spiritual' senses (hearing, word, thought, 'I').

In Steiner's recommendations for three main phases of education – nursery, lower school and upper school – we can glimpse a remarkable kind of nurture of the twelve senses. He wanted the nursery and kindergarten to be full of practical activities – baking, cleaning, washing up, making things out of simple materials – but activities filled with reverence and care for the substances and things of the surroundings. Here the qualities of the substances, materials and furniture matter greatly – perhaps more than at any other time.

Small children, Steiner sometimes said, are completely united with the whole sphere of their sense-perceptions, which is less differentiated than in adults. Because of this they are deeply imitative – everything in the surroundings makes a deep inner impression. Small children have no possibility of 'alienating' themselves from their surroundings (except in tragic disorders of autism and the like). Thus they 'imitate' the very qualities of the things around them, so it is crucial that these should be 'honest'. An object which is a kind of a lie – which is in any way fake, or made of materials estranged from nature – brings a kind of immorality to the child through his senses. The traditions and instincts of true *craftsmanship* are needed above all in the creation of the environment to nourish the senses of young children. The children, Steiner once said, should be able to experience at this time 'the world is *good*'. This is the source for true security and inner certainty in the world in later life, and for the birth of the real creative moral being of the individual working in the will.

In the lower school, from six to fourteen, a great demand is made on the class teacher. He or she must strive to be above all an *artist*. For the emotional life of children is awakened in a new way, with a sense for drama, the battle of good and evil, beauty and ugliness. Here all the arts are needed, and here, too, lie the strongest and most comprehensive possibilities for a nourishment and therapy of all twelve senses. The plastic arts – sculpture, modelling, woodwork, etc. – engage particularly the will senses, but relate these activities also to the life of feeling. The arts involving music and language (including drama and poetry) engage particularly the spiritual senses of hearing, word, thought and 'I' but again embracing them into the sphere of feeling. Quite centrally stands painting, the art which lives with colour, but into which play subtly our senses of taste, smell and warmth.

It is at this time, above all, when a kind of bridge can be created, so that the child learns to breathe freely between himself and the surrounding world. And it is in the arts that the most crucial therapy for the enlivening and healing of the senses lies. In the middle school, Steiner said, the child must experience 'the world is *beautiful*'.

In the upper school, the pupils are faced with a new kind of challenge. They meet teachers in a new way, as 'knowers', as 'scientists' in the true sense, specialists in different fields of knowledge. The task here is to open the world to the pupils as it lives in the experience and enthusiasm of adults. In adolescence, a more detached perception begins; the spheres of sense perception and inner life begin to be more distinguished, and among other things pupils begin to take a more objective look at their teachers and parents, and to realise that they are by no means perfect. But adolescents are always searching for true perceptions mediated by the spiritual senses of word, thought and 'I', for the truth in the human beings around them.

The confusion of untruthful images and violent or chaotic music with which our culture assaults adolescents at this time is a direct attack on the senses, but particularly on the spiritual senses which are most crucial for building a true understanding between man and man. Here again, we must seek for therapies in all the arts, but perhaps particularly in drama, poetry and song.

A deeper understanding of the senses will also open the way to new science, in which the senses can be trusted because they are known in their different functions and qualities. In the upper school, adolescents will be greatly helped by teachers who can show them a path of devoted and exact observation of natural phenomena. In this connection, Steiner pointed often to the path taken by Goethe, which enabled him to discover the 'Ur-plant', the archetypal plant present formatively in the plants around him – an Idea perceived in reality. This is the path for the healing and overcoming of alienation. In the upper school, Steiner said, the pupils should come to experience 'the world is *true*'.

I began this essay by exploring the role of the senses in waking up, a birth out of the womb of sleep into the light of day. Growing up entails a related birth and awakening, for which home and school provide a womb. If human beings are to awaken to themselves in the world, they need the freedom of a healthy sphere of twelve senses. To help this is one of the central tasks of the education initiated by Rudolf Steiner. But it is a task which needs to continue throughout adult life. In practical terms, it means working for an environment in which the 'goodness' of the crafts, the beauty of the arts, and the truth of the sciences interweave.

The birth of our true humanity thus depends on the right nourishment through the 'well-springs' of our senses as essentially as on air we breathe and the food we eat. But we need also to become aware of the 'monsters' which lurk in these well-springs. I have already mentioned the kind that would enslave us in greed and addiction, and fetter us permanently to the world of bodies. But there are also the monsters that would alienate us, abstract us from reality and take us wandering in worlds of private inner fantasy because we can find no secure relation to the surrounding world and other people, or do not wish to come down to earth.

In the whole spectrum of the arts, which (as we have seen) can weave through all our senses, we can begin to bring the different spheres of perception into a more living and weaving relationship, as the rainbow makes a bridge between heaven and earth. We need to bring something of the realism and certainty which is given naturally through the body-senses into the world of our spiritual senses, while these need to lend some of their essential 'selflessness' to the will-senses.

Through our four feeling-senses we are linked quite particularly with the world of nature: with colour, the warmth of the sun, the tastes and smells of the plants and animals which feed us. We have developed a civilisation which in its knowing is estranged from nature, and in its doing is destroying nature. The therapy must begin with a sense of gratitude and wonder to the nourishment that is given by nature, through our twelve senses, so that we may awaken to ourselves, and to our responsibilities on earth.

1975

[1] In *Anthroposophie: ein Fragment* (Rudolf Steiner Nachlassverwaltung,1970). Not yet translated.

[2] We may object that we hear birdsong 'coming from a bird'. But that is an interpretation, added by thinking, to the sensation itself. The actual percept is simply 'given', as are all sense-perceptions, simply by waking up and becoming open to sense-experience. For a fuller discussion of this crucial point, see Rudolf Steiner's *Philosophy of Freedom*. (Rudolf Steiner Press, 1964).

[3] It is extremely difficult, and a subject of much current scientific debate, to disentangle the physiological and the psychological components of pain experience.

[4] *Man as a Being of Sense and Perception*,three lectures, Dornach, July,1921. (Rudolf Steiner Press; out of print).

Meaning and the Human Soul

As the ninth century saw a denial of the spirit in man,[1] so the special crisis of the twentieth century is the denial of the human soul. This was Rudolf Steiner's prediction more than half a century ago, and the signs of its truth are all around us.

The soul is the inwardness of the human being, and cannot live without finding the inwardness – the meaning – in other human beings and the world. Thus a first attack on the soul was to drain nature of inwardness by filling our minds with abstractions – molecules, atoms, impersonal forces. So the rocks and plants are no longer a manifestation of divine creation, but little more than raw material for technological exploitation. In factory farms, animals are well on the way to being seen as mere quantities of flesh, and during this century there are determined efforts to extend this bleak world to the transactions between human beings themselves. You think your friend is smiling? No, some facial muscles are contracting, thus widening the oral aperture. A mere conditioned response.

The central citadel of inwardness, around which the battle for the soul is being fought, is language. We still assume that what people say *means* something. Their words are more than mere warm air and noise. In language, the inner worlds of human beings meet. And the life which sustains language, which makes it more than an exchange of verbal stimulus and response, is imagination.

Here, at the heart of the battle, Owen Barfield has made his life's work. He once remarked plaintively, in an autobiographical aside, that this work had consisted mainly in thinking and writing. But his pen has been a true sword, and he has fought, with great vigour and effectiveness, a battle for meaning and imagination that has attracted to his banner a growing circle of supporters and like-minded combatants, especially in the United States.

It will therefore be a great joy to all his friends and admirers that the collected volumes of his essays has now been published.[2] Three of the essays appeared originally in the *Golden Blade* but many have been published in journals not easily accessible to British readers, which makes this collection particularly welcome.

All the essays have in one way or another to do with language, and with meaning in language, and so provide a thread which leads back to the starting-point of Owen Barfield's work. He once indicated how this arose out of his experience of lyric poetry. How can words, combined in particular ways, stir the soul life and a deeper perception? (This is clearly related to the question of how a smile can be more than the widening of a facial aperture). Such questions led him a long way. Quite soon he met the work of Rudolf Steiner, which has been his chief inspiration and guide for many decades. But he has always travelled on his own feet, found his own language and made his own observations. This is the strength of his work, and through it he has also opened a road to Steiner for many others.

There is a story that Rudolf Steiner once showed a friend a printer's dummy of a new edition of his book *The Philosophy of Freedom*. All the pages were blank. 'This' Steiner is reported to have said, 'is my favourite copy of this book. Everyone should write his *own* philosophy of freedom'.

This, so it seems to me, is essentially what Owen Barfield has been doing over the years. He has been thinking and writing. But this has entailed a strenuous spiritual activity which helps to create a free space in which the human soul can live – not only for himself but for our present times and times to come. It is part of the attack on the soul that the need to fight essential battles *in thought* is barely understood today, (except, strikingly enough, in totalitarian countries, where the really dangerous people are seen to be those who think for themselves).

The notion that there is a gulf between 'theory' and 'practice' is simply one more facet of the Cartesian dichotomy between mind and matter, or between inner and outer experience, which is at the root of the present crisis. History shows well enough that the assumptions and attitudes which shape society are half-conscious versions of what lives in clarity among contemporary philosophers. So it is only in the light of the spirit that the essential issues can be properly seen, and there that the most essential battles have to be fought (one of the main weapons in the attack on the soul is to engulf culture in a damp mental fog).

It was here that Steiner began his own public work. Living and working in Central Europe near the turn of the century, he saw that his central task in *The Philosophy of Freedom* (which he once recommended should be rendered in English as 'The Philosophy of Spiritual Activity') must be to transcend Kant, and in particular to overcome the idea of fundamental limits to knowledge. For Kant made evident and apparently permanent a kind of imprisonment of the soul, first heralded formally in our culture by Descartes. The inwardness of the human being, the soul, the mind, was placed in a cell of private experience, cut off from direct access to surrounding realities, an onlooker at mere appearances.

In his own life and work, Steiner sprung the lock of this prison cell, and showed a road open to all human beings to find a way to the inner realities of the soul and spirit in nature and in man. And he demonstrated in practice how the needs for a renewal of practical life can be found on this path. But the battle for the soul was far from won.

In the English-speaking world, through the middle part of this century, the attack on the soul took a further step. It is well known that prisoners in solitary confinement may begin to doubt their own identities and even their real existence. Locked in its cell by Kant, the human soul, prompted by the logical positivists and then by the linguistic philosophers, began to argue itself out of existence. The line of argument is now quite familiar. It is a close relation of that behaviouristic psychology which would ban all reference to 'inner' states of mind or soul because they are 'unobservable'. So 'hunger' is replaced by 'eating behaviour', and smiles by the widening of oral apertures.

Correspondingly, some linguistic philosophers argued that all language which refers to 'inner' realities is meaningless. We can speak only of what is verifiable by the senses. The soul is thus not only imprisoned, but gagged. Thus the soul is finally isolated not only from nature, but from other human souls. The natural conviction that human beings can meet through language is undermined. The 'problem of communication' becomes the central neurosis of social life (and grotesque and often desperate efforts at non-verbal communication spring up in myriad weekend encounter group workshops).

This is where Owen Barfield has been at work, and the collection of essays is well titled. The rediscovery of meaning – in language and in life – is a most central need of the human soul. And there is a particular way in to this discovery, a golden key. It is the same key we find in Steiner, and which Goethe, the pioneer of rediscovery of meaning in nature, also knew very well. It is the idea of evolution – but an evolution not of one half only of the Cartesian dichotomy, of matter, but of the other half also, of mind. The moment we take this up, it works like a magic wand on the landscape of history, and a transformation scene began to take place before our eyes.

Put in the most abstract possible way, the point is this: The

Cartesian dichotomy was itself produced by mind. Moreover, we ourselves reproduce it every morning as we awake from sleep and dream to look at the world 'out there' (and to become aware of ourselves 'in here'). Yet by realising how this experience *comes into being*, whether historically, or each morning, out of another state of consciousness, we must realise that the duality of our experience cannot be a dichotomy (in the sense that there are two different kinds of universe which somehow abut), but must be a *polarity*, and therefore must contain an inward unity.

One of Owen Barfield's central contributions has been to show that in the history of language, in the meaning of words, there is a kind of script, a fossil record of the evolution of the human soul. In this record, the gradual polarisation of experience out of an earlier dream-like clairvoyance can be followed at least in its most recent phases (that is, through the past three or four thousand years). The earlier essays in this collection are particularly concerned with this theme, which Owen Barfield announced so clearly in his first book, *History in English Words*.

As he has so often described, all our present abstract words – 'courage', 'disastrous', 'perceptive', 'humour', and thousands more – all once had 'outer' as well as 'inner' meanings ('disaster', for example refers to the stars). At the same time, words which now have only outer meanings once also had inner meanings. *Pneuma* meant wind *and* spirit.

For the Cartesian intellect, it is not rational for words to refer to both sides of the dichotomy at once. As a consequence, the twentieth century has tried to persuade us that all use of words to refer to 'inner' experiences (including, of course, anything that could be called poetry) is at best misleading, at worst a 'disease of language'. But once we see language as an expression of a developing polarity of the human soul and nature, we have to see that the residual inner meanings of today's 'outer' words (and of course the residual outer meanings of today's inner words) are remnants of what Barfield calls 'original participation', a mode of experience when the life of the soul and of nature were experienced not as a dichotomy but as a unity. (There are some interesting words into which the dichotomy has as yet barely entered. We still speak quite naturally of a 'warm room', and a 'warm welcome', of a 'heart-attack' and of a 'hearty welcome'. Under the chilly scrutiny of the linguistic analyst, we should probably confess that when we attach 'warm' and 'heart' to 'welcome' we are speaking metaphorically, and hence about something unverifiable by physical means. But we go on doing it all the time, and cling to the conviction that a 'warm smile' expresses a reality more fundamental than an extended widening of the oral aperture).

To recognise language in this way, woven into the evolution of the soul, has far-reaching consequences. Above all, as Owen Barfield puts it in the title essay of this volume: ' . . . the positivists are right in their conclusion that if (they would say "because") nature is meaningless to the human mind, most language is also meaningless. But the converse is equally true, that if language is "meaningful", then nature herself must also be meaningful. In fact, as Emerson pointed out long ago, "It is not only words that are emblematic; it is things which are emblematic"'.

In other words, through seeing in language the record of the evolution of an 'onlooker' consciousness out of 'original participation', we are led to realise that we are, as human souls, neither insubstantial ghosts nor strangers to nature, but that in observing the 'outside' of nature we are meeting that whose inwardness we can seek in unconscious realms of our own souls.

As Owen Barfield points out, the twentieth century has brought forth a partial recognition of this polarity in fields apparently as far apart as particle physics and psychoanalysis. With quantum physics, it has to be accepted that what we see in 'nature' depends on how she is conceived in our souls (e.g. particles or waves). Psychoanalysis has long recognised in dreams an inner experience of nature in the human organism. But the ghosts of positivism haunted the minds of both Freud and Jung, since both seem to have conceived the 'unconscious' as produced, fundamentally, *by* the physical organism. Even Jung's collective unconscious seems to have, in the end, the status of a common property of generations of material organisms. He never seems to have taken the explicit step of seeing that organisms may equally well be understood as being born out of the collective unconscious – or out of what Steiner more directly called the world of the soul and spirit. Yet this step is now almost staring us in the face. The dualism of mind and body still stands stubbornly in the way, and this accounts for the crucial importance of the idea of polarity in the works of Goethe, of Steiner, of Coleridge, and of Barfield. For once the idea of polarity is properly grasped, organism and mind, inner and outer realities, can be truly distinguished without being divided, and we can see them as expressions of our present mode of consciousness.

All this vividly illumines the past and the present – but what of the future? Some aspects of the story which Barfield tells have been dawning on many people. The sense of a lost participation, of an abyss which has opened between man and nature – or even more far-reachingly between everyday consciousness and awareness of spiritual worlds – shows itself in the wave of interest in occultism, astrology, Eastern religions, 'ancient wisdom' and past spiritual practices. Those in whom such interests awaken often see correctly, that the success and power of modern science and technology depend on the Cartesian dichotomy. Only by experiencing ourselves as divorced from nature, as detached onlookers, could we have embarked on the kinds of investigations and manipulations which have dominated our lives in recent times.

This diagnosis is now widespread among those seeking 'alternatives'. But the remedy is usually to regard the whole dichotomy as as aberration, a wrong turning, which can be undone by a denial of intellect, by 'tuning in and dropping out', by reviving a variety of ancient attitudes, ways of life and spiritual practices. It is seldom clearly seen that this can be as drastic an assault on the soul as positivism, even if launched from the opposite direction. For it denies all meaning to the evolutionary process which has led to the dichotomy. Yet this dichotomy is the primary fact of experience of every modern human soul which awakens in any way to attempt a critical appraisal of the human situation. To deny it is like denying adolescence to a child. To seek a way back beyond the 'wrong turning' is like an attempt to regress into a world of lost innocence (indeed psychoanalysis claims to detect a powerful urge of this kind in all human souls).

Rudolf Steiner seems to have been almost alone in seeing the full meaning of this evolution and its consequences. He saw the dichotomy, for all its tragedy, as the birthplace of individual freedom (a freedom, incidentally, which all those who would choose to regress to a pre-Cartesian way of life claim as a birthright without thinking much about it). Without the experience of complete separateness from nature, the human soul could never awaken to its present and future responsibility *for* nature (a responsibility whose actuality is underlined daily by the so-called environmental crisis). And within this freedom for responsibility lies the seed of love – not a love inherited from or determined by nature, but germinating and unfolding freely in the shrine of the heart as the essential being of man.

Here again, Owen Barfield has shown how we can seek within language for this birth of freedom. It is announced most explicitly by the Romantics as imagination. Barfield has sometimes contrasted 'inspiration' and 'imagination' as words which point to past and future forms of 'participation' . The poet inspired by his Muse is a *vehicle* for a creative process. The poet who labours inwardly for imagination begins to become responsible for it.

What this means in life has begun to be disconcertingly clear in the sciences. The sources of experiment and technology are in the imagination (otherwise known as the capacity to form hypotheses). It is now rather obvious that what scientists imagine (or hypothesise) has far-reaching consequences – and should entail a more serious sense of responsibility. For in imagination, we reach across a threshold. It is a matter of common experience in science that crucial advances emerge more often than not quite dimly at first, as inner apprehensions which can barely be shaped in language, mathematical or otherwise. How are we to become responsible for such a process?

Clearly, the first step is to *take seriously* what is very nearly explicit in quantum physics and implicit in all science. As Owen Barfield puts it in the essay *Science and Discovery*, if we had truly left behind the idea that the mind of the scientist is totally detached from the world he investigates, 'we should have become naturally, unforcedly and unremittingly aware that the mind *cannot* refer to a natural object without at the same time referring to its own activity. And this in turn would require an equally unforced awareness not only that scientific discovery is always a discovery about language, but also that it is always a discovery about the self which uses language'.

He goes on to show that the scientific process itself is demanding that its much-prized objectivity about objects (not, as Barfield remarks, really such a difficult feat!) should really be seen as a kind of schooling for a much more difficult feat, namely objectivity towards that which is to be found within the soul itself. We should not be surprised to find that the moral qualities of a human being colour the world of his imagination, or expect the scientist to be any more insulated than the poet from the powerful forces which live at the threshold of the unconscious. Thus science itself is beginning to speak an old language in a new form. It is an adventure into mysteries. But at the threshold of every past Mystery temple the neophyte was confronted with a warning and a demand that he attempt the most thorough self-knowledge. This warning reappears in all Rudolf Steiner's work on the modern 'path of knowledge', most directly and simply as the warning that every spiritual step should be accompanied by three moral steps. This is an obvious requirement of any responsible exploration into mysteries, once we recognise that they embrace both the human soul and the inwardness of nature, as a polarity.

Here then is the starting point for future endeavour. But the fullest depth of meaning in this evolution of the human soul is indicated in the final essays of this volume. One of them, *Philology and the*

Incarnation, was reprinted from its original home, *The Gordon Review*, in the Anthroposophical Quarterly (Spring, 1969). Owen Barfield there compares an old and a new phenomenon of language. The first is the one already mentioned – the fact that 'inner' experiences were in the past described by words which referred also to the 'outer' world. The second is a recent phenomenon, the use of words which describe qualities of a nature in terms of their effect on us. He cites 'charming', 'depressing', 'entrancing', 'amusing' and several others. These usages are very recent, not earlier than the seventeenth century.

In this there is a complete change of direction in the relation between man and nature as embodied in language: in the past 'outer' words used to denote 'inner' qualities; very recently words for inner experiences used to denote outer qualities. This change of direction, Barfield says, can be located philologically quite exactly, with seven or eight centuries on either side of the reign of Caesar Augustus. A philologist studying this period could rightly feel that here 'was the moment at which there was consummated that age-long process of contraction of the immaterial qualities of the cosmos into a human centre, into an inner world, which had made possible the development of an immaterial language. This, therefore, was the moment in which his true selfhood, his spiritual selfhood, entered into the body of man . . . '.

Quoting thus briefly and out of context from this beautiful essay does not do justice to the way in which the thread of evolving language leads Owen Barfield into the Christian mystery. When I first read this essay, it brought for me an enrichment of the mysterious phrase, 'The Word became Flesh', for which I shall always be grateful. In this volume, it introduces two final essays, *The Psalms of David*, and *The Son of God and the Son of Man* which should be read in their completeness.

These essays are thus a kind of summary guide to Owen Barfield's work, and will, I hope, prompt many new readers to read the books in which the themes of the essays are developed in greater depth and detail. It is a work which needs to reach as widely and deeply as possible into the English-speaking world, where on the one hand positivism is still enthroned in many realms, while on the other there is a growing dalliance with a regressive solution to the dichotomy which is positivism's source. And I shall only be echoing Barfield's own almost-too-modest sense of proportion if I conclude by saying that one can hardly climb seriously the hills of Barfield (and some of them are quite steep) without seeing ahead, as a necessary continuation of the adventure, the mountain ranges of Steiner.

[1] Formalised at the Eighth Ecumenical Council, 869 AD.   1978

[2] *The Rediscovery of Meaning and Other Essays*, by Owen Barfield. (Wesleyan University Press).

EDUCATION FOR LIVING
The Man Who Wants to Scrap Schools

We are all in favour of education. We usually assume that, like economic growth the more there is of it the better. Governments all over the world, in rich and poor countries, and whatever their political complexion, share these assumptions. Quite recently, doubts have begun to creep in about economic growth. It is beginning to look like a dangerous idol, delivering most of the goods to a small minority, while driving humanity towards some kind of planetary catastrophe. Now there are doubts emerging about education, too.

The gap between the educationally affluent and the educationally deprived shows little sign of closing. And even rich countries can barely afford the education system they believe they need. What if our assumptions about education should prove as wrong-headed as our assumptions about economic growth? This is the question now being explored by a number of radical writers, particularly in the United States.

One of the most controversial and disturbing voices is that of a brilliant, ambiguous stormy petrel of the Roman Catholic Church, Ivan Illich, who is in London this weekend for the publication of his latest book, *Deschooling Society*.[1] For his onslaught on the citadels of established education, Illich brings to bear twenty years of experience as a turbulent Catholic priest. Now forty-five, lanky, dark, aquiline, with glittering eyes and a frequent but enigmatic smile, he displays enormous erudition, command of a dozen languages, and boundless energy.

At a philosophical congress in Cyprus last month he acquired a working knowledge of demotic Greek in seven days from a teach-yourself book and the hotel gardener. He would jump into the sea and head for the horizon at amazing speed, and later take thirty-five mile walks across open country in the heat of the day. His contribution to the congress, a typical Illich social commentary – clever, elusive, challenging and poetic – caused more talk, and more anger than anybody else's.

Illich was born in Vienna; his father was an engineer from Dalmatia, his mother a Sephardic Jew. They had to leave Austria in the 1930s because of the Nazis, and the young Illich completed his education in Italy. By the age of twenty-four, he had degrees in theology and philosophy from Rome, a doctorate in the philosophy of history from Salzburg, and a successfully completed research project in crystallography in Florence. Offered a place at Rome's Collegio di Nobili Ecclesiastici where the Church's stars are trained for the Vatican diplomatic corps, Illich went instead to Incarnation Parish, New York City, and plunged into the Puerto Rican slums.

Within three months he spoke fluent Spanish and knew more about Puerto Rican problems than any other priest in New York. In 1955, Cardinal Spellman, who had become one of Illich's most constant supporters and friends, appointed him vice-rector of the University of Puerto Rico, and a year later he was made, at the age of twenty-nine, the youngest Monsignor in the US.

By this time, Illich was becoming radically critical of the smug bureaucracy of his Church in America, and of the rigid and uncomprehending attitude of its 'Yankee' missionaries towards other cultures. Within a year of arriving in Puerto Rico, he had founded an 'Institute of Intercultural Communications' to give crash courses in Spanish to American priests and to steep them in Latin American culture.

His centre began to attract progressive clergy from all over the US, but he was soon in deep trouble with the conservative Catholic hierarchy on the island. In 1960 his bishop packed him off back to New York, to a still sympathetic Cardinal Spellman. During the subsequent winter, Illich walked and rode 3,000 miles through South America, from Santiago to Caracas, looking for somewhere to re-establish his work. Early in 1961 he chose Cuernavaca, Mexico, and set up his Centre for Intercultural Documentation, with brave support from the local bishop.

The Centre is now famous for its language courses, which teach fluent Spanish in twelve weeks. But it is also a place where students can go deeply into Latin American history, culture and politics. At first, most of the students were clerics, but their numbers diminished as Illich sent back at least half of each intake, on the grounds that they could never be sufficiently 'de-Yankified' to serve Latin America. By the mid-1960s, eighty-five percent were secular students, and it is now a kind of free university in the style of a medieval monastery.

Progressive priests expecting to find an outpost of nonconformist underground Catholicism – mass in a Tee-shirt, wine in a plastic mug – are often surprised to find a vein of severe orthodoxy and adherence to the rules which is a part of Illich's complex character. He is up at six each morning to say his breviary, goes to confession in a conventional booth, takes communion every Sunday, and observes a whole array of holy days and saints' days.

During the 1960s, Illich and CIDOC came under increasingly vicious attack from right-wing Catholic organisations in Mexico. Illich energetically fuelled their hostility with radical speeches and articles, contrasting the institutional Church ('the Church-as-It'), which he regarded as a tottering bureaucracy, with the true Church ('the Church-as-She').

In June 1968, Illich was summoned to a bizarre interrogation in the bowels of the Vatican, conducted by three Monsignors representing the Congregation for the Doctrine of the Faith, a direct descendant of the Inquisition set up in the eleventh century to suppress heresy. Illich kept quiet about these proceedings until January 1969, when the Vatican issued an order forbidding Catholic priests and nuns to attend CIDOC. Illich promptly rang the religious editor of the *New York Times* and gave him a scoop; the extraordinary mishmash of questions with which he had been faced in Rome 'What did you have to do with the kidnapping of the Archbishop of Guatemala?' 'Is it true that you would like to see women go to confession without a grate in the confessional box?' 'What do you think of Heaven and Hell, and also of Limbo?' And there were many more.

Two months later, Illich announced his decision 'to retire from Church service, to suspend the exercise of priestly functions, and to renounce totally all titles, offices, benefits and privileges which are due to me as a cleric'. At the same time, he stated that he would retain two of his priestly obligations – to say his breviary each day, and to remain celibate. He had arrived at a typically elusive Illich position, half in and half out of the Church. In his own eyes, he is presumably within the Church-as-She but out of the Church-as-It.

The ban on CIDOC (which Illich had disregarded and which had immediately generated a flood of applications from progressive priests and nuns) was revoked by the Vatican in June 1969, on condition that it be supervised by the Conference of Latin American Bishops. But meanwhile Illich, not a supervisable person, has been swinging his formidable firepower round to aim at a new target, the established church of Education. *Deschooling Society* is his first book-sized barrage.

He attacks on several fronts – economic, functional, ideological. Rich countries, he says, are developing an education apparatus which they can barely afford, and which can never be afforded by poor countries. In all countries, the cost of education is growing faster than national income, and faster than the numbers being educated. To educate all pupils equally in the US through secondary schools would increase current costs to $80,000 million a year – well over twice the total spent now. University education is still more expensive: to produce an American college graduate costs about $35,000, ten times what is spent on the poorest ten per cent of the US population.

In poor countries, the discrepancy is much wider. Graduates in Latin America cost between 350 and 1,500 times what is spent on the average child. All over the world, Illich says, rich and poor nations are busy creating educational caste systems, in which a minority at the top rests on a broad base of 'failures' at the bottom.

This is one recurrent theme in Illich's critique. Schooling, he argues, serves to control and perpetuate a meritocratic hierarchy, which itself reinforces the assumptions of an acquisitive and growth-oriented society. For schools, he maintains, also teach young citizens to equate the acquisition of more schooling with access to more money and goods in later life, and to regard both as unquestionable virtues.

The most generally acknowledged function of schools and colleges – to purvey knowledge and skills – is one which they do badly, Illich says. The actual content of twelve years schooling represents no more than one or two years' work for an adult. Specific skills like languages can be briskly and more economically learned with a few months' intensive drill. Most aptitudes directly applicable to most jobs are learned on the job. Paper qualifications, except where they record the acquisition of narrowly definable skills like shorthand and typing, seldom have much to do with a person's competence to do a particular job. Such qualifications are more often used to restrict entry into trades and professions, in the interests of those already in them.

Illich therefore argues that questions of competence to do a job should be completely separated from a person's educational history: 'Inquiries into a man's learning history must be made taboo, like inquiries into his political affiliations, church attendance, lineage, sex habits or racial background.'

All this is good radical stuff, couched in Illich's vivid aphoristic style. But the argument becomes more complex, and in parts more dubious, as he goes on to discuss other functions of school, and to propose alternatives.

He quotes statistics which indicate that eighty per cent of most teachers' time is occupied with 'custodial' functions – keeping the pupils in the school, and in some sort of order. Illich remarks that fifty years ago no country in the world had even ten per cent of its teenagers in school. Mass education of adolescents is a new phenomenon and an unsolved problem in almost every industrial country. For all too many inmates, a rise in the school-leaving age means receiving a longer sentence. But even for those who go with the system, their eyes on the higher rungs of the ladder, much of school experience is a journey through impersonal, exam-shaped abstractions, remote from the real questions, passions, ideals and inner concerns of the candidates.

Illich's remedy would be to abolish schools and replace them by education 'utilities'. He characterises schools as essentially 'manipulative' institutions, which process young people, on a par with jails (which process criminals), and hospitals (which process patients). It is characteristic of such institutions, he says, that the people in them are not there of their own free choice, but have been coerced or bribed to enter. He contrasts these with 'convivial' institutions, such as telephones, parks, sewerage systems and water supplies. The customers for these services, he argues, do not have to be coerced into using them, and the rules governing their use are mainly concerned to ensure full and fair access for all.

Illich, therefore, envisages a variety of 'convivial' education services. One service would help people to gain access not only to libraries and museums, but to factories, farms, airports, laboratories and so on, for educational purposes. Another would provide an educational version of marriage bureau, bringing together people with common interests for study and discussion. Such services, he recommends, should be administered by an independent education profession. This would include 'pedagogues' who can give advice to parents and students on learning difficulties, and 'masters' – gifted tutors capable of stimulating, guiding and opening up a field of learning for a student. The personal relationships which this entails, Illich believes, are seldom possible in modern schools.

It is an appealing notion, but has a good many weaknesses. Illich seems to have had little first-hand experience of schools or of children, and his book is that of a radical outsider looking in (through spectacles tinted by twenty years of rows with the Catholic Establishment). For despite all the ills that he mentions – and they are real – schools contain very many teachers who are dedicated heart and soul to pedagogy in the sense that Illich describes: not the imposition of abstractions on captives, but the finding and meeting of real needs of young individuals, and the fostering of the human relationships without which the job is impossible.

There are very good reasons why such work needs to take place in a special setting, the main one being that technological urban society has created an inhuman environment. The romantic notion of an education acquired simply by living, knocking around asking questions, observing adults at work, may have had some reality in small scale rural communities of the past, but the impersonal, fragmented activities of the modern city are something quite different. Schools don't have to be factories for manufacturing citizen-consumers. They can be places where young people find some experience of the wholeness of nature and human society, and of their own humanity – schools as microcosms of mankind.

Illich is also attached to the notion that children and adolescents, left to themselves, would be better at deciding what is good for them than adults. This belief has a deep appeal for modern romantic intellectuals, who feel themselves divorced from nature, life, instinct, etc., and from youth. It assumes that the ills of human nature are manifest only with adulthood, that the Fall of Man coincides with the acquisition of the vote.

'Deschooling Society' is almost wholly devoid of any discussion of human development from infancy. Yet one of the outstanding features of man is that he depends more on learning than on instinct and owes much of his special status in the kingdom of nature to his prolonged childhood and youth, during which he is guided and cared for, not by instincts, but by adults.

The everyday urban environment, which adults are beginning to recognise as uncomfortably inimical to themselves, does not offer adequate support for growing up. Children are natural artists – but their imaginations need nourishment. Office blocks and traffic jams are starvation rations. Adolescents seek some unity and meaning in knowledge; cities are agglomerations of specialists.

Good teachers can nurture a much wider and richer experience. Schools could and should be places where they can work more freely than anywhere else, where windows can open to a wider inner and outer world. The fact that examination and other pressures often cramp this ideal is a reason for removing the pressures, not for treating education in the same way as sewerage.

These shortcomings apart, the Illich onslaught could do good. 'Fundamental social change', he writes, 'must begin with a change of consciousness about institutions.' (I think he should have said 'about people', but no matter). We are witnessing now such a change of consciousness about the impact of industrial institutions on the planet. Unthinking pursuit of educational growth needs questioning too. Illich's bombardment of Education-as-It – the schooling industry – makes a good beginning. It may encourage more attention to Education-as-She.   1971

The Social Meaning of Education

I would like to start by telling a story that illustrates a problem – a problem that anyone who tries to talk coherently about the meaning of Waldorf education will have to tackle. It has to do with making an appropriate relationship with what we call 'science'.

A young friend of mine is at present working in a small day school attached to a hospital in the country. It is a tough job: The school population is always changing as children come and go. Some of the children are very ill – some are terminally ill. The project is funded by some local organisation, and my friend has to negotiate her needs for the school with an official who is well disposed, but unimaginative – and certainly without any concept of a Waldorf approach to education.

One of the things she wanted to do with the children was to bake cookies. She needed some simple equipment, and so she had to discuss the idea with the administrator, who was at first quite baffled. What, he asked, could be the educational value of baking cookies? They talked around the problem for a while, and then light dawned: In baking cookies little Johnnie would *learn to weigh flour*. Weighing flour is a skill that can be objectified and measured, and cookie baking can thus be evaluated as a method of teaching weighing. Relieved, he gave the go-ahead.

On a later occasion, my friend had another problem. She wanted to make a little garden with the children, and she asked for the funds to buy seeds and a trowel. 'What, she was asked, 'is the cognitive value of planting seeds?' This time she exploded. 'For God's sake,' she told the administrator, 'this may be the last spring that several of my children will experience.' The administrator was also a human being, and so she got her seeds. But I do not need to elaborate how a particular interpretation of what constitutes education – in this case, shaped by the notion that valid educational practices must centre on the performance of measurable skills – can lead, at the least, to some bizarre conversation, and, at the worst, to a meager, thin, and dehumanised perspective on education as a whole.

But the problem goes beyond negotiating funds from an administrator. My friend had to find an appropriate language to account
for her wish to bake cookies with the children, but she did not
even attempt to describe to him what cookie baking implies for her.
She could, of course, share with her contemporaries some general
thoughts, such as that in baking cookies, the children learn to be
creative with their hands, to work together, to produce something
useful for themselves and others, and so are being educated for
society in some way. As I am supposed to offer you some thoughts
on the social meaning of Waldorf education, I could proceed on
similar lines. But you would not be satisfied with worthy generalities
of this kind, nor would I.

One of the things my friend would probably have liked to say
about cookie baking is that it brings the children to a direct experience, in everyday life, of great and deep archetypal processes and
activities, in which they are themselves immersed at several levels
in their own development, and which are at work in the world
around them, processes that an earlier language might have called
'earth', 'water', 'air', and 'fire'. You start with flour (earth), an inert
and formless substance. You add water, and get dough, which can
seem to move and writhe in your hands as though it were alive.
You add yeast – air begins to work in the dough, and it rises. It
becomes sensitive, and will collapse in a cold draught or if clumsily
handled. Then it is exposed to fire, and transformed into bread,
which can be eaten for lunch.

For a reductive science, we are dealing with a bit of applied physics and chemistry, and Johnnie learns to weigh flour. Structuralists
would of course have no difficulty in seeing other levels of meaning
in the process (Levi-Strauss, in *The Raw and the Cooked*, does, in effect, just this). But it is in any case apparent to an observant teacher
that the activity of baking cookies can mean to children rather more
than messing around with dough or weighing flour, or even making
something nice for lunch. It can have a ritualistic quality, speaking
to levels of experience that not even adults, let alone children, can
adequately bring to consciousness or articulate. Yet there can at least
be an empirical question: To what do such early childhood experiences lead in the adult?

I thought that I would start with this story, and with this question,
since when I came to think about this talk, and to dip into a few
bits of recent investigation on aspects of social education, I realised
how formidable a problem of language is built into current discussion of education. I am not a scholar in this field, so there is probably a great deal going on of which I am not aware. But it seems

that quite a bit of investigation of questions concerning social education is strictly cognitive: Research is done on such questions as 'When does a child, looking at an adult, realise that the adult may have a different picture of the child than the child has of the adult?' And then, a little bit more advanced: 'When does the child begin to ask if the adult realises that he is being looked at by the child from a point of view different from that which he is looking at the child?'

It is not my intention in any way to downgrade the interest of such questions, or to deny the value of studying them. I was educated in the sciences, and am very much concerned that even if we question some of the more restrictive and stultifying presumptions of a purely positivistic and reductive approach to the world, we do not throw away the central virtues of science, the attempt to achieve integrity of thought, clarity and accuracy of observation and description. Yet I am very much aware that what I now want to describe is not at present empirically verifiable in any rigorous way. It demands a certain readiness to make intuitive connections between phenomena and experience, and must also remain, in a short talk, on a very general level. Yet I think that many people can begin to see an immediate 'meaning' in certain principles of social education, originally put forward by Steiner, and if they are meaningful, we should obviously take them very seriously in educational practice.

I will take as a starting point three words already introduced into discussion at this conference, words that were used to denote three social ideals, the ideals of the French Revolution: Liberty, Equality, Fraternity. Most of us, if asked about liberty, equality, and fraternity, would probably say 'I'm *for* them'. They seem to describe worthy aspirations we all share. But they pose a question – a question to human nature itself: If they have any meaning, they must refer to definite social capacities in the human being. Without such capacities, they are empty words. The events of our times have shown us that we evidently have these capacities, if at all, in a rather rudimentary form, or are even dominated by opposite ones. So if we are in favour of these social virtues, we must ask an obvious question: How may they be *educated* – that is, developed and strengthened for use – in adult life?

Before pursuing this, I would like to look at these qualities in a little more detail, although still in a very general way. I want to relate *liberty* to something that has been emphasised by two previous speakers, namely our capacity to be *creative* beings. For true creativity, liberty is essential. A creative act brings something new into the world, and therefore changes it. The old is thereby modified or even destroyed. As creative beings, we are true revolutionaries, and a first necessity for us to function in this way is freedom of speech. Through speech, we first begin to utter what we want to put into action.

Freedom of speech is the most dangerous liberty for any totalitarian system. Many of you will know Solzhenitsyn's *The First Circle*, which centres around a group of scientists imprisoned by the regime. For their creative scientific work, they have to have freedom of speech. But to prevent this freedom from contaminating others, they have to be locked up, so that they can talk only to each other. At one moment, one of them says: 'We are the only free men in Russia!' The reason is that they are free to talk to one another. And they have to be allowed this freedom, since otherwise the life and progress of science itself – even if the main interest in their creativity comes from the military – would wither and die. As a problem of education, though, we can ask how are we to work with children so that the *capacity for liberty*, for freedom as an inner quality that allows the fullest possible expression of a person's creative potentiality, may be nurtured? Or how, to put it the other way round, are we to avoid imprisoning these capacities in disabling inhibitions and hang-ups?

We can put similar questions towards *equality*. This is a word about which we all tend to become very confused. Liberal and leftist political discourse in England has come to appropriate this word almost exclusively for material equality, for 'fair shares' in goods and services. Quite apart from the fact that no society with a uniform standard of living has yet existed, it is doubtful whether this was the fundamental meaning of the word for the French Revolution. A very little imaginative reflection on the word will show that it also refers to another, but nonmaterial, sphere of experience, namely the relations between human beings *as human beings*, which come to expression in terms of arrangements for upholding what we call fundamental human rights. Formally, this emerges as an aspiration for equality before the law: It must be possible to arraign even a president or a prime minister. We have deep feelings not so much for fair shares as for fair dealing. Equality thus refers to a human capacity to be fair in relations with other human beings *purely in respect of their humanness.*

So what does *fraternity* mean? In the British trade union movement, you call your fellow trade unionist 'brother'. (In Russia, you call him 'comrade.') It is true that actual behaviour in trade union life in Britain at present is not always all that fraternal. But what does the use of the word, in an ideal sense, mean? It can become a reality only through the exercise of another human capacity, which is to take account of another person's needs. Fraternity demands goodwill that is more than sentiment, that is *perceptive*. Quite apart from the depressing struggles of the modern industrial scene, blindness to real needs may live where there seems to be abundant goodwill. Missionaries used to go to Africa full of fraternal goodwill. They were quite incapable of seeing the meaning of the structures and rituals of the tribal societies they encountered. They saw the ritual dances to celebrate festivals and seasons of the year as fertility rites, and as rather disgusting. They took away the dances, and gave the women knitting. This is what can happen if goodwill is not awoken to become a capacity for social perception.

So these three words point to capacities for creativity (which can live only in liberty), for 'give and take' among equals, and for perceptiveness of the real needs of others. So we can ask: Can they be educated?

I must perhaps apologise at this point for the fact that I am still not going to tackle this question directly, but want first to lead it into a still wider context. Reductive science inevitably loses much sense of the validity of questions about meaning because it has to *narrow* the context in which it works. But we see the meaning of a limited sphere of experience only if we see it within a larger one. So baking cookies can be seen as a rather laborious way of teaching children to weigh. Or it can be seen as a means of participation in certain archetypal experiences (into which I cannot go further here). Similarly, we can tackle the question of how to educate capacities for liberty, equality, and fraternity as a problem of how to ensure that certain forms of social behaviour of which we approve will take place. Or we can try to look more widely and more deeply. And here I want to make a short, very tentative excursion into history (which I do with some trepidation, as I am not a historian either).

Now if you visit, today, a fairly remote and untouched tribal culture – and there still are a few – you can expect to find a very complex society whose structure is supported by customs and rituals to a degree to which we can barely conceive. An English district officer who worked in some islands in the South Pacific in the early part of this century, W. Grimble, describes this beautifully in his book *A Pattern of Islands*. There are, for example, the most elaborate rituals of greetings, which vary according to whether you are a stranger, a relative, younger or older. There are rituals for entering a house, for leaving, for walking down the village street, for drawing water, preparing food, going to sleep, getting up, and so on.

As far as I know this complex fabric of customary ritual is always found in such cultures, and is experienced as ultimately God-given. The rituals will also be experienced as the way to make proper relationships with *beings*, both human and supernatural. We call such cultures 'animistic', and our reductive explanation is that these are primitive ways of dealing with what we now know to be 'laws of nature' that are really both abstract and impersonal. Yet it is worth realising how we, too, live within these laws, much as a person would live in a primitive culture in a much richer and more personal way, within the divinely ordered hierarchy of Beings around him. When we hold a glass in the hand, we do not just let go of it. We 'obey' the law of gravity and hold on. This is our 'ritual'. It simply does not occur to us, in ordinary life, to question this fabric of law into which we are woven.

We can speculate that some such relationship to 'law and order' as is found in tribal societies goes back a very long way. But we do know of further developments. When such a society begins to get large and complex, additional means of ordering its affairs develop. In particular, the law is vested in a person, who is perceived as the representative of Divine Law within the society – a chieftain, a priest, a king. Think of King Solomon. When order broke down – when people quarreled, and could not order their affairs by custom – they turned to the king: a human being not merely in a position of power, but vested with the divine ordering-power of the universe, bringing life among the people as the sun brings light to the planets.

Later still, when the sun goes in – there seems to be a shortage of leaders of the same divinely inspired stature – the law begins to be written down and codified. It dies into books, and is consulted as tradition. Then human beings have to begin to debate what the books really mean. The legal profession is born (the judge is the last remnant of the priest king). The ordering of society has increasingly to be sought through the exercise of reason.

It is fairly easy to see that these three modes of ordering society – customary ritual, inspired authority, and reasoned insight – depend on definite human capacities. The first depends on a capacity to imitate your surroundings, to pick up the customs and follow them, the second depends on the capacity to recognise and be guided by a human authority figure, and the third on the capacity to understand arguments – both one's own and those of others. I realise that I am making some fairly bold assertions at this stage, but I have not time to elaborate on them now, and I hope they can be accepted as broadly self-evident.

I want now to return to education and to children. Here I should say that I must speak not so much as an experienced teacher, but as an experienced parent – we learn quite a lot about child development, too, if we are at all observant. And one of the things we learn

– or are taught by our children – is that they pass through profound changes in their relationship to social life and to law and order in the family.

Suppose you visit a group of four-year-olds, rolling their cookie dough on the kitchen floor. You can try saying 'don't', you can explain that the rules direct that cookie dough must be rolled on the table, not the floor. Four-year-olds will take very little notice. You can also try reasoned debate, and embark on laborious explanations about the unhygienic state of the floor compared to the antiseptic state of the surface of the kitchen table. They will not take any notice of this either. So you have failed as a divinely inspired lawgiver, and as a reasonable lawyer. At this point, I am sorry to say – and I must obviously speak only for myself – parents may occasionally resort to brute force, and simply clear the floor of dough and squealing four-year-olds in one fell swoop.

But what *does* work to bring order to the lives of this age group? Parents usually get to know the secret very well: You need custom and ritual. The skilled kindergarten teacher will make a little ritual of every activity, and will establish a familiar and sustaining rhythm each day (only adults experience repetition as routine). She will speak on behalf of the whole group of children as 'we' – 'when we arrive, we take off our shoes and put them on the shoe rack; when we do modelling, we first put on our aprons; when we roll out cookies, we first dust the table top with flour'. In such an ordered society, a new arrival is immediately taken up and borne along, through the force of imitation, with the customs of the group. Such a kindergarten will move through the year with birthday rituals, end- and beginning-of-term rituals, seasonal rituals (chestnuts, Christmas decorations, planting crocuses, spotting the first birds' nests), and so on.

At home, you have to do the same thing. I remember a period of getting small boys up to bed, not by announcing 'it's bedtime' but by hooting to announce that the engine was ready to leave the station. The boys hitched on behind as trucks and we chugged up the stairs (one boy liked to be the engine, and I was a truck, but I still initiated the ritual by hooting).

You have to understand what games are right, too: You cannot usually expect four-year-olds to 'take turns' on the swing or the seesaw. You can be fairly sure that the biggest and the strongest will take the longest turn. But games with a ritual – ring-a-ring o' roses, songs that give each person a turn, and so on – are rituals into which a whole group will enter without friction, and with a sense of being securely supported in their 'society'.

I hope I have described phenomena that are recognisable to anybody who has had anything to do with young children. But I realise that in the context in which I have been speaking, I am implying something that should now be made explicit. It is a fundamental concept that runs through Steiner's thinking about human development, and hence through Waldorf education: It is a concept that turns up in other contexts, but it is, quite simply, the proposition that in their development children pass through stages that repeat, or echo in a recognisable way, stages through which the adult cultures of humanity have passed over very long periods of time in the past. Such a proposition entails a further thought, which does not feature very largely in contemporary thought at present, although the work of people like Owen Barfield and others is leading in this direction: It is the thought that we can recognise through history a definite and coherent process of development, which can be adequately understood only as a development of human consciousness – not just of the thoughts people have about the world, but of the mode of awareness itself – which had undergone a coherent process of change and development through various distinguishable phases.

If such thoughts are entertained at all, they begin to bring into one's perception of the meaning of education that wider perspective of which I spoke earlier. Indeed, the perspective begins to become almost unnervingly wide. Yet it can give meaning to our own work as parents and teachers in the most immediate and practical way. So I would like now to look at two further phases of childhood in this context – lower school (about seven to fourteen), and high school (adolescence).

In infancy, there is a profound capacity for imitation, which brings an affinity with ritual and custom. The security and familiarity offered by the rhythms of life in a well-ordered family, play group, or kindergarten echo the ordered security, the sustaining rhythms and rituals of tribal societies of the past, in which the order was experienced as God-given. This puts a rather awesome responsibility on the kindergarten teacher, as the giver and sustainer of the order, to which I will return.

What happens when school proper begins? Irrespective of school, observant parents will begin to see that the social capacities and expectations of the children begin to change. New faculties are coming awake. Eight-year-olds are very aware of and interested in the *rules* of their social order. You can sometimes hear wistful conversations about home life: 'Are you allowed to stay up late on Fridays? I'm not. No, I can't come out this morning until I have made my bed. I'm not allowed to.' It is not that the rules are necessarily obeyed. But the *existence* of rules is expected and taken for granted. The children understand that part of the school or the home is 'out of bounds', even if they break the rules (often a main source of excitement in life). It is also taken for granted, and expected of adults, that they know what the rules are and try to enforce them. But together with this expectation is another, absolutely crucial one: It is that as a law-maker and law-enforcer, the adult shall be *fair*.

The classroom at this time is the scene of complex social dynamics: Various minitribes form and reform, and squabble with one another. Individuals fight and dispute ownership of property, rights to the next turn on the seesaw, and so forth. They turn quite naturally to the adult as administrator of the law, and ask for a judgement. But woe betide the adult unskilled in this very difficult art. He is immediately dubbed as 'unfair'. The teacher of this age group who gets a reputation of being unfair, who seems to have favourites, who picks on scapegoats, soon forfeits all affection, respect, and authority.

But the adult – whether parent or teacher – who understands the fundamental social needs of this age, and the unfolding capacities in which they are rooted, will recognise, behind the questions of the social order in the classroom and home, a need to find adults who can stand among the children as wise lawgivers stood among their people in the past. It is another daunting perspective: Modern adults do not feel very much like King Solomon. Yet if they are at all perceptive, they will recognise in children a deep need and hope that they can be sustained by adults who are both fair and knowledgeable, who not only know the rules, but know the answers to their endless questions. When you answer the question of an eight-year-old, it is, whether you like it or not a *pronouncement*, not something the child wants to argue about. (As we shall see, adolescence brings a drastic change in this respect.)

So we are taught by children of eight or nine that they need from us qualities of which most modern adults are both uncertain and afraid: They ask for *authority* – not tyrannous or dogmatic authority, but the kind of sun-filled wisdom of a Solomon, representing the heavenly order on earth, permeating his culture with an ordering light.

Then, at adolescence, a further profound change takes place. Adults and young people alike have to begin to seek this ordering life in the awakening intelligence of the adolescent – the 'reasonable' solution to problems, the understandable ways of ordering society. Woe betide anyone dealing with adolescents who tries to fall back on his authority as an administrator of established rules: 'Okay, that may be your rule, but now you just tell me *why*. If you can make me *understand* the rule, then maybe – just maybe – I will go along with it this once . . . '

Parents and teachers know very well that if they shy away from debate, they are sunk, they forfeit respect. You must know why you require something of an adolescent. And what is more, you will be asked whether this idea is a mere abstract convention, or is an ideal by which you live yourself. Most adolescents have an uncanny nose for hypocrisy – one rule for teenagers, one for adults. They also have a great capacity to respect real integrity, even when they see someone living by guiding thoughts they do not intend to make their own. Yet they can begin to enter into the point of view of others, and compare it with their own. Indeed they are deeply interested in doing so, and disappointed when adults will not do the same. They expect their point of view to be understood also.

I am afraid that these may seem to you to be a string of commonplaces. Yet it is also commonplace to see parents reverting to forms of creating social order that belong to earlier stages of development: In despair at the legalistic debates that seem to be necessary to arrive at the simplest agreements with a teenage son or daughter, how often do we ourselves revert to the role of divinely inspired lawgiver: 'Well, that's the rule in this house, and as long as I'm in charge, the rule stands'. Except that the teenager realises very well that the lawmaker is far from divine, and is inspired largely by fear, insecurity, or simply a tyrannous rage. We may even regress still further, and sink to brute force. But then we finally forfeit respect and affection.

If we dwell on these phenomena, and also try to acquire a little sense of history, we can begin to get a deeper and fuller perspective of the social meaning of education, and of the changing social capacities that awaken in children to which we need to respond appropriately. But this does not adequately answer the question implied by my theme. It may be that we can learn to work more appropriately with children and young people by awakening to the depth and meaning of the phases of social development through which they pass. But how does this work out for *adult* life? How are we to educate those social capacities that we need – and perhaps feel that we need rather badly – for adult society? What is the connection between what I have been saying and what I started out with: How may we educate the capacities for liberty, equality, and fraternity?

In a course of lectures given in 1919, Rudolf Steiner came out with something, in his rather aphoristic way, on which I want to reflect for the remainder of this talk. He said, in effect, and quite simply: A child who does not *imitate* thoroughly in his first seven years will not be able to develop an adequate capacity for *freedom* as an adult. The child who does not experience real *authority* in his second seven years will not develop an adequate capacity for *equality* – I would say fair dealing – as an adult. And the child who does not experience people in whom ideas live as *ideals* in adolescence will not develop an adequate capacity for *fraternity* as an adult.

If Steiner is right, he is obviously saying something of profound importance for educationists and for parents. So I want to see if I can make sense of this, in a quite simple way. I do not want to attempt here to make links with any particular schools of developmental psychology, although I think that this would be an interesting and important thing to attempt. Indeed, there may have been such attempts, for all I know. But I have repeatedly found it extremely fruitful and illuminating to reflect on these things that Steiner threw out near the beginning of this century, and that have now been worked with quite intensively in Waldorf education throughout the world for more than fifty years.

Imitation and freedom: What can Steiner mean? In their first years, children learn most fundamentally by doing. As Alan Howard said in his talk, children 'play their way into knowledge'. They are always at play, and their play is work. In this activity, you can sense an enormous force, a force of *will* (you know what happens when you tear a four-year-old away from baking cookies because his mother is at the door). This 'will' activity is a force at once creative and revolutionary: Bricks are piled up into great castles, which are then demolished with equal determination. We meet tremendous revolutionaries working at a quite basic physical level.

Without the support of appropriate social form, this force of will can run wild and become merely destructive. Some of the more extreme experiments in 'progressive' education, where very young children were let loose exclusively for 'self-expression', could lead to a state of exhausted lostness. A tribe that loses its structure, its customs, its sense of living supported and sustained with a God-given order, can rapidly fall apart. There have been many tragic examples of this in our times, as such cultures have met ours, which is structured in quite a different way.

It is not too difficult to see that this same will, revolutionary and creative, begins to rise up into more awakened modes: as imagination in the young school child, as idealism in the adolescent, as the creative spirit in the adult – that spirit which is most dangerous to tyrants and totalitarians, but which, as in *The First Circle*, they cannot live without.

So we may begin to see in imitation that which first socialises the creative will, that which helps the child to gain confidence and strength as a being of action in the world into which it is newly arrived. We can even speculate as to whether there may be living – quite unconsciously – a kind of question from the child to the adult world: Can you make surroundings that offer for imitation an order that echoes, if rather remotely, the divine order within which I lived before birth? Steiner once said that children of this age hope to find 'goodness' in their surroundings. Perhaps he meant something of the goodness a tribal society could experience in the God-given order of their lives. In the kindergarten, the teacher has the responsibility for creating a world, and can perhaps pray that if God inspected it, he would see that it was good. In a more general way, we can see that as adults we need inner and outer freedom for effective expression of our creativity. We cannot be creative if we are excessively burdened by inner hang-ups and inhibitions. It is a modern commonplace that such inhibitions may have their roots in childhood experiences. Here is something of a meeting point with Steiner's aphorism, but a bit flat and dull compared to the perspective we have been trying to portray.

So what about equality as a social faculty that needs for its full unfolding an experience of true authority in the middle years of childhood? As I said earlier, we tend to be in a muddle about equality. Yet we understand very well that we want, in some sense, in our society, to be treated as equals by other human beings. The muddle comes, rather naturally, from the fact that most of the obvious ways of comparing human beings reveal inequalities, whether we look at natural endowment or at what has been acquired in life. If we mean anything by human equality (on which depends the idea of equal human rights), we must mean something apparently paradoxical, namely that by virtue of all being different, and yet being human, we are all equal.

I do not think that this idea will acquire substance as long as we consider ourselves to be products of heredity and environment alone, since we all have different heredity and are differently treated by the environment. But I think that the strength and persistence of the idea of equality points to an *experience*, not fully conscious and not capable of adequate articulation in a reductionist culture, that we are most fundamentally *spiritual* beings, dwelling in an organisation subject to heredity and environment, but not totally determined by these.

If some such idea of the human being begins to live (as it does in some modern schools of humanistic psychology), then we can make a deeper sense of what it may mean for a school child to meet a true authority as teacher or parent. Solomon stood among his people as both human and divine. He could illuminate their lives with a light not derived from heredity or environment, but from the spirit.

When a teacher or a parent deals with a dispute in classroom or family so that the children experience it as truly fair – can we not imagine that such an experience of true authority can live on as a sense that human beings can live in human society also as spiritual beings? For the sense of equality among adults – the source of fair dealing, of equity in society – needs roots in some awareness that within each person we meet there lives also a shaft – however obscured or dimmed – of a spiritual light. As terrestrial beings, we are unequal. As spiritual beings, we are in a fundamental sense equal before God. The social issue is whether anything of this reflects itself in social life and practice. The capacity for such awareness – so we seem to hear Steiner saying – is nurtured or denied by the experience of authority in the middle part of childhood. When an adult makes judgements not out of favouritism or prejudice, but out of a recognition of the emerging spirit in each child, he thereby confirms for the child that an equal spirit lives in his teacher.

Finally, what of adolescence? Steiner speaks of this time as crucial for nurturing a capacity for fraternity, the quality that can begin to open the way to social relationships based not on custom, or rules, but on insight into the needs of others. As I have already said, fraternity is not a matter of sentimental goodwill. If this were so, the word *do-gooder* would never have acquired its pejorative meaning. No, fraternity depends on true insight – on being able to apprehend the realities of another situation. For this to be possible, we must accept that the human being is capable of engaging in a very remarkable and mysterious activity, which we call thinking. For a strictly behaviouristic view of human nature, thinking does not exist, since in the sense in which I am using it, it means being able to grasp in one's own mind what is at work in one's surroundings, including the minds of others. To say 'Aha! I see what you mean' does not mean anything to a strict behaviourist. For building a free social life it means everything.

Steiner frequently emphasised that the central task of educating adolescents is to help them to *think*. But by thinking he did not mean simply the acquisition of certain narrowly defined cognitive skills or the ability to operate in a few analytic and logical modes. He meant the fullness of that activity by which we gradually understand the world, including each other. As science itself has come to recognise, insight often begins as an *imaginative* act – a hypothesis – that is only gradually shaped into a rigorous, but then often narrower, tool for knowing some aspect of the world. But we have only to look at how real living science actually works, at its frontiers, to grasp something of what Steiner meant when he said that adolescents need to meet teachers in whom knowledge lives as ideals.

Observant parents and teachers can soon see how deep is the need for such experience, and how often it is disappointed. What we see as alienation in adolescents is often a sad but realistic perception that the adult world has not attained that freedom of insight for which the young person longs, but thinks in stereotypes, in habitual categories, in conventions. 'Knowledge' then degenerates into learning a conformist programme of intellectual behaviour patterns. The alternative is to drop out. At the same time, every undergraduate knows how boredom gives way to interest when he meets a teacher in whom the quest for knowledge is alive with enthusiasm and wonder, where it is an adventure into the unknown, not a mere rehearsal of safe and familiar territory.

The liberation of the human will into its own adventure of knowledge is quite recent historically – indeed it is the basis of true science. It has not only opened the way to immense journeys, both inner and outer, but is bringing into being a social order that is still full of uncertainties – and yet where there is one certainty, which is that social life can no longer be built on customs or commandments alone. There have to be meetings of minds (or else we shall create more sinister alternatives, which deny that we have minds at all).

In education, we face here a very great challenge. Another aphorism from Steiner, part of which I have already mentioned, is that while infants hope to meet goodness in their surroundings and children need to meet beauty (i.e. fairness), adolescents are engaged in a deep search for *truth* – and they need to find teachers who are fellow searchers, and who can show the way. In such experiences, we can perhaps see how seeds of the capacity for brotherhood can be planted: where the adult is experienced as 'brother' on a journey, a quest for insight. Only in the meeting of minds can there be founded the beginnings of a social order that includes freely made fraternity.

If we understand this, we can also hold on to something else in dealing with the upheavals of adolescence: If adolescents are, at a deeper level, searching for truth, they need also to be truly perceived. The people who work most effectively with them are usually those who can see the real but often struggling being emerging amidst the turmoil, who can hold on to the ideal even if it is surrounded by a good deal of chaos. Here again, an enormous amount must depend on whether teachers and parents bear within them a conviction that other human beings are, so to speak, *really there*. If they are merely trapped in their own mental images, uncertain of their capacity to see anything other than their own habitual patterns of thought, they cannot work into the realm of experience where true insight, and true freedom, can begin to be born.

Perhaps I should draw to a close here. I have been trying to explore an apparently simple question, which is how we may educate, not particular forms of social behaviour, but social *capacities*, which by implication must live as possibilities in human nature when we acknowledge the social ideals of liberty, equality and fraternity. I have made an excursion into history, in the hope that this may enrich our possibilities of grasping the dimensions of Steiner's aphoristic assertion that the capacity for liberty (I would say creativity) is to be nurtured through imitation in early childhood; the capacity for equality (I have said, fair dealing) needs an experience of luminous authority between seven and fourteen; and the capacity for fraternity needs a meeting with ideas that live in adults as ideals, with true thinking.

For myself, Steiner's indications resound with experiences I have made empirically and repeatedly as an experienced parent, and also in my somewhat limited experience of teaching children. But I am very much aware that just as my young friend, whom I mentioned at the beginning, had the greatest difficulty in explaining to an administrator why she wanted to bake cookies with her children, so what I have been saying may seem half-baked, or not even baked at all. But if this is so, I will dare to attribute it, somewhat arrogantly, to the fact that much modern educational discourse tends to be conducted at present within so narrow a frame of reference that any journey across a wider territory can seem like a trip in a hot air balloon. But I hope that this audience, at least, has been with me, and has found the journey meaningful. A good deal depends, for our social future, so I believe, on our grasping the meaning of education in a way that is true to the fullness of those capacities of which the human spirit is capable.

1980

Mindstorms in the Lamplight

In this short review, I shall attempt an evaluation of Seymour Papert's *Mindstorms*,[1] and the approach to the use of computers in education it embodies.

This commentary cannot be exhaustive. The virtue of Papert's work is that it is not trivial. It impinges on fundamental questions of education, psychology, philosophy, and epistemology, and a full analysis would require a much longer treatment. My purpose here, in response to the mainly enthusiastic and uncritical reception of *Mindstorms* by teachers and parents, is to sound a sceptical note, and to justify it.

Papert's achievement is to devise a programming language, LOGO, that enables children to construct their own programs, and to control a small robot, the turtle (or an equivalent on the video screen). They can make the turtle, for example, draw shapes. The kinds of things LOGO enables children to do with turtle embody 'powerful ideas' (notably mathematical and physical ideas). Thus, says Papert, the child learns through doing, is in control all the way, has fun, and is ushered into the mathematical and computer culture with confidence. 'The new knowledge is a source of power and is experienced as such from the moment it begins to form in the child's mind' (p.21).

Papert is not naïve about the potency of the realm to which he is introducing children. Computers are tools. Tools are never neutral, but create a culture of tool users who have to operate them on the tools' terms. Computers embody a mechanised version of thinking. Will they make children think mechanically? Papert's answer is yes, they will. But LOGO enables them to *choose* to learn to think in this way. 'I have invented ways to take educational advantage of the opportunities to master the art of *deliberately* thinking like a computer . . . By deliberately learning to imitate mechanical thinking, the learner becomes able to articulate what mechanical thinking is and what it is not' (p. 27).

The LOGO approach is underpinned by Piaget (with whom

Papert worked for some time). But it is a 'new' Piaget, setting aside his framework of natural development in favour of a more 'interventionist' approach. In particular, it is claimed that LOGO makes it possible for children to 'concretise' formal operations well before Piaget's threshold of eleven to twelve years. Furthermore, they can enter these realms with enjoyment, and avoid creating for themselves the blocks to mathematics that easily form at this stage because formal operations seem so remote from real life. In a world shaped by the powerful ideas of mathematics, we are told, the mathematical illiteracy engendered by such blocks must be overcome, and with the help of LOGO, children may be initiated early and painlessly.

I shall question this program on three grounds: its tendency to experiential impoverishment; its uncritical 'head-start' philosophy; and its idolatry of 'powerful ideas' and computer thinking. While Papert acknowledges, briefly, that there may be situations in which thinking like a computer is *not* appropriate or useful, he claims that by deliberately learning mechanical thinking, children will become aware that this is just one 'cognitive style' and that they can choose others. He does not say what others he recognises, or how children might learn to discover, practice, and value them. He merely glances sidelong here at issues of great importance, which I shall consider briefly at the conclusion of this discussion.

Leaving aside the theoretical underpinnings, what actually happens in a LOGO learning environment? Examples are given in the book. The child sits at a keyboard with a screen, typing instructions. With the help of LOGO, the machine is programmed to draw a 'flower' (Figure 1.), then a lot of 'flowers' in a 'garden' (Figure 2.). Next, the child may devise a program to draw a bird (Figure 3.), then a flock of birds (Figure 4.). Then the birds can be put into motion. 'The printed page,' says Papert, 'cannot capture either the product or the process; the serendipitous discoveries, the bugs, the mathematical insights, all require movement to be appreciated' (p. 93).

Now let's hold on a moment. Flowers? Birds? Movement? There is not a flower or bird in sight, only a small screen on which lines are moving, while the child sits almost motionless, pushing at the keyboard with one finger. As a learning environment, it may be mentally rich (even if the richness is rather abstract), but it is perceptually extremely impoverished. No smells or tastes, no wind or birdsong (unless the computer is programmed to produce electronic tweets), no connection with soil, water, sunlight, warmth, no real ecology (although primitive interactions with a computerised caterpillar might be arranged).

Building Up

Figure 1.

Figure 2.

It's a bird

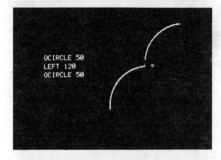

Figure 3.

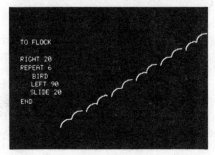

Figure 4.

Granted, we are not discussing the teaching of botany, meteorology, or ecology, but the mastery of 'powerful ideas'. Yet the actual learning environment is almost autistic in quality, impoverished sensually, emotionally, and socially. (All right, children have fun, and sometimes work together on programming, a social and affective plus. But compare the scene with any traditional children's playground games, or their involvement in the ancient and wise psychodramas of fairy stories.)

In this respect, computers in classrooms are simply extensions of television in classrooms. Evidence of any profound educational value in television, except as an adjunct for good teachers (any profundity then comes from the teachers, not the television), is not known to me. It feeds us with brief stimuli and surrogate reality. All the energy that has gone into debating the effects of the content of television programmes has obscured the question of sheer impoverishment of life, the effects of simply sitting still for hours, absorbed in an artificial image world.

Computers, of course, are not entertainment, but LOGO makes them entertaining as a means of introducing children to powerful ideas. These are the ideas that are really shaping adult life, we are told, so why not meet them early? Put away childish things like making sand castles, feeding real turtles, playing tag in a playground rather than on a video screen and with other children rather than an electronic mouse, collecting real flowers, painting with a real brush and paints. But if you do not learn to control computers early, the earnest voices whisper, they will control you. You must give your child every chance.

If I seem intemperate, it is because of the loss of real connection with childhood of which the whole temper of *Mindstorms* is a symptom. Papert himself cannot be blamed for this. He is a brilliant exponent and champion of the dominant cultural tide, technological and instrumental in spirit and soul. When he was two, as he describes in his Foreword, Papert knew the names of lots of automobile parts, notably from the gearbox and transmission. He soon became adept at turning wheels not only in the external world but in his head (and indeed in his heart: 'I remember there was *feeling, love*, as well as understanding in my relationship with gears'). Gearwheel models later helped him into mathematics. It is a fascinating glimpse into the inner life of a man with a touch of genius.

However, there really is much else in childhood besides gearwheels. No doubt young Seymour did more than turn wheels in his head. And the focus of his book has been deliberately narrowed to the question of achieving earlier, deeper, and more effective entry into some powerful ideas of mathematics. But if adopted uncritically, the message of *Mindstorms* will reinforce the tunnel vision that afflicts education, servile as it is to technocracy and easily alienated from the fullness of human experience.

Piaget, of course, made his observations and discoveries in rather richer environments (although even he had to impoverish them a little for experimental purposes). His genius was to see deeply into largely spontaneous childish operations, and to draw out of the children themselves, through conversation, a glimpse of childhood consciousness. Like many important insights, basic Piagetian realisations are often fairly obvious once articulated. The childhood skills of managing see-saws and swings are exercises in applied physics. The physics is enacted, not thought; known intuitively, not intellectually. Yet it is experience that can later be lifted into more abstract and conscious experience as a grasp of mathematical laws, calling for skills in formal operations.

The progress from sensorimotor through concrete to formal operations was regarded by Piaget as a real, natural developmental rhythm. Certainly, its unfolding calls for appropriate environmental correlates. In particular, the capacity for formal operations may scarcely develop at all if not exercised when it awakens around the age of eleven or twelve. But the idea that we are here dealing with natural developmental rhythms is challenged by Papert. As an 'interventionist', he sees Piaget's stages as capable of being concertinaed into early childhood. LOGO allows us to introduce a first practice of formal operations to seven- or eight-year-olds. The computer way of thinking can thereby come 'to inhabit the young mind', providing a head start in coping with the adult world.

The results of all kind of head-start programmes should in any case lead us to be cautious in expecting clear long-term benefits from meeting LOGO at age seven. It is too early for empirical evidence to exist, so the question must be left open. But even if positive evidence did exist, it should not lead us to neglect other questions. While Piaget explored some other aspects of development and education (for example, the child's relation to moral questions), his main focus was on cognitive development. And because most educational discussion is about cognition and intellect, this is what Piaget is best known for. Since even the most goggle-eyed computer enthusiasts scarcely argue for computers as tools for affective or moral education, Piaget can be summoned to support a case that is from the beginning a kind of caricature of what education is really all about.

In *Mindstorms*, Papert tells touching stories about children intimidated by mathematics, who then learn to love learning with the help of LOGO. Their love is for the machine and the games they can play with it, echoing Papert's own infant love of gearwheels. All this would be funny if it were not so sad. It is well-known that autistic children can make close relationships with things that they cannot make with people. It could be interesting to explore whether LOGO might help some autistic children develop confidence enough to venture to play with people. But we are talking about pathologies and therapy, not education. What kind of a culture are we developing if people have to meet its most powerful ideas through machines rather than through people? If people – that is, teachers – consistently work in such a way that they block access to these ideas, should we not be looking at how teachers work rather than selling them a prosthesis? At the heart of real life is working with people, being with people, understanding people. (Does this have to be argued?) As long as classrooms include real teachers, cognitive development cannot, in the nature of the situation, be divorced from emotional, social, and moral experience. Particularly in the period before puberty, while engaged in Piaget's concrete operations, children are fundamentally involved, if they are in good health, in gaining social and emotional experience. It is prime time for imaginative and artistic education. Their relationships with adults at this time influence profoundly how they relate to adults in high school –including mathematics teachers. There are here very large areas of educational concern that are far more significant than demonstrating some kind of early competence in formal operations.

I should say here that I do not want to devalue computers in education altogether. That would be absurd and foolish. I take it as obvious that proper education in computer science belongs in high schools. LOGO will have real interest and value here. But there are further issues that need attention. LOGO is a sophisticated language, requiring considerable computing capacity. It may help entry into powerful ideas, but is it the best way to understand computers themselves?

Much has now been written about the ease with which we project aspects of ourselves onto these machines (and indeed, we really meet aspects of ourselves, notably our own capacity to 'think like a computer', in the programs we use). The potential for obsession, delusion, and confusion is now well known, but no less a cause for concern for all that. The best medicine would surely seem to be proper insight into both the principles by which the machines operate and, still more fundamentally, the essential features of the 'style' of thinking that computers embody and demand. For this, we need 'transparent' systems, right down to the level of machine language. The force of development is to make sophisticated systems cheap enough for schools. There is little commercial incentive to sell transparent systems. But there is a significant intellectual interest and challenge. How can one open up for fifteen-year-olds the history of thought from which emerged Boolean algebra, information theory, the Turing machine? What tools would help? LOGO is, in its own terms, a brilliant achievement. But it uses this background to learn to operate within certain realms of powerful ideas. The interest in these is presented as power. The inner background, the spiritual choices that are actually being made when we think like a computer are not illuminated by playing with LOGO, since they are not grasped in any wider historical or cultural context.

Yet without concern for this context, LOGO and its like can only serve deeper idolatry of that 'instrumental reason' which Joseph Weizenbaum, in his famous and penetrating polemic,[2] rightly identifies as one of the most serious illnesses of the computer age. Despite Papert's (unsupported) claim that early thinking like a computer will promote awareness of other styles of thinking, the entire temper of his work is in the spirit of instrumental reason. This is revealed very clearly in his argument that as learners, we are all fundamentally *bricoleurs* – structuralist jargon for 'tinkerer' – assembling bits and pieces of materials and tools, which one handles and manipulates. Learning is learning to operate, to control, to be competent instrumentally. It is pragmatism in action. Truth is what can be made to work, the means are the ends. It is a tide of thought that runs so deep and strong through our technocratic society that one challenges it at one's peril. So it is worth looking at two more examples from *Mindstorms*.

To get a digital computer to draw a circle, one must break down the curve into many small straight lines. The LOGO program makes this explicit to the user. As Papert rightly says, this introduces children to the powerful idea of differentials. Essentially, this is the technique developed by Newton and Leibniz whereby continuous but variable processes can be mathematically grasped by breaking them down into infinitely small discrete steps. It is an abstract and very powerful method, a most fundamental tool in mathematics and physics. It is also a kind of essence of instrumental reason. With it, we can manipulate a biological growth curve mathematically. This can easily obscure the fact that if we 'differentiate' an actual living plant, it will not grow any more. We have killed it.

Papert gives, in another context, the example of learning to understand the flight of birds. He argues that his approach is not ordinary reductionism, because we get nowhere with the problem by studying feathers. Our grasp of bird flight came from grasping mathematical aerodynamics and by building aircraft. By analogy, Papert argues that computer systems and artificial intelligence can 'act synergistically with psychology in giving rise to a discipline of cognitive science whose principles would apply to natural and artificial intelligence'. (p. 165).

This disguises the circular problem buried here. No one denies that computer systems can throw light on aspects of human intelligence. Quite obviously, the systems themselves are products of this intelligence, and so by studying them, we study aspects of ourselves. The emphasis needs to be on *aspects*. Leaving out, now, the emotional and moral questions touched on earlier, the very force and success of computer systems, and the powerful ideas of physics and mathematics, easily allow them to occupy the whole ground. We take a limited truth for the whole truth, because this particular style of thinking gives such power.

Our culture is quite extraordinary in this combination of idolatry of a particular kind of power, while floundering fundamentally in helpless anomie. A good part of the problem, in my conviction, lies in the tendency of instrumental reason to prevent our asking important questions. This can be illustrated by pursuing Papert's bird flight example a little further.

While Papert sees himself drawing on the stucturalist tradition, in which we owe much to Piaget, his structures are those of received mathematics (more exactly, the 'mother structures' of the Bourbaki school). There is no discussion of how complete a description of the universe might be based on these structures. They 'work' for the realms of powerful mathematical ideas with which Papert is concerned. There is a structuralist version of reductionism going on here. This is the more striking in that some biologists, also concerned with things like birds and bird flight, and realising that received Darwinism is preventing our asking a lot of rather important questions, are also looking to structuralism for new progress.

Yes, aerodynamics throws light on how bird flight is physically possible. But such insights tell us nothing about why birds fly from place to place. Aerodynamics enables us to see more deeply into the 'adaptations' of birds for flight. All living organisms are adapted in very 'intelligent' ways to their environments. We have to expend much intelligence (using a form of intelligence closely allied to instrumental reason) to understand these adaptations. Yet the concept itself is quite problematic,[3] since the the word presupposes a 'niche', a keyhole for the key. But neither can actually be meaningfully defined without the other. At the same time, our functional biological questions easily obscure nearly all recognition of the fact that we actually have no understanding of biological forms in themselves. Birds are seen as devices for flying, whales as devices for the consumption of krill, but we lose sight of the question of why birds and whales exist at all.

Goodwin, Webster, and others have recently been arguing for a stucturalist theory of *biological* form.[4] Such a theory would have its own 'mother structures'. Certainly, there would have to be some relationship with the Bourbaki structures, since the universe is coherent. But the mathematics for biological forms may be very different from the mathematics for computers. There is an important frontier of modern thought here, which can only be crippled if these exploratory apprehensions are seized, limited, and treated merely as tools for instrumental reason.

Computers, by their very nature, and whether operated with LOGO or otherwise, are potent training grounds for thinking about thinking in purely functional, operational, and instrumental terms. This is the explicit philosophy of what Weizenbaum calls the 'artificial intelligentsia'. Within this framework, *Mindstorms* is a powerful and significant contribution. My contention, though, is that its brilliance is the brilliance of the pool of light beneath a street lamp at night, which features in what is evidently Weizenbaum's favourite drunk joke: The drunk is searching for lost keys in the pool of light. A policeman asks him where he lost them. 'Out there' , says the drunk, gesturing vaguely into the darkness. 'Then why are you looking here?' 'Because the light's better', says the drunk.

If we are scientifically honest, the real mysteries of human consciousness are still shrouded in darkness. They do not cease to exist because we learn to operate brilliantly in a confined and tightly defined cognitive mode. Do we do our children any service by gathering them into the lamplight, and suggesting they forget the rest? The light is flat, and there is little room to move around. Compared to the mysteries of hide-and-seek among moving shadows, it is a limited world, and modern adults are not having all that much fun living in it. And suppose the real keys to our future are not in the pool of light, but somewhere out there?

Even in mathematics there are mysteries. High-level pure mathematicians tend to complain that the realm where new mathematics originates is obscured for most students by instrumental reason. They are taught to manipulate the tools – hardened specialised devices needed to operate at the level of definitions, axioms, notations. But their origins are more mysterious, intuitive. Mathematics used to be called 'the Queen of the Arts.' It is not the same world as that of flowers drawn step by step by an electronic turtle.

Mindstorms deserves every appreciation in its own terms. It is those terms I have questioned in this brief review, especially if they are treated, by implication or by default, as sufficient for education or for life. And if it seems that I am making a mountain out of a molehill – after all, *Mindstorms* is a short book, with a limited aim – it is because, if it is a molehill, it is sited on the slopes of the mountain of instrumental reason. And embedded in the issue of truth as power, or truth as wisdom, is a fundamental spiritual crisis of our time.

1984

[1] Seymour Papert, *Mindstorms: Children, Computers, and Powerful Ideas* (New York: Basic Books, 1980).

[2] Joseph Weizenbaum, *Computer Power and Human Reason* (San Francisco: W.H. Freeman, 1976).

[3] Richard C. Lewontin, *Adaptations, Scientific American 239*, No. 3 (September 1978): 212-30.

[4] G. Webster and B.C. Goodwin, *The Origin of Species: A Structuralist Approach*, *J. Social Biol. Struct 5* (1982): 15-47.

The Movement that Everyone Tries to Forget

Some 40,000 pupils attend the ninety-odd Rudolf Steiner schools all over the world. They are all fully comprehensive coeducational, unstreamed schools taking normal children from kindergarten to eighteen. (They are quite distinct from the many homes and schools for handicapped and maladjusted children and adults run on Steiner lines).

The movement is strongest in Germany, where the first Waldorf School was founded in Stuttgart in 1919 for the children of employees of the Waldorf-Astoria cigarette factory. The German schools were closed by the Nazis, but reopened in 1945, and now number more than thirty. The movement has spread to most European countries, as well as to the United States, Canada, Australia, New Zealand, South Africa and South America.

The six schools in Britain which form the Steiner Schools Fellowship feel themselves somewhat out on a limb in their own country. They are all growing, or at least holding their own, in spite of severe economic pressures. They have no endowments, and none of the snob appeal which attracts wealth. Nor do they promise high-octane A level performance. Their examination results are adequate in relation to an entry which is not selected on academic ability, but the specialist demands of the British examination system have forced serious distortions of the kind of work which the schools really want to nurture in their senior classes, and no one is fully satisfied with the resulting compromise. Yet interest grows. There is a steady stream of visitors and inquiries. The teachers themselves have a pressing sense of the relevance of their ideals and practices to many current educational conundrums. Nevertheless, the schools were never intended to become the preserve of a mainly middle-class minority which can pay fees. So they are asking themselves, with some urgency, what place this kind of education will be able to find in Britain in the next few years.

Not many educationists or teachers in this country know much about Steiner education. This is partly the fault of the movement itself. There is very little literature in English, and Steiner teachers have been too busy to spend much time making their work more widely known. There are, though, some other obstacles. The somewhat empirical temper of British cultural life means that most practising teachers approach their work as a craft, and – often wisely –distrust theories and systems. But Steiner's aim was to found an education on a detailed understanding of child development – and his account of this development quickly leads beyond the usual frames of reference in which most people are accustomed to discuss these matters.

This means that whoever begins to study Steiner's work seriously will quickly be led into deep waters. He may begin to scent whiffs of what seems like mysticism or occultism, and he will certainly need to make some relationship with the extraordinary figure of Steiner himself. People may come to terms fairly easily with someone who claims to speak, as Steiner did, out of direct spiritual experiences, so long as he or she pronounces mainly about some other world, or about religious or inner matters safely insulated from practical life. It is different when such a person begins to describe his activities as spiritual research and to bring the results to bear on such humdrum problems as the teaching of arithmetic.

Steiner himself, who as a young man had many friends among leading artists, philosophers and scientists in Vienna, Weimar and Berlin before the turn of the century, was largely ostracized by his circle from the moment he began to speak directly of his personal spiritual experience. Yet he did not begin to do so until he had, at least to his own satisfaction, fully understood the relationship of this experience to the familiar functioning of the human mind in thought, feeling and action, and had formulated this as a clear theory of knowledge which he published first as a doctoral thesis (*Truth and Science*) and soon afterwards enlarged and developed ,as a book (*The Philosophy of Freedom*).

Nevertheless, it was another twenty years before he began to be approached seriously by teachers, doctors, farmers, scientists and others, asking not merely for help in their personal lives but for a renewal in their practical work. (During this period he lectured and taught, at first mainly to members of the German Theosophical Society, and later within the Anthroposophical Society which he founded in 1913. This led to work in drama and the arts.)

To his work with the first group of teachers in Stuttgart after the First World War Steiner also brought a certain amount of teaching experience of his own. He had not worked in a classroom but, coming from a very poor Austrian family, he had had to work to support himself, while studying for a science degree at Vienna's Technical Univerity, by extensive private tutoring.

Steiner wished the Waldorf schools to be judged by their work. He intended them to be, quite simply, good schools. Waldorf teachers are not expected to inculcate a particular world outlook into their pupils but to equip them to find their own ways as adults. Of course the phrase 'good school' begs a lot of questions, which, if they are pursued at all, quickly become very large questions indeed. Few people who think seriously about education would measure the real value of a school's work by its examination results or by the income and social status of its pupils in later life. What matters is whether the pupils go on to realise their full potential and make fruitful relationships with others. Success, in these terms, is barely measurable. Nevertheless, as a general statement of aims, this would apply well enough to Steiner schools. But for teachers and educationists the significance of this form of education must lie not in such generalities but in the details of concepts and practice.

What is the basis of a school curriculum? Why do we teach what we teach? The simplest answer is that an educated person should have acquired certain knowledge (the 'subjects' of established school tradition) and learnt certain skills (notably the three Rs). Fortunately this is seldom satisfactory today. We know that the conventional subjects, treated simply as bodies of knowledge, lead all too easily to the aridities of chalk-and talk, to boredom and deserts of abstraction. The selection and teaching of skills no longer seems such plain sailing either. The behavioural sciences are beginning to offer more powerful techniques for training and shaping behaviour – but this is making us aware that all training embodies certain social and moral assumptions. The radical response is that all education is a device for perpetuating various kinds of tyranny.

Between these two extremes there has grown the search for a truly child-centred education, a search in which all Steiner teachers also feel themselves to be most deeply engaged. To this search, Steiner made two main contributions: first, a detailed account of child development (many features of which have subsequently been confirmed and supplemented by the work of Piaget, Gesell and others) and second, an approach to a curriculum designed to support this development which is still, in its conception and detail, unique.

It is characteristic that Steiner emphasised the physical development of the child as much as the psychological (Tanner's recent work is relevant here). This accounts for the emphasis on chronological age, as opposed to developmental age, which often surprises visitors to Steiner schools. Yet it would be strange, unless we really believed in the Cartesian dichotomy divorcing mind wholly from matter, if the maturation of the organism were not linked with maturation of the mind.

Children, Steiner said, do not grow up – they 'grow down', from head to limbs. And as they grow down physically, they wake up, psychologically, from limbs to head. The new-born baby is all head; the limbs are more or less appendages. The adolescent, by contrast, often goes through a stage when he seems to be all limbs, before reaching final adult proportions.

Yet waking up proceeds, in a sense, in the opposite direction. Babies and nursery-age children learn mainly by doing (Piaget's 'sensori-motor' and Bruner's 'en-active' stage of development). Not until adolescence does the individual begin to use his head in an adult way, when he becomes capable of more abstract intellectual criticism and analysis of his surroundings.

During the all-important middle years, which Steiner placed explicitly between two stages of physical maturation, change of teeth and puberty, the inner and outer growth processes cross, so to speak, in the heart of childhood. The rhythms of pulse and breathing begin to approach the adult's, movements become more rhythmic and graceful, and the child is for a while beautifully balanced until the awkwardness of adolescence begins. At the same time, a rich inner life of imagination, fantasy and feeling begins to unfold – everything becomes heartfelt.

For Steiner, this was not a mere figure of speech. He regarded the rhythmic functions of the body, which are embodied most explicitly in the heart and lungs, as the organic basis of our emotional life, as the limbs are the basis for action and the brain for thought. Thus while the pre-school child lives essentially in the immediate events around him, the seven-year-old begins to dispose of a freer life of imagination and feeling, with which he can enter into painting, story-telling or games in a new way. At this time, thought is not naturally critical and analytic, but pictorial and dramatic. The stories enjoyed by under-fives are mainly a series of happenings; but then there begins to awaken a sense for stories filled with drama, triumph and tragedy, laughter and tears, good and evil, and a meeting of reality with mystery and magic.

For this stage of childhood Steiner wanted teachers above all to work as artists, not to teach art as a subject, but to bring into classroom activities all the living imagery, colour, poetry and magic of which they are capable. Classroom practice, too, should have a living organic balance between listening, speaking, doing, between humour and seriousness, impulse and patience, taking in, transforming and giving out. To work with children in this way, to learn to know them as a social group and take accounts of individual needs, demands a great deal of time.

This led Steiner to recommend that each class in the junior school should have a class teacher, who moves up the school with the group, spends at least two hours of each day with them, and is responsible for a substantial part of their work for the eight years from six to thirteen (although languages, games, eurhythmy, crafts, etc., may be taken by specialist teachers). This is obviously a great challenge and a great opportunity for the teachers concerned. They are not bound by a strict timetable, and can shape the work to the needs and progress of their group. Thus for nearly fifty years they have had in their classrooms the flexibility and scope which the more progressive primary schools in this country are now attempting to establish.

But Steiner recommended the class teacher system for a further reason, which seems at first less in tune with the times. Maturation from infant to adult includes, Steiner said, a development in the child's natural relation to authority. The small child is essentially imitative, and is supported above all by security and routine. The adolescent is essentially critical, and is best guided on the one hand by reason, on the other by integrity. But in the middle years, Steiner insisted, the child expects and needs authority, not didactic or autocratic, but the chance to repose confidence in an adult as a source of wisdom and guidance. It is the relationship which led adults in other cultures and other times to expect authoritative guidance from the elders of a family or tribe.

The crucial experience for children at this stage, Steiner insisted, is not knowledge as such, but how knowledge lives in individual human beings. The chilly notion of impersonal truth, which stems from the sciences (and is now being recognised there for the dangerous myth that it is), is quite foreign to childhood. It comes quite naturally to an eight-year-old to expect his teacher to know almost everything. He brings an instinct and capacity for trust which can be a precious gift for later life, and feels betrayed by the adult who offers only scepticism and self-doubt. When an eight-year-old is encouraged to 'find out for yourself', often by reference to books and films, the implication is that these impersonal resources for learning have an authority which the living human being lacks.

This is not to say that children in Steiner schools are never encouraged to look up things or make use of books. But such work takes second place to the sharing of first-hand experience and exploration between teachers and children. By moving up the school with his class, the teacher is having to grow constantly himself, and from his enthusiasm and energy for this work there can flow the natural authority which Steiner hoped for, an authority of a life's work, not of a dead hand.

With puberty, a new relationship is needed. The adolescent begins to have a more detached and critical view of the adults around him, but can recognise and respect authority based on mastery of different fields of work. In the upper school, therefore, pupils work with specialist teachers, although the format of a main lesson, lasting two hours a day in block periods of four to five weeks, is retained. This allows all pupils to follow a broad curriculum of common studies in humanities and sciences until eighteen (although in Britain, the demands of A level work compel much modification of the programme in the sixth form).

Perhaps the most interesting field for detailed study by teachers and educationists are the suggestions Steiner made, not only for the general approach to different age groups, but for the actual content of the curriculum to support successive stages of development. To appreciate Steiner's thinking here, it is necessary to look more closely at his view of these.

As already mentioned, Steiner emphasised chronological age as much as mental age. The physical development of the child is looked after by nature; the doctor intervenes mainly to correct conditions of imbalance caused by illness or malnutrition. Children in advanced countries now grow bigger and come into puberty earlier than a century ago. (Whether this is in any way an advantage is disputable. We can be thankful for the disappearance of deficiencies caused by too little good food, but they are in danger of being replaced with disorders caused by too much bad food.)

However, it is accepted that there is a normal path of physical development from birth to adult, which is fairly constant. A proposal to manipulate this development, for example by inducing puberty at five, would not find much support. A long maturation process is clearly associated with the unique capacities of the human species.

In a competitive society, though, in which there is a premium on certain kinds of intellectual skills, psychological maturation is often viewed differently. Although it is somehow linked with physical maturation, it appears to be rather more mobile and malleable, so that under-fives may be trained to perform what look like adult intellectual feats (not only reading and writing, but various logical and mathematical operations). At the same time, the crucial and formative nature of the pre-school years has increasingly impressed child psychologists, with the result that a growing weight of educational research and technology is beginning to focus on the nursery and even on the cradle.

Steiner was emphasising the extreme importance of the first five years of life, more than fifty years ago. This arose from his view that this first stage of development is dominated essentially, by imitation in a very fundamental sense of the word.

The distinction between 'I' and 'the world', which adults take as given, awakens only gradually. The infant, Steiner said, at first experiences himself as inwardly and outwardly united with all that happens around him. He should, for example, be surrounded by rich and well-formed human speech, irrespective of whether he understands all that he hears. But it does not follow that this openness should be exploited to achieve precocious performance of specialised forms of behaviour currently valued by adults, and to do so, Steiner claimed, might seriously impoverish other aspects of development (even leading, much later in life, to physical and constitutional weaknesses).

Behind Steiner's approach to this question lies a view of the human being which goes right outside the usual framework of educational discussion. For he regarded growing up as the gradual incarnation of an individual human spirit into a physical organism, and education as essentially concerned to support this incarnation process. And the gradual maturation of new faculties and modes of awareness he regarded as intimately linked with the process of growing into various functions of the organism, as these themselves mature.

Thus during infancy the human being is growing especially into his digestive and metabolic functions, and is nourished by every aspect of his surroundings as directly as by his food. After the change of teeth, he is growing more particularly into the rhythmic organs of heart and lungs, which awakens an inner experience swinging between expansion and contraction, laughter and tears, and brings a relationship to the world which is neither imitative unity nor detached observation, but a consciousness which has some of the drama and variety of vivid dream.

Then at adolescence, according to Steiner, the human spirit begins to unite itself more deeply with the parts of the organism which are, so to speak, nearest to death – with the functions of nerves and senses, and with the skeleton. Out of this grow at their proper time the adult's capacities for detachment, clear observation and objective thought.

This account of childhood needs to be looked at in conjunction with Steiner's view of history. He did not accept the notion that human beings of earlier cultures shared the same detached apprehension of nature as ourselves, while simply entertaining more confused theories which they then projected as myths. He regarded these mythologies rather as entirely valid descriptions of real experience, associated with a different mode of consciousness.

What we know as our modern consciousness is essentially a dualistic apprehension of ourselves *vis-à-vis* the world (and which generates nowadays varying degrees of alienation). This began to awaken, according to Steiner, among the Greek philosophers, and more generally in Europe with the Renaissance. Modern science was born out of just that sense of detachment which gradually overtakes each modern child around adolescence. Behind the historical development, too, according to Steiner, we should learn to see a gradual process of incarnation of the human spirit.

This is the essential background out of which Steiner began to make suggestions for building a school curriculum – a curriculum through which the organic process of becoming at home in the body can go hand-in-hand and be supported by an education which leads the human being to be at home in the world. There is space here only to pick out a few examples.

With the younger children, Steiner urged teachers wherever possible to proceed from the whole to the part, from living to non-living, from action to knowledge, from man to nature. Thus writing precedes reading in Waldorf schools, and the former will emerge out of imaginative experience and action.

For example, before introducing the letter W, the teacher may tell a sea story full of wind and waves. The children will learn a watery, wavy poem, and paint waves. Out of the painting, the teacher will lead into a more formal exercise of the letter form – an abstraction, but one born out of a living experience. The child thus follows, essentially, the same process as the historical development of writing, from pictograms to our present skeletal but convenient alphabet.

The children will also both hear and speak many stories and poems in their own language, and in at least one foreign language (more often two), before there is much emphasis on solitary reading and writing. The music and rhythm of words are important experiences for young children, as most parents know, long before their meaning is fully grasped.

Throughout the first school years, the children's imaginative life and grasp of language will be nourished by hearing, re-telling, acting and illustrating stories. For the six-year-olds the teacher may draw mainly on fairy stories, moving on at seven to fables and legends, to Old Testament stories at eight, Norse stories and sagas at nine, Greek myths and legends at ten. In using a sequence of this kind, the teacher leads children through different qualities of imaginative experience, gradually 'down to earth', preparing the way for history proper.

By the eleventh year, children have begun to have a sense of time more like the adult's, while the intellect is become more awake and critical. At this time, Steiner suggested, teachers could introduce Greek history, which begins as myth and ends as fact, while Greek culture and consciousness move from mythology through philosophy, and prepare the way for the more prosaic world of Rome.

It is generally recognised that the first experiences of arithmetic are crucial, and here Steiner made some interesting recommendations. By starting with 'two plus two equals four', the child meets (i) a completely abstract proposition, (ii) a reductionist view of the universe in which wholes are made up of parts, and (iii) a problem with only one answer. If he explores instead how to divide an apple or a cake and share it round the class, he starts from real life, from wholeness and from a problem with several answers. Similarly, the teacher may first introduce children to Roman numerals, in which II arises by dividing the wholeness of I, instead of launching straight into the Arabic system with its powerful but highly abstract concept of zero. The children will also find their way into number through old-fashioned chanting of tables, as well as through musical rhythms and stepping games. As in so much else, at this age the children need to learn by heart before they learn by head.

The way into the sciences also follows a gradual path from imagination to observation and abstraction. For six-year-olds it seems perfectly natural for animals, plants and rocks to talk to each other, as well as humans. By the ninth year, though, there comes an important transition on which Steiner placed much stress (in Gesell's account, this age marks the emergence of 'self-motivation'. One symptom is moments of sudden private loneliness, feelings of detachment from parents and home, often coupled with sudden rebellion. It can be like a premature glimpse of adolescence. To weather this crisis, the child needs to become at home in the world in a new way.

Here Steiner suggested that the children should come to know various forms of human work where craft, skill and knowledge of materials and the environment are important – the farmer, fisherman, builder, blacksmith. The children may churn butter, build a wall, and perhaps, if they can find a cooperative farmer, cut and bind a small amount of wheat before the impersonal combine takes over. A period on house-building can include many realistic exercises in plan-making, calculation of areas and quantities.

Many schools embark on elaborate projects of this kind nowadays, with most valuable results. But the notion that house-building, in particular, has a special value in the ninth year must seem abstract and strange without some appreciation of the child's inner situation at this time – his need to make himself at home in the world and in his body in a new way. Steiner suggested that this period could be accompanied by a first introduction to formal grammar, to the construction and building-bricks of language. Here again Steiner teachers will tend to start with activities (the verbs) before going on to things (the nouns).

From the crafts and trades, the class will probably move on, in the tenth year, to local history and geography, including first exercises in map-making (for example, a detailed representation of the way from home to school). Gradually, the children move from their immediate human environment into natural history and the sciences, beginning with the kingdom closest to man, the animals. Here Steiner recommended teachers to start with studies of the form and ways of life of some characteristic higher animals – eagle, mouse, lion, cow, octopus, etc. In particular, he hoped that children would experience the specialised adaptations of such animals in relation to the versatile and in many respects unspecialised form of man.

Next will come botany, introducing more emphasis on careful observation of the surroundings, and some first discussion of ecological questions (Steiner was already emphasising the importance of educating children to care for the earth in 1919). Geography will expand beyond the locality to take in, for example, a whole region or continent, and in their twelfth year, the class will begin to look at climate, meteorology, astronomy, mineralogy, to awaken gradually a sense for the life and structure of the earth within a wider universe.

As puberty approaches, the physical sciences are first introduced more formally. Steiner anticipated a good deal of modern thinking about science teaching in recommending that a strong element of observation and discovery should precede theoretical explanation. But he also, less fashionably, urged that the artistic experience of earlier classes should not be banished from the laboratory, but welcomed. Thus Steiner teachers may begin physics with acoustics, which can be introduced through music, the making and tuning of bamboo pipes and demonstrations of the remarkable forms on a vibrating Chladni plate. Likewise, an exploration of the phenomenology of colour (including, for example, after-images, coloured shadows and other phenomena usually better known to artists and psychologists than to physicists) will precede optics.

The great changes which overtake young people at puberty are familiar enough, and do not need to be rehearsed here. Many teachers probably share Steiner's hope for a final four years of schooling to help the emerging individual find and test his own powers of discrimination and judgment in relation to every aspect of modern life, an education for freedom. A great many of the difficulties of adolescence have to do with inner and outer unfreedoms, and here Steiner predicted that the effects of environmental and educational inadequacies in earlier years would at this age begin to make themselves sharply felt.

The imitative needs of the infant, if not appropriately met, can re-emerge at puberty and make the adolescent helplessly vulnerable to every passing fashion. And the natural need of the first school years to look up to some adult with affection and confidence as trustworthy authorities, if not adequately fulfilled, can manifest in the adolescent as over-dependence or indiscriminate worship of cult heroes.

Steiner also emphasised the enormous importance of sustaining work in the arts and crafts right up to school leaving age as the most essential help for adolescents struggling to integrate their turbulent new life of feeling and will with an awakening critical intellect. A number of features of adolescent culture which have become familiar since Steiner's time seem to confirm his warnings of the trouble which imaginative deprivation and over-intellectualisation in early school years would bring. (Is it possible that in turning to drugs and Tolkien, teenagers may in part be attempting to make good a lack of fairy stories in infant school?)

There is no space here to describe Steiner's many suggestions for the last four years of schooling, which he held should be available to every young person, whatever their academic abilities. Conditions in the world are very different from the Stuttgart of 1920 and particularly in Germany, some Steiner schools have recently inaugurated interesting experiments in secondary education, notably attempts to combine continued liberal studies and artistic work with industrial apprenticeships and various forms of craft and vocational training.

In Britain (one of the few European countries where Steiner schools get no state aid), such developments are unfortunately blocked at present. School-centred apprenticeships do not fit into the British scheme of things, while the highly specialised academic demands of A levels are quite foreign to the broad experience of many aspects of the real world which Steiner wanted. The current doubts about A level specialisation and the whole pattern of higher education may gradually lead to a situation in which the British Steiner schools will be able to realise more of their full potential.

There is not space here either to describe Steiner's account of the four 'temperaments' in children and adults which the teacher should learn to recognise, nor to go into his recommendation that each school should be run by a community or college of teachers, without a headmaster. In the relatively short time in which Steiner worked with the first Waldorf school, before his death in 1925, he produced a great wealth of suggestions, many of which have still to be fully tested and worked out.

Ultimately what matters about Steiner education is not only whether the schools work, but whether the premises on which they are based are true. Much of what Steiner was saying about child development in 1919 now looks remarkably prescient in the light of work done since. But his account of the meaning of this development is still barely discussable in polite intellectual society. Educational debate tends to skirt round the central question of the essential nature of the human individual. Steiner teachers build all their work round a conviction that each pupil is the bearer of an evolving human spirit with a past and a future leading beyond birth and death. It is not a fashionable view in a sceptical age. But it brings a natural sense of affinity with all other teachers – and luckily there are quite a number – for whom education means caring for the essential humanity of each individual as it emerges and matures in every child.

1973

CARING FOR THE PLANET
Prophet of the Convivial Society

Labelling people so as to paralyse serious attention to what they are saying is a familiar device of our shorthand society. The word 'Doomster' is a case in point. It is now applied to almost anyone who sees a fundamental ecological crisis approaching, irrespective of whether his central concern is the effect of DDT on wildlife, the supply of oil, the contradictions of capitalism, or a theological conviction that Judgement Day is at hand. There is an added implication that Doomsters are a gloomy lot, compared with their upbeat critics who believe that the world can work its way out of its troubles with a bit more science, technology and economic growth.

If he can be categorised at all, Ivan Illich, the rebellious former Roman Catholic priest turned radical social critic, certainly belongs in the first. He does not *argue* that our present kind of industrial society, whether capitalist or Communist, cannot survive much longer; it is a premise he starts from (thus annoying both Communists and capitalists). He is more concerned, as he says in his latest book[1], to outline 'an epilogue to the industrial age' to sketch the conditions for a new 'inverted society'. His vision is far from gloomy (although he recognises that the collapse of the present order could usher in either savagery or Big Brother): it is predicated, in fact, on a view of the potentialities of human beings that is much less limited than that of those critics who resign under the slogan, 'You can't change human nature'.

Illich is hoping for something more fundamental than political or social reform. We must start, he believes, with a kind of cultural revolution, a deep shift of assumption and outlook: 'Fundamental social change', he wrote in *De-schooling Society*, 'must begin with a change of consciousness about institutions'. *Tools for Conviviality* continues to work for such a change.

He has chosen the word 'tool' to denote both technological inventions, and the social and political institutions that use them. His central thesis is that these tools now dominate rather than serve human life. (The phallic connotations of the word reinforce his point. We have fallen prey, he remarks, to an idolatry of 'infinitely swelling obelisks' that we have erected for the worship of speed, growth, consumption etc.) The institutions and inventions of a truly 'convivial' society, by contrast, must enhance rather than destroy real human relationships.

In itself, this is not a particularly novel thesis. The originality lies in the sweep and detail of his argument, and in the remarkable personality of the man himself. Now forty-eight, thin and aquiline, with a curious tentative charm and enormous physical and intellectual energy, Illich's future seems likely to be as interesting, and probably as turbulent, as his past.

As a priest, he seemed set, at the age of twenty-four, for a brilliant career in the Catholic hierarchy. But instead of accepting a place at the Vatican's diplomatic college in Rome, he took over a parish of Puerto Ricans in the New York City slums. In 1956 he was appointed Vice-Rector of the University of Puerto Rico, and a year later Cardinal Spellman made him the youngest Monsignor in the United States. Soon in trouble with the Catholic authorities in Puerto Rico, he was recalled to New York, and then set off on a 3,000-mile journey on foot and horseback through South America. Early in 1961, he founded CIDOC (Centre for Intercultural Documentation) at Cuernavaca, Mexico.

Starting as a centre for teaching Spanish and Latin American history and culture to American priests, it has evolved into a kind of free university at which a drastic critique of industrial society — and particularly of its relations with developing countries – is nurtured. Illich himself, anxious that CIDOC should not become a 'place of pilgrimage', has severed all formal connections with it. But, as is open to anyone else, he regularly books a room and announces a seminar, and he cannot easily escape being one of the major attractions of the place when he is in residence.

The present book is essentially a collection of extended notes arising out of a series of seminars at the Centre. It is aphoristic and condensed, and will not satisfy anyone looking for a carefully argued treatise. As a stimulating radical cocktail, though, it packs a real and sometimes unexpected punch. This was enhanced in a long conversation I was able to have with Illich recently. We went over some of the points of his book; delivered in his slight Austrian accent, accompanied by vivid gestures of his thin brown hands, the argument springs to vivid life.

He starts with a discussion of the 'watershed' where many modern institutions and technologies turn from benign to malign. In his earlier onslaught on 'schooling', he argued that education becomes malign as it turns into an increasingly expensive commodity, and begins to replace learning by compulsory subjection to a meritocratic pyramidal obstacle race erected on a broad base of academic failure. Now transport (soon to be the subject of a separate book) and medicine get some of the same treatment.

Illich on mechanised medicine: 'Only the very rich in the United States can now afford what all people in the poor countries have – personal attention around the death bed.' And quoting a recently retired US Secretary of Health: '80 per cent of the US health budget now goes to produce iatrogenic illness [illness caused by doctors] or to treat it.'

Illich on transport: 'In the United States, 22 per cent of the energy converted drives vehicles, and another 10 per cent keeps roads open for them. The amount of energy is comparable to the total energy – except for domestic heating – required for the combined economies of India and China.' Transport crossed a watershed 'when vehicles had created more distances than they helped to bridge; more time was used by the entire society for the sake of traffic than was saved.' Illich believes, in fact, that he can show that fundamental social disorder begins to be generated as soon as transport accelerates much beyond 'bicycle speeds' (15-20 m.p.h.).

Our growing enslavement to humanly counter-productive technologies, services and institutions leads him on to distinguish between 'work', 'labour' and 'machine operating'. He illustrates this in conversation by quoting a recent study in the US showing that traditional work and crafts, where the individual retains some creative autonomy – weaving, field work, wood and stone carving, even hauling ropes on a sailing ship – are commonly accompanied by song, whistling or humming. The labour of mining and heavy industry, by contrast, bring 'jerky verbal behaviour, cursing and obscenity' – work becomes a kind of torture. Finally, the passive machine watcher or operator neither sings nor curses, but retires into day-dream and consumes Muzak.

The politics of the future, Illich says, must be primarily concerned not with allocating and maximising the means of production, but with 'the design criteria for tools' that will allow a more convivial society. It might be necessary, for example, to limit the maximum horsepower available to any individual for a particular form of work. The need for some 'labour' would not disappear, but in a world where the creative autonomy of work is protected, labour would be faced as a necessity, not forced.

He goes on to survey six different ways in which our present tools frustrate our humanity and dominate our lives. He calls them

Overgrowth, Radical Monopoly, Overprogramming, Polarisation, Obsolescence, and Frustration.

Overgrowth, leading to biological degradation of the environment, is staple doomster fare, and needs no elaboration here. But it also brings 'radical monopoly'. By this he means not only monopoly of a product by a firm, but of a service or activity by an institution. Thus cars monopolise roads and destroy the environment for feet or bicycles. Schools increasingly monopolise learning by transforming it into a commodity, education. Funerals are expensively monopolised by undertakers, medical care by doctors.

He quotes with approval a major 'inversion' achieved very recently in China with the training of one million 'lay health workers' or 'barefoot doctors', who have responsibilities for health education, sanitation, immunisation, first aid, birth control, etc. This is in contrast to trends in the West, where 'an American can now spend in two days of private nursing the median yearly cash income of the world's population'. Wherever radical monopoly imposes consumption of a standard product or service, personal autonomy is restricted and conviviality suffers.

Linked with radical monopoly is 'overprogramming', a growing dependence on specialist expertise acquired by expensive training. This creates 'knowledge capitalists' and a competitive market in education commodities. To maintain this market, an elaborate structure of professional restriction and control grows up. A Latin American shanty-town dweller is prevented from building a home out of simple materials by regulations that refuse to consider plans not signed by a qualified architect (while only the rich can afford to live in the latter's tower blocks). Self-help is stultified in all kinds of ways by a rigidifying apparatus of professionalised services and regulations.

Overprogramming brings 'polarisation', the growing sense of helplessness and deprivation of any form of individual participation created by large-scale organisation of all kinds. Widening gulfs open between those who control the power and the rest (whether it is the bulldozer operator replacing the gang of spade-workers, or the entrepreneur who controls a corporation).

Finally, all this apparatus generates a pace of change and obsolescence that deprives people of what Illich calls 'the right to tradition'. He is particularly interesting on the destructive effect of losing roots in the past (the 'generation gap' is just one example). The consequence is a gradual breakdown of law and order, inviting more imposed social control.

These five malign dimensions are linked with measurable features of industrial growth and social change. But the sixth, 'frustration', is in a different category. It arises, Illich claims, from the conflict between what people value and what they actually experience in their lives: over-work amid labour-saving devices, stress amid time-saving devices, medicine that makes you feel ill, education that makes you feel a failure, transport that adds four hours' commuting to a working day.

Such frustrations may be deeply if dimly felt, but they are obscured, when political and economic decisions are made, by addiction to growth. Withdrawal from this addiction, he warns, will be difficult and painful, and hindered by three main obstacles: obstacles of inner habit of thought, feeling and attitude.

He cites first a familiar target of radical doomsters, 'idolatry of science', but gives the critique a special twist: 'Science is now used to label a spectral production agency which turns out better knowledge just as medicine produces better health'. Both generate increasing dependence on the specialist producers of these commodities, at the expense of personal effort and responsibility. 'The institutionalisation of knowledge . . . makes people dependent on having their knowledge produced for them. It leads to paralysis of the moral and political imagination.'

More subtle, and less familiar, is the gradual corruption of language, which he epitomises in the growing dominance of nouns over verbs in many common usages: The phrase 'I want to learn' becomes 'I want to get an education'. 'I want to walk' becomes 'I need transportation'. Instead of working, loving and enjoying oneself, people *have* work, sex, fun, etc. Accumulation and possession of things gradually replaces creative human activity and cripples the imagination, so that the possibility of a convivial society can no longer be understood, let alone discussed.

Finally, Illich warns of our 'loss of respect for formal legal and political process'. The forms (not the current content) of common law embody a shared social language, a 'deep structure' for human relationships, for the equitable balancing of conflict and regulation of change. Revolution that ignores such processes denies at the outset the possibility of a truly convivial society.

Only here does one begin to become aware of Illich the rebellious priest, who would have us look for the Law within. The Word once given as commandments from without now struggles to live within the deep structure of human relationships. 'I feel almost unbearable anguish', he concludes, 'when faced by the fact that only the Word recovered from history should be left to us as the power for stemming disaster. Yet only the Word in its weakness can associate the majority of people in the revolutionary inversion of inevitable violence into convivial reconstruction.'

In such reconstruction, he clearly believes that the poorer countries, not yet so far advanced on the path of growth addiction, may have the better chance of showing the way. Nevertheless, it is in the rich countries that he is striking, with growing insistence, the tense chord of frustration stretching through them.

I doubt very much whether he will actually get us all out of cars and on to bicycles unless catastrophe compels it (in which case we would probably lose the means of making bicycles as well). But his determination that we imagine anew and with vigour what makes for 'conviviality', and that we contrast this clearly with the inhumanities we impose on ourselves in the name of growth, efficiency and progress, is necessary and wise. I shall look forward to the next book on transport – and I may even dust off my old bicycle in the shed.

1973

---

[1] *Tools for Conviviality* by Ivan Illich (published on 27th September, 1973 by Calder and Boyars).

Menace in the Silent Spring

Six thousand birds died on one Lincolnshire estate in the spring of 1961, after eating seeds dressed with poisonous chemicals. There is now a 'voluntary ban' on using these seed-dressings for spring-grown wheat, and last year casualties were fewer. But birds are still dying – and many biologists are deeply disturbed.

Their anxieties extend far beyond the birds. For toxic chemicals that have come into use since the war have exploded with megaton impact into the complex interactions of living things. They are part of a process, according to Sir Julian Huxley, 'by which man is progressively ruining and destroying his own habitat'.

It was not forseen that seed-dressings would kill birds. And the full repercussions are still not clear. It is certain that several British birds of prey are declining; there is a strong suspicion that they are accumulating insecticide residues by eating large numbers of other birds which have fed on dressed seed – and the residues may be sterilising their eggs. The decline of the hawk removes one of the main checks on the woodpigeon.

This is merely one example of the complex chain reaction that can follow from the use of these potent chemicals. There may be others, more subtle and still undetected, and the extent of this biological uncertainty lends weight to the vaguer and more general anxieties among the public at large.

These anxieties will be sharpened by the publication here last week of Rachel Carson's book *Silent Spring*, which has been a bestseller and a focus of furious controversy in America for months. Miss Carson quotes several examples of grossly irresponsible use of insecticides and, still more disturbingly, argues that traces of these poisons in food may be linked to the increase in cancer and other diseases.

The book draw almost exclusively on American experiences. In Britain, in many ways, the position is much better. Toxic chemicals are used less, and with more care; the pesticide firms are generally responsible and together with Government Departments concerned are acutely sensitive to public opinion.

Central to the control of poisonous chemicals in Britain is the Notification of Pesticides Scheme. It is voluntary – but appears to work well. Under this scheme, manufacturers notify the Ministry of Agriculture of each new toxic product before it is marketed. A dossier is supplied on such things as its composition, toxicity, proposed method of use and possible hazards. Results of experiments to check long term effects of small doses must be provided.

The dossier is examined by two committees, on neither of which the industry is represented, but which include Government and university scientists. The committees produce recommendations for 'safe use' of the product, or if they have doubts, press for further tests.

These arrangements are supplemented by the Agricultural Chemicals Approval Scheme. Chemicals are eligible for approval only after they have been cleared under the notification scheme. Approval is granted by an independent committee of scientists if they decide that the manufacturer's claims are valid.

In practice, virtually all new products are now notified, and the larger firms bring strong pressure on smaller firms to conform. The current list of Approved Products lists 566 individual preparations, made up from 75 basic chemicals. A number of the latest ones are considerably less toxic than their predecessors.

In most cases manufacturers start consulting the scientific committees informally at the research stage. The last thing they want is to have a product turned down when it is ready to be marketed – by which time up to £1 million may have been spent on it. (A few years ago ICI spent £400,000 on a product called 'amiton', and then abandoned it because it looked too poisonous to man.)

A different kind of check is provided by the Agriculture (Poisonous Substances) Act, which regulates the use of some of the more acutely toxic chemicals. Its main purpose is to protect the sprayer, and it lays down rigid specifications for such things as protective clothing.

But an 'approved' insecticide can be – and often is – intensely poisonous. It is 'cleared' for use only in carefully defined circumstances. And here is a snag: there is nothing to prevent the sprayer, safe behind his gas-mask, from giving the brussels sprouts a lethal dose in an absent-minded moment. In America, new laws prescribe the maximum residues of various poisons on products sent to market. In Britain, it is argued that an action could be brought under the Food and Drugs Act against a grower whose goods had 'excessive' residues; that a law compelling sprayers to follow manufacturers' instructions on the tin would not be enforceable; and that in any case farmers are more likely to spray too little than too much, as the stuff is expensive.

However, some scientists believe that there is a strong case, as the confusion of poisonous farm chemicals multiplies, for some kind of scheme to ensure proper instructions and training. This could require farmers to attend a one- or two-day course at some local centre in winter. There they would be instructed in the uses and hazards of the latest products, and reminded of regulations and safety measures. A certificate of attendance at such a course would be needed to purchase pesticides.

That pesticides are doing no gross human injury in Britain is shown by the fact that while 140 farm workers are killed each year in various accidents, none has died from toxic chemicals since 1956. There were eight such deaths between 1946 and 1953, before the regulations to protect sprayers came into force. Out of 20,000 non-fatal accidents annually on British farms, about five are due to chemical poisoning.

Accidents affecting the public have been few – the best known was when seventy people fell ill in Wales after eating flour that had been transported in a railway wagon contaminated by endrin, an insecticide. All recovered. There are no established cases in Britain of people being poisoned by spray residues in food.

In other countries, there have been considerable casualties, usually due to gross misuse of sprays. Parathion, a viciously toxic insecticide related to the wartime 'nerve gases', has probably caused most deaths. In India, 1,000 people were poisoned and 100 died when a leaking container contaminated food in a warehouse.

Parathion became a common method of committing suicide in Germany, Denmark and Finland; it was available in small, convenient ampoules and was reputed to be rapid and painless. (It is certainly rapid: Rachel Carson tells of a chemist, experimenting on himself, who took a minute fraction of a gram and was paralysed before he could reach the antidote.)

In general, though, the immediate situation is comparatively reassuring. Despite the vast quantities of potent poisons distributed over the earth each year, casualties are few by any reasonable standards, and are minute when the substances are used as recommended.

Yet no one can read without unease Rachel Carson's statement that enough parathion is sprayed on Californian farms annually to kill five times the world's population, And a nagging anxiety remains about possible long-term and cumulative effects.

What evidence is there of such effects? An objective inquirer must conclude that there is so far very little. This does not mean, though, that there is no cause for concern. People in the South of England now carry about one-twentieth of a gram of DDT, and one-tenth this amount of the more potent dieldrin, stored in their body fat.

There is no definite evidence that these chemicals are doing any harm there. Citizens in the States of Georgia and Washington, United States, are carrying five times as much. In one experiment, volunteers ate over one three-hundredth of a gram of DDT every day for eighteen months until some 14 grams was stored in their body fat, without apparent ill effects.

All this would be more encouraging if it were known why DDT and related poisons are poisonous. But nobody does. They act on the nervous system in some way, but the details are obscure.

It if is proved, as N.W. Moore, a Nature Conservancy scientist, suspects, that traces of dieldrin and DDT are reducing the fertility of bird's eggs, it will be vital to discover how. For traces of these poisons can also reach the human foetus and the baby through breast milk. Any likely dose would be minute – but there can be no complacency in the face of basic ignorance.

The hazards of the other major groups of pesticides, the 'organo-phosphorous' compounds which include parathion and its relatives, are different. These compounds do not persist in the body or in the soil as the DDT family does, but break down quickly.

Nevertheless, they can have cumulative effects, by gradually reducing the level of an enzyme in the blood, and at a critical level sudden collapse follows.

More tricky is the fact that two different organo-phosphorous compounds may 'potentiate' each other – a minute dose of either may be harmless, but a dose of the two together may cause a subtle interaction with a lethal effect. Such interactions appear to be very rare – but obviously there could be nasty surprises round the corner.

For people in Britain, there can be some cold-hearted reassurance in the fact that if long-term effects show up, they are likely to appear first in spraying teams combating mosquitoes and other pests in the tropics. So far, although these teams are more exposed than anyone else, there is no firm evidence of such effects. But there is a case for regular and compulsory medical examination of all who work regularly with sprays, if only to amass data which would be invaluable if anything should go wrong later.

In all, it is fair to say that there is no immediate cause for clamorous anxieties about hazards to humans in Britain – but there is certainly no cause for complacency. There can be no question of giving potent poisons the benefit of the doubt – they should be under permanent suspicion however innocent they look. And medical research should be persistently and vigorously inquisitorial.

But the case against pesticides does not rest only on their potential threat to human health. The most sinister fact is that insects are learning to resist them. On a recent count, 137 different species of pest were found to be resistant. As a Dutch expert has remarked: 'A resistance is being developed which in the long run will make the control problem insoluble'.

Some houseflies and mosquitoes can now shrug off not one but several of the most lethal poisons. A species of red spider mite is reported to be resistant to 80 different types of chemical.

Some experts believe that many insect species will learn, in time, to resist every new poison the chemist throws at them. This reinforces the argument for more subtle methods of attack. It is already clear that insecticides are palliatives only, like aspirin for headache: they remove the symptoms for a time, but not the cause.

This does not mean that there have not been notable successes. 'Eradication' campaigns have banished mosquitoes and the malaria they carry from areas containing 300 million people. Current campaigns aim to free another 697 million from this scourge. But the World Health Organisation is deeply worried lest the ingenuity of the mosquitoes should outrun that of the chemists, and races of super-mosquitoes surge back on an epidemic scale. If this happened, the effects could be appalling, since natural resistance to the disease has dropped sharply in the cleared areas.

Pesticides can also claim impressive agricultural successes. In Britain, one of the best documented examples has been the gain of one million tons of sugar beet a year since 1959, following spray control of aphids which transmitted a virus disease called 'yellows'.

Intensive modern agriculture, with huge areas under one crop, represents a highly artificial biological situation. Just as urban humans become dependent on central heating and other services to mitigate the struggle for existence, so sugar beet can flourish only under a chemical umbrella.

But this protection is bought at a cost. Apart from resistant insects breaking through the chemical barriers, sprays can clear the way for new pests by killing off natural enemies. The red spider, a fruit-tree pest, increased enormously when tar-oil sprays depleted its natural enemies. A Dutch entomologist, H.J. Huek, has suggested that DDT actually stimulates the spider to breed faster.

The full effects of this upheaval in natural insect communities may take time to show. But nearly twenty years of using the modern insecticides as a blunt instrument have produced situations like that in American apple orchards, where twenty-two sprays are now needed each year to control a single pest, the codling moth.

Some of the persistent insecticides, such as DDT and dieldrin, accumulate in soils with serious effects. In Britain, severe attacks of cabbage-root fly have broken out on land treated in previous years with these poisons. The poison residues kill off small beetles that normally eat most of the cabbage-root fly's eggs. There is also evidence that these residues are killing off tiny creatures that play an important part in forming healthy soil by breaking down plant matter.

Residues can also taint crops. One field examined recently by Government scientists had received a heavy dose of BHC (an insecticide related to DDT) in 1947; in 1958 potatoes grown on the field were still too severely tainted to be sold.

As a result of all this, biologists arc nowadays talking urgently of the need for 'integrated control'. This means using chemicals with the greatest discrimination – as a rapier rather than a bludgeon – and backing them up with other methods.

The simplest methods are cultural practices. It has been found, for instance, that cabbage aphids, which suck about £1 million off the value of British brussels sprouts each year, don't like heights. They can be controlled by growing sprouts 100 ft. or more above sea-level.

In Israel, a serious virus disease of maize which affected 70 per cent of the crop has been virtually wiped out simply by planting four to five weeks later, when a hopping insect that spread the virus had become scarce.

Many other 'biological' methods are being tried. In America, twenty-two different pests have been controlled by importing other insects which eat or parasitise them. Ironically, one of the most successful predators, a ladybird which controlled scale insects in Californian orchards, was wiped out by chemical sprays and the pest surged back.

Another method is to sterilise large numbers of male insects with chemicals or X-rays, and release them. They mate with females, who then lay sterile eggs. In 1954, this method eradicated the screw-worm fly, a pest which ravages cattle, from Curaçao.

Other biological methods include breeding resistant crop varieties, spraying bacteria which attack only certain insects, and luring male insects into traps with concentrated sex hormones extracted from females.

All such methods call for an intimate knowledge of each pest and its relation to the creatures around it. Out of such understanding can grow control methods of far greater subtlety and power than the crude blanket spraying of chemicals. With sufficient biological knowledge, new and *lasting* balances may be established between crops, pests, parasites and predators.

Certainly the most serious charge against post-war pest control is that it has been dominated by chemists, not biologists. The research laboratories of the big firms employ hundreds of scientists to mass produce new chemicals and 'screen' them for insecticidal action. Fundamental biological research is largely confined to universities or Government laboratories. But Government scientists, already hard pressed to assess the new pesticides as they appear, are few and poorly financed and can only nibble at what ought to be done.

Some of the criticisms of pesticides have certainly been exaggerated. Angry bird-lovers and anxious citizens have given vent on occasions to lurid accusations about pesticide hazards to health on very inadequate evidence. Unfortunately, though, the responses from industry and Government are often at least as alarming in their complacent dogmatism.

A question in the House of Lords recently elicited the fact that various foods were being checked for residues of poisonous chemicals – mutton, milk, butter, imported apples and wheat. Lord St. Oswald, answering for the Government, said baldly: 'The results of these surveys showed that there was no hazard to consumers of the crops sampled'.

It is possible – even probable – that no hazard does exist. But no one can be *certain*. It is impossible to clear any biologically active chemical *finally* of harmful effects. A dash of proper humility before huge acres of ignorance, together with a larger scale, more aggressive effort to minimise the use of toxic chemicals on the land and supplement them with biological methods, would provide more real assurance than any number of soothing 'authoritative' statements.

As the Director of the Nature Conservancy remarked at a scientific conference: 'It must be understood that it is an out-of-date approach to beat up nature with every conceivable modern machine and chemical and to seek to get the best results by short-cuts. In farming and forestry, as in nature conservation, we must learn to work with rather than against nature, and we can only do this if we understand how nature works and if we adopt a somewhat more humble attitude'.

1963

Polluting the Planet

A few centuries ago, men used to plant oaks which would take 500 years to mature. They must have had a quite different relationship to time. Today, we peer a mere thirty years ahead through a haze of unreality. The plan-span of most Governments extends no further than the next election, and more usually not beyond the next Budget. For the average citizen long-range planning means looking at holiday brochures in January and dreaming about next August.

A few uneasy paragraphs appeared in the newspapers recently following the revelation that North Sea gas may run out in two or three decades. The idea of looking so far ahead – let alone four or five centuries, as the oak planters did – now preoccupies only the science-fiction writers. Yet within the next thirty years, not only North Sea gas, but a vast variety of more easily accessible resources on which we now depend will be running low. This assumes that we survive the more immediate problems of land, food, population and water supply which show every sign of compounding a major planetary crisis within the lifetimes of everyone under forty-five.

Most people perceive that we live in a must unusual period of history, that we have become quite remarkably inventive in technology, that there are a lot of cars and aeroplanes about, more noise and fumes, that life is crowded and somewhat tiring. But it is not easily realised, with full imaginative force, what we are doing to the planet.

Five hundred years from now, one thing is quite certain. Historians – if there are any – will look back on the twentieth century as a time when men plunged into a reckless transformation and exploitation of their global environment quite without precedent. They will study with awe our incredible confidence that something would turn up – new techniques, new resources, new discoveries. They will survey, with cold shivers running down their spines, the insouciance with which we exposed the delicate, and to us largely mysterious, balances in nature and in our own bodies to new and ingenious stresses and environmental insults each year. They will examine, dumbfounded, how we blundered somehow into the twenty-first century, and contrived, by means which are still obscure to ourselves, to preserve a world capable of supporting future historians.

But they may also ring with a red pencil the 1960s and 70s as a period when growing numbers of men, including a swelling proportion of respected scientists, began to perceive with full clarity the need for urgent action.

Last September, delegates from all over the world attended a UNESCO conference in Paris to debate 'the scientific basis for the rational use and conservation of the resources of the bioshpere'. In other words, they were wondering if we know how to keep the earth habitable. Soon there seems likely to be a monster UN conference to survey the same ground. The immediate effect of conferences of this kind is to provide remunerative employment for typists and generate stacks of paper. But they also have two less tangible but positive effects. They help to create a climate of opinion and intention which supports campaigners trying to get their Governments to take these problems seriously. And they gather together a formidable bulk of information which, though often bogged in almost unreadable prose, has a sobering cumulative effect.

For it is the accumulation which needs to be appreciated. The water engineer perceives that his problems of the next ten years are difficult, but apparently soluble. The agriculturist sees a chance of stepping up production which may just fend off mass starvation for the next generation. The municipal engineers hope they can just about dispose of a rising tide of sewage. It is when these and many other environmental problems are surveyed as a whole, in a 30- or 40-year perspective, that some sense of the effort needed to keep the earth habitable emerges.

The population explosion is the most familiar of these looming planetary stresses, and it is fundamental to the rest. For while twentieth-century man would undoubtedly have done drastic things to his environment with a static population, he is doing a lot more with an exploding one. In 1860 the world's population was probably about 1,000 million, and it is thought to have taken 200,000 years to reach that figure. Sixty years later, it had doubled. By 1975 it will have doubled again, to reach 4,000 million. By the end of this century 6,000 million citizens are confidently expected to be living or partly living on earth, and if there is no pause, children now being born could spend their old age among 12,000 million others.

If the earth were all covered with earth, so to speak, they would be no immediate problem. But it isn't. Three-quarters of the globe is covered by sea. Half of the land is uninhabitable, being covered with snow, ice, deserts, rocky peaks, etc. We have to share what is left – about 25 million square miles. British citizens live in one of the most crowded corners. Evenly shared out, we could each expect about one acre of the British Isles; Americans would get twelve acres each.

We are eating into this land at an alarming rate. In the United States, a baby is born every twelve seconds and a car every five seconds. The two together set up a new demand for living space and road space which eats away two acres of countryside every minute. Urban expansion may swallow up a sixth of Britain's farmland between now and the end of the century. This is the land – a foot or so of fertile topsoil with a few more feet below – on which our terrestrial existence ultimately depends.

The soil is being treated pretty roughly in many parts of the world, although this is not a new phenomenon. Centuries ago, goats were eating parts of the Middle East bare; Merino sheep gnawed away at the hills of Spain; iron smelters cleared Scottish hillsides of trees, and millions of tons of fertile soil were washed steadily into the sea. However, the American dust bowls of the 1930s set new standards of environmental destructiveness. Partly as a result, the whole problem of 'conservation' of the environment has attracted more energetic attention in the US than anywhere else.

Meanwhile, greedy and ignorant farming and timber felling, coupled with urban growth, are spreading to sub-tropical regions, where both the soils and the populations are far worse equipped to cope with the stresses that result.

The soils of tropical forests, accustomed to warm semi-darkness, collapse and disintegrate when trees are cleared, and wash away in the next rains. And urban growth often means malignant expansion of shanty towns and settlements. The advanced nations of the world are deeply preoccupied with preserving some kind of habitable conditions in their cities. The shanty towns are growing up with none of the services which are just enabling European and American cities to hold their own.

Yet it has been estimated that urban growth in undeveloped regions is now going ahead far faster than in developed regions. Between 1920 and the end of this century, the urban population of the developed countries is expected to quadruple; the urban population of undeveloped countries will multiply twenty times, so that nearly twice as many people will be town dwellers in poor regions as in rich.

The rich are now discovering the enormous overheads of city

living, the vast investment and maintenance involved in keeping the great conurbations functioning at all (and even then, there is horrible decay in the centres of places like Chicago). There seems little prospect that the poor regions will be able to invest even a fraction of what will be needed to prevent the development of tropical slums which will make Chicago's ghettos seem like a Garden of Eden.

To appreciate the problems, it helps to look in more detail at one or two of the urban problems of advanced countries. Take the generation of waste, an activity pioneered with special energy in the US which shows the shape of things to come.

Each American citizen produces some three-quarters of a ton of solid refuse per year, and this thriving industry is growing at four per cent per year. Los Angeles alone dumps twelve million cubic yards of refuse each year into tips and landfills. The wonders of the modern packaging industry mean that a growing proportion of this refuse is virtually indestructible – 48,000 million aluminium cans are discarded annually, 28,000 million long-lived jars and bottles, and uncounted plastic containers and wrappings. If they are incinerated, there is an air-pollution problem.

Giant car-dumps are a familiar feature of the landscape, and have prompted the development of colossal plants which grind up old cars into small bits (the first of these has now arrived in Britain, and is installed at Willesden). Mining companies are said to be eyeing certain American scrap-heaps as a potentially richer source of minerals than those provided by nature.

Even more formidable is the US sewage industry, which by the year 2000 will be dealing with almost 37,000 million gallons of municipal sewage a day, or about 132 gallons per head per day. In Britain, the current flow is about 10 gallons per head per day, to which are added 1,300 million gallons a day of industrial effluent.

It is currently costing us some £133 million a year to treat and dispose of the country's sewage and industrial effluent, and the cost is expected to double within a few years. In Britain we are exceptionally fortunate in that no city is very far from the sea and we have relatively abundant water to sluice away our wastes. Even so, a survey in 1958 showed that over 5,000 miles of rivers were polluted, often grossly.

The Water Pollution Laboratory is just completing a second survey, and preliminary indications are that there have been some improvements (notably in the Thames, following a gigantic £40 million treatment and disposal scheme recently completed by the GLC). But even so, rivers near cities are often dead, smelly and totally unfit for bathing.

The latest sewage problem comes from the urbanisation of farming. Instead of depositing their manure as precious fertiliser on fields, animals on factory farms have the equivalent of running water and flushing toilets. The result is vast quantities of odorous slurry, which is becoming a major disposal problem. The National Farmers' Union recently protested that if the river authorities enforced current anti-pollution regulations, British farmers might have to invest £250 million by 1972 to control their farm wastes. Thus we have the weird spectacle of farmers buying in subsidised fertiliser from the chemical industry, and operating a subsidised farming system which may need more subsidies to dispose of the unsubsidised fertiliser produced free by the animals.

The rivers are not our only sinks. We use the air as well. It is estimated that into the air over the US there are dumped annually sixty-five million tons of carbon monoxide, twenty-three million tons of sulphur compounds, fifteen million tons of oil and sooty substances, twelve million tons of dust, eight million tons of acrid nitrogen compounds and two million tons of other gases and vapours. It is predicted that even with severe controls, these amounts will more than double by the end of the century.

In Britain, there is a parallel situation, with an emission of one and a half million tons of grit and ash, two million tons of smoke and five million tons of sulphur gases annually. The Ministry of Technology estimates that resulting corrosion, soiling and other damage is costing £350 million a year.

These are some of the gross features of the situation. They add up to a very expensive and messy problem. But they also add up to something more. For despite our best efforts, we are releasing into the environment substances and processes never before encountered by the living organisms of the planet including ourselves. A great many subtle balances, with millennia of evolution behind them, are being changed with quite unprecedented speed.

Some of the effects we understand. Detergents have fouled our waterways with foam, and are still liable to block the bacterial digestive processes in sewage works. 'Soft' detergents, which can be attacked by bacteria, are solving the first problem, and a solution has also been found to the second. But many effects we do not fully understand.

People in towns get more lung cancer than people in the country, irrespective of how much they smoke. Air pollution may be involved, but the details are obscure.

Rainfall over parts of Europe has become increasingly acid, almost certainly because of pollution by sulphur gases from oil burning.

Acid rain appears to be depressing the yield of Scandinavian forests. It may be having other effects. We don't know.

Traces of pesticides are now found in virtually all animals and man, including Antarctic penguins. Some animals, particularly birds of prey, accumulate large amounts through food chains. Their eggs may be sterile.

In the US 400 new chemicals come on the market each year. They are commonly tested for direct health hazards. But after use they are disposed of – and sooner or later they or their breakdown products become involved in biological processes of one kind or another, most of which we know little or nothing about.

It is no help to go round prophesying doom. The fact that we survive at all in an urban environment is a demonstration of the rugged resilience of biological systems, which have a built-in ability to resist stresses and bounce back after injury. Nevertheless, there have recently been some unpleasant environmental surprises, and there are certainly more in store. The sheer variety and scale of things we are doing to the planet suggests that a variety of biological balances must be near breaking point.

A growing number of biologists and ecologists (whose speciality is the interactions between communities of living things) have begun to utter serious warnings about these trends – some of which could conceivably upset not only local but global balances. Next week I shall report on some aspects of this threatening situation.

1968

Time to Stop the Plunder

We tend to think of the impact of our technological civilisation on the planet in terms of large-scale effects – traffic, roads, sprawling cities, deep mines, intensive agriculture, clouds of smoke and fumes, huge dams and power stations.

But we owe our survival on earth to much subtler phenomena – biological processes of delicate complexity in which small shifts and changes can have slow, unforeseeable but sometimes catastrophic consequences.

The industrial revolution has gradually created industrial medicine, a vast sphere of research and regulation, in which discovery hobbles along behind tragedy. Consider the alarming, and still unfinished, story of asbestos. Large numbers of people probably died of lung disease before asbestosis, caused by inhaling dust and fibres from this rugged silica-containing mineral, was recognised in the 1920s. Legislation was passed in 1931 requiring dust suppression and ventilation in asbestos factories.

Nevertheless, in 1955, Dr. Richard Doll, of the Medical Research Council, demonstrated that men who had worked twenty years in a large asbestos textile factory were eleven times more liable to lung cancer than the population as a whole. Two doctors at Queen's University, Belfast, have recently published a survey showing an incidence of lung cancer among a group of male asbestos workers twenty times that of a comparable group in the community. New regulations have just been published tightening up control, and extending it to workers on building sites and other places where asbestos is being used regularly. British Rail has stopped using asbestos insulation in passenger coaches and is using fibre-glass instead.

But this is not the end of the story. Work in South Africa, confirmed by studies at the London School of Hygiene and Tropical Medicine and elsewhere, has traced a fatal kind of tumour, mesothelioma, to exposures to asbestos forty years earlier. Eleven patients in the London study were not asbestos workers but had lived within half a mile of an asbestos factory, while nine others were relatives of asbestos workers. One woman who died from the disease had brushed down her husband each evening when he returned from work covered with asbestos dust.

In 1910, world production of asbestos was 30,000 tons a year. Today it is four million tons. It is used for roofing and tiling, insulation, filling in plastic tiles, ironing board covers, building boards, brake and clutch linings, paints, plasters and myriad other products. Asbestos is everywhere, as the Asbestos Information Committee is currently emphasising in an advertising campaign which announces that '50,000,000 people in Britain are protected by asbestos.'

It takes a long time to identify some of these hazards. Still longer to control them. But we are increasingly exposed to all kinds of substances which were previously locked up in the earth or did not exist in nature at all.

Measurements of snow samples taken near the Poles have indicated that there is ten times more lead in the atmosphere today than 200 years ago. It comes from lead smelting, and more recently from anti-knock compounds in petrol. Measurements in Los Angeles show an average concentration of lead in the air fifty times that in rural areas, and possibly 5,000 times that existing in the pre-industrial age.

Lead is a cumulative poison, commonly used in the Middle Ages to do people in by stealth. There is no evidence that it is doing anybody in now, and careful studies suggest that concentrations in people's bodies are still well below danger levels. Dr. P.J. Lawther, of the Medical Research Council's Air Pollution Research Unit, emphasises that air pollution measurements can mislead: 'We should measure what's in people's bodies, not in the environment'. Nevertheless, he concluded a recent analysis of the situation with a warning that it should be kept under 'close review'.

Meanwhile, we have all been accumulating more exotic poisons, notably the persistent pesticides like DDT, traces of which are now found even in the bodies of Antarctic penguins. Here again, the present levels appear to be well below what might be hazardous, and in this country we can take some cold-hearted comfort from the fact that any new chronic effects are likely to show up first in workers engaged in anti-malarial campaigns in tropical regions, who are exposed to much larger doses.

Nevertheless, the possibility of nasty surprises is underlined by the fate of the peregrine falcon. These are at the end of a biological 'food chain' – they are particularly fond of pigeons, which may in turn concentrate pesticides by eating treated seeds. Both in the United States and Western Europe populations of peregrine falcons and other birds of prey have crashed in recent years, and their decline is associated with the introduction of persistent pesticides.

There is now evidence that the pesticides upset liver functioning and calcium metabolism, leading to thinner egg-shells which are pecked and eaten by the parent birds, with disastrous effects on their numbers. On present trends, some of these species will soon be extinct in Western Europe and the US. This is a dramatic example of the queer and wholly unexpected effects of releasing an exotic chemical into the environment.

Some less exotic chemicals which for some years have been generously sprinkled on farmers' fields are now showing signs of backfiring on the environment. Increasing numbers of lakes and reservoirs are now 'dying', through excess loads of nitrates and phosphorous compounds deriving from sewage and from fertilisers washed off fields. Most of the phosphates originate in detergents, and emerge in sewage effluents. Nearly half the nitrogen compounds are washed off fields which are being dosed with twice as much nitrate fertiliser as ten years ago.

These substances can lead to explosive growth of water plants, often blue-green algae which can release toxic substances poisonous to fish. Decaying plant matter consumes all the oxygen in the water, which becomes lifeless and often foul-smelling. This process of 'eutrophication' (or over fertilisation) has overtaken at least forty lakes in Europe and the US.

In Britain eutrophication problems are attracting increasing attention. Lake Windermere could become vulnerable, as may new impounding reservoirs which gather up polluted water from rivers. Professor Barry Commoner, of Washington University, Missouri, recently warned that the use of nitrate fertilisers in farming might have to be curtailed, which could cause a 'massive dislocation'. But the alternative, he said, could be a series of 'biological cataclysms' in various parts of the world.

Finally, there are some global effects of our rampaging civilisation which may turn out to be extremely hazardous. Over the past 100 years we have begun to consume fossil fuels at what is now a breakneck pace. During this period, we have as a result poured 360,000 million tons of carbon dioxide into the atmosphere. It has been estimated that the flights of jet aircraft landing at New York alone now emit some thirty-six million tons of carbon dioxide into the air annually.

This gas is responsible for a 'greenhouse' effect which allows in heat from the sun but prevents it from escaping back into space. Space probes indicate that the atmosphere of Venus is extremely rich in carbon dioxide, with the result that its climate near the surface may be, in the words of one American scientist, 'very like hell'. Our industrial activities may be heading us in the same infernal direction.

By the end of this century, we may have released enough carbon dioxide to raise the atmospheric temperature by two degrees centigrade. Quite soon, this trend could begin to have drastic climatic effects, including melting the ice caps, which would eventually flood many of the world's major cities.

Perhaps, fortunately, another global activity of *Homo* not-so-*sapiens* is to pump all kinds of dust and grit into the air. Recent measurements show that this is cutting off a noticeable quantity of sunshine and reflecting it back into space, thus offsetting the carbon dioxide warming effect. Indeed, we might even be in a position to cool the earth and extend the ice caps by continuing to use the atmosphere as a dustbin in this way.

One could extend almost indefinitely this list of ways in which we are playing around ignorantly and often brashly with our planet – the only one we know of that is remotely habitable for organisms like us.

But perhaps the point has been made. If we do not apply the brakes quite savagely to a number of current environmental trends, and acquire a lot more ecological wisdom, there will be some major and possibly irreversible catastrophes in the century to come.

Certain remedies are obvious – more research, more education, more conservation. But in one sense, this is a trivial answer, for the problem has much deeper roots. It is closely linked with a central dogma of our civilisation, which asserts the overriding necessity and desirability of 'growth'.

Obviously, growth is a good thing in so far as it helps to feed, clothe, and house people, and reduce hunger and misery. But we are now being forced to realise that we are buying growth by squandering planetary capital at a frightening pace – fuel capital, mineral capital, water capital, soil capital, even animal capital (many whale and fish populations, for example, seem likely never to recover from our triumphs of fishing technology).

In this connection, it is perhaps worth remembering other kinds of growth. In a medieval context, the word has very sinister associations indeed. A tumour is a highly efficient, expansionist biological enterprise, recklessly exploiting the resources of its living host. With unswerving entrepreneurial drive, it soon establishes subsidiaries throughout its environment, which grow as industriously as the parent company. The result is familiar – suicide for the tumours through death of the host. During the past couple of centuries we have been very busy creating a civilisation which is now looking dangerously malignant. We have got to find a cure.

We shall be compelled, I think, to look not only to more research and investment, but also within ourselves. Exploitation as such is not new – earlier civilisations have plundered their environment and one another with persistence and energy. Nevertheless, these peoples felt themselves, in the last resort, to be servants rather than masters of natural and supernatural forces in the universe. The scientific and technological age was launched, in effect, when Francis Bacon recommended that men should 'torture nature's secrets from her'.

His use of the feminine gender echoes a very old relationship to the life of the planet (we still speak of 'Mother Earth'. But his proposal foreshadowed a technocratic society in which a personalised nature has been replaced by a depersonalised 'environment' – the surroundings of the entrepreneur on which he operates to his own satisfaction. Bacon also prophesied the streak of violence which runs through our technology, with its break-throughs and revolutions, its power stations, atom-smashers and shattered sound barriers, its ruthless competition and aggressive marketing, its whole ethos of mastery and conquest.

This may have been a necessary phase. If we had not learned to kick nature in the teeth, we might never have emerged from the medieval womb. The development of scientific technology was intimately involved in an assertion of independence, a rejection of authority and tradition, a new habit of experiment and (in the broadest sense) free enterprise, which has transformed the whole fabric of life, irrespective of what has emerged from the laboratories.

What is striking, and hopeful, about the past century or so, is the emergence, hand in hand with rugged technological individualism, of a new kind of social concern. Boys of five are no longer driven up soot-filled chimneys. We have Factory Acts, laws about violence and cruelty, provisions (however patchy and inadequate) for the old, the sick, the poor. Slowly, haltingly, we have been trying to check the neglect and exploitation of man by man.

The next great step in civilisation – which in our own interests we shall *have* to take long before we have solved many of our other problems – will be to make effective provision for the welfare of the planet. We shall *have* to move from a violent exploitation of the environment to a knowledgeable and non-violent practice of human ecology.

This will demand a much more critical look at our assumptions about 'technological advance'. Entrepreneurial technology regards it as both virtuous and compulsory to 'exploit' each new discovery in the market place as soon as possible. This must be balanced by a much more vivid perception of real social and planetary *needs* and clearer concepts of social and human goals.

We have demonstrated our technological potency to ourselves clearly enough. It is time we realised that, just by virtue of this potency we are now *in loco parentis* to the planet, and caring for the life of the earth is part of caring for ourselves. And, just conceivably, the effort to avoid destroying the 'environment' may prove good practice for finding ways of not destroying one another.

1968

Small and Beautiful World

Just over twelve years ago, Fritz Schumacher (who died aged 66, suddenly and unexpectedly in Switzerland last week) launched his idea of an 'intermediate technology' for the Third World in an article in this newspaper.

He argued that advanced technology was having disastrous effects in developing countries, and a quite different approach was needed. We described his views as 'startling' and many experts were scornful.

Last March, in Ann Arbor, Michigan, I heard him speak on a cold Sunday evening, at the tail end of a university vacation, to a rapt audience of 5,000 students. He had become a hero of the alternative society, a spokesman not only for some radical ideas about development in the Third World but for the groundswell of frustration and despair, especially among the young, over the miseries of life in advanced societies.

His American tour drew huge youthful crowds. But he was also received by State governors, prominent academics and industrialists, and by President Carter. The ecological crisis and the energy crisis, of which he was an early prophet, are now the conventional wisdom of a multitude. Mr. Desai's new Government in India has publicly embraced intermediate technology. The American Government has set up a $20 million fund for research in alternative technologies. And in Britain official support is at last forthcoming for the Intermediate Technology Development Group, which Schumacher founded in 1965.

The title of his best-selling book, *Small is Beautiful*, has passed into the language. No man, it would seem, could ask for his life to be crowned with more success. So why did I find him, after his lecture, in a curiously uncertain mood?

In part, he was doubtful about his own success. He wondered how much real will for change lay behind the enthusiasm. He saw a danger that his words could be inflated into gas balloons, which would carry people gently over the landscape of the world's problems at a considerable height, in the illusion that their trip was changing life below. He was deeply sceptical of panaceas and blanket solutions. He saw real hope for the future in many small-scale but concrete initiatives (in his own domestic life, this included milling wheat by hand and baking bread, thus bringing a therapeutic balance into the life of a busy intellectual, and providing his family with a product much superior in quality to any available in the shops).

But his real concern went deeper. He died just before publication of his latest book, *A Guide for the Perplexed*. He was convinced that the real answers to our problems would come not from new means – intermediate technology included – but from new ends. Technological society, he held, was a product of a crippled and impoverished view of human beings and of the world, which goes back in intellectual terms to Descartes, and the subsequent conviction that all important realities are measurable.

He began to ponder these questions thirty-five years ago, as a farm labourer in Northamptonshire. Born in Bonn, he had been a Rhodes scholar in Oxford in the 1930s and then, having decided that to live and work in Nazi Germany was impossible, emigrated to England permanently. The war brought a brief internment, then farm work until 1943.

After the war he worked with Beveridge; he was also a prominent member of *The Observer's* editorial team. From 1945-50 he was economic adviser to the British Control Commission in Germany. There followed twenty years as economic adviser to the National Coal Board in London, when he began to perceive vividly that our industrial way of life is built on a profligate expenditure of natural capital, namely coal and oil.

During this period he was seconded to advise the Government of Burma, and managed to include some serious study of Buddhism. This influenced the now classic essay *Buddhist Economics*.

In 1962 Schumacher spent time with the planning commission in Delhi to advise on rural development. There he saw the appalling effects of pouring in aid in the form of advanced technology. Often, plant broke down and could not be maintained. But where it worked, cheap goods undercut rural industries. Unemployment in the villages brought migration to the shanty towns spreading round the big cities. The Western technologies could be operated only by an elite. The rich got richer, the poor, poorer.

From these experiences came the concept of 'intermediate technology', of the kind that in Europe allowed the long slow transition from the Middle Ages to the twentieth century. The traditional village tools were too primitive. Western products too complex. There was a gap in the middle – a need for simple pumps, improved building materials and storage techniques, packing machinery and tools that could be understood and maintained by a village blacksmith.

Such technologies were almost forgotten. One of the first tasks of the Intermediate Technology Development Group was to compile a catalogue of suitable products – 'Tools for Progress'.

The group now has forty full-time employees, a series of expert panels, and consultancy and development units with contacts and projects all over the world, many of them highly successful. But the problems are formidable. The educated elite in developing countries, usually trained in Europe or America, tend to have been brainwashed into the same uncritical enthusiasm for technical sophistication which produces so much idiocy in the West.

Schumacher was the first to acknowledge that without human and social development, technology – intermediate or otherwise – can achieve nothing. Thus it remains to be seen how far and how deep the intermediate technology idea can reach into the problems of the Third World.

Meanwhile Schumacher's work attracted growing attention in the advanced countries. We too have unemployment generated by labour-saving technologies, decaying cities and depersonalised work. Schumacher was convinced that we are witnessing the end of a way of life that will destroy itself by its own contradictions within half a century.

In recent years, among his many activities Schumacher also presided over a society to promote organic farming and gardening, the Soil Association. This body, once widely regarded as the resort of cranks, is now clearly a respectable pioneer of ecological sense. Schumacher had seen the havoc which agri-business can create in developing countries. Now its gross inefficiencies, in global terms, are becoming clear in advanced countries.

One of his latest enthusiasms was for food-bearing trees, which can achieve three-dimensional protein production with solar energy. He launched a project to breed improved varieties, build seed stocks and promoted planting, in the interests of our children, to help them survive the food crisis which he expected to be the inevitable companion of the coming energy crisis.

He was recently confirmed into the Roman Catholic Church (making legal, as he put it, a long-standing illicit love affair). For his *Guide for the Perplexed* he had been reading Thomas Aquinas, and often quoted his saying 'The slenderest knowledge that may be obtained of the highest things is more desirable than the most certain knowledge of lesser things'.

On his American tour, his youthful audiences frequently tried to draw him into a denunciation of the giant corporations. He refused to be drawn. 'I never deal with corporations', he said. 'I deal only with people. And I have actually found some very able people even inside big corporations'. He met everyone as though they really mattered. And he lived his own life with consistent humanity. He will be missed – and remembered.

1977

AFTER LIFE

The Evidence for Life After Life

In the early morning of 20 December 1943, a twenty-year-old private soldier, George Ritchie, collapsed in front of an X-ray machine in an army hospital at Abilene, Texas, and was rushed into an isolation room with a diagnosis of acute double pneumonia.

Twenty-four hours later, the ward orderly found Ritchie apparently dead: breathing had stopped, there was no pulse or blood pressure. The duty medical officer checked, and told the orderly to prepare the body for the morgue after he had finished his rounds. He straightened Ritchie's arms along the blankets and pulled up the sheet to cover his face.

About nine minutes later, the orderly returned, and thought he saw a hand on the 'corpse' move. He fetched the doctor, who again pronounced Ritchie dead. Against all military and medical etiquette, the orderly suggested that the doctor should try giving a shot of adrenalin direct into the heart. Surprisingly, as he had twice pronounced Ritchie dead, the officer did so. The heart resumed its beat. On Christmas Eve, Ritchie recovered consciousness, and was back on his feet two weeks later.

He recovered consciousness, that is to say, as far as the doctors and nurses around him were concerned. But three days earlier, he had been standing beside his bed looking down at his own body with a sheet drawn over the face. He had been hunting frantically through the hospital after a hectic journey across a large slice of the United States lasting an interminable period of time. When he came in to the small cubicle where his body lay, he recognised it only by the ring on the middle finger of the left hand, a small gold owl on black onyx.

As he looked down at his body, the light changed and brightened, a figure came into the room and with it an altered experience of space and time, so that Ritchie found himself surrounded by a living panorama of all the events of his life in complete clarity and detail. The entrance of the figure of light ushered in a still more far-reaching journey, from which he returned to the pain of his lungs and high fever, when the adrenalin jolted his heart back into action. Then he relapsed into complete unconsciousness until Christmas Eve.

Modern techniques of heart massage and electric shock are making this kind of resuscitation almost commonplace. When someone's heart stops, he is not treated as 'dead' but as suffering from 'cardiac arrest'. There are some minutes during which there is a chance to stir the heart back into action. Every cardiologist in a modern hospital will now have patients in his care who have spent some minutes of their lives without a heartbeat.

It probably occurs to few doctors dealing with cardiac emergencies to ask their patients what they remember of the experience. After all, the patients have been 'unconscious'. But if they do ask, and can persuade their patients to talk freely, the chances are that half or more will remember those minutes very well indeed, and will begin to describe some very remarkable experiences.

George Ritchie tried to tell the doctors and nurses of his experiences, but he was met with incomprehension and soothing remarks: 'Get some rest now. Don't try to talk'. So he fell silent. But he went on to qualify as a doctor and psychiatrist. Now fifty-five, and in excellent health, he practises in Whitestone, Virginia. He has behind him a successful and utterly respectable career: twenty-seven years of practice in Virginia; President of the Richmond Academy of General Practice; Chairman of the Department of Psychiatry at Towers Hospital, Charlottesville. He is solid and reassuring, direct in thought and speech, but with a warmth in voice and eyes which speaks of a vigour of inner life not obvious in his conventional exterior. The only oddity, when we met and talked during a visit to Washington, was a small lapel badge with a pentagram and roses. It is the insignia of the Universal Youth Corps of which Ritchie is founder and president, which works with juvenile delinquents, and to which he devotes an increasing amount of his time. The origins of this foundation lie in a religious experience, about which he was somewhat reticent, which had visited him thirteen years after his illness in Texas. But he felt this experience to be a further step in the meeting with the figure of light and the 'journey' on which he was taken while he lay without heartbeat in the army hospital at Abilene. Since then, he has spoken of these experiences occasionally, to parents, to friends, to groups of students, and only last year published a fuller account. [*Return from Tomorrow* by George Ritchie, MD, with Elisabeth Sherrill (Chosen Books 1978).]

One of his students, a philosophy graduate beginning medical school, was Raymond Moody, now qualified and teaching in Charlottesville, Virginia. Moody lives in a modest house on the edge of the town with his wife and two children. He is a burly and beaming man, with a philosopher's forehead, who converses with visitors in a rocking chair which he keeps in constant motion, as though oscillating with the ripples which have swept round the world from his best-selling book, *Life After Life*. For Moody was prompted by hearing Ritchie's story to seek for similar accounts. With a good deal of astonishment, he quickly realised that he was touching a hidden but not uncommon vein of experience among his fellow human beings.

'I had only to mention "out of the body experiences" to a lecture audience, and I could be sure that some people would come up to me afterwards and tell me of similar experiences, either their own, or of close friends and relatives'.

His book has brought these experiences out into the open – he has now collected many hundreds, and begun some simple classification of their variety. But when we met, Moody said, 'I have done as much as I am going to do in this field' . He considers he has established the existence of these experiences, shown their astonishing consistency, and provided a basis for further work by others. Although this research has had a considerable effect on his life, both outwardly (he is inundated with correspondence and requests for broadcasts, articles and interviews, which he now fends off with determination), he will not be drawn into public debate on the significance of his findings.

Spiritualists and all kinds of esoteric groups are constantly knocking on Moody's door. 'But I've no interest in mediums and all that.' Of one thing he is certain: 'The medical profession must now confront these experiences clinically. The doctors must realise that some of their patients are having these experiences. Even boy scouts are now taught cardio-pulmonary resuscitation. These things will be all around us.' Meanwhile, he is moving on to research in other fields.

Moody's book, and its sequel, *Reflections on Life after Life*, continue as best sellers. But they have begun to prompt further studies among a small group of doctors in entirely orthodox medical circles in the United States.

In 1976, a young nurse at a colloquium in the medical school at Gainesville, Florida, mentioned Moody's work. Dr. Michael Sabom, a cardiologist at the university hospital (he is now Assistant Professor of Cardiology at Atlanta, Georgia) was present, and became interested. He began to ask his own patients some questions. He has now published several papers in medical journals, and others are pursuing similar inquiries. Their results are uncovering the same astonishing situation. The results of these investigations are summed up in the cool and cautious language of scientific medicine by the preface to a recent publication by Dr. Sabom.

It is worth quoting in full:

'Numerous reports have appeared in the non-medical literature of unique experiences occurring in people near death. To document the existence, nature and clinical implications of these near-death experiences, patients who had been unconscious and near death were interviewed. At the time of unconsciousness, twenty-nine patients experienced amnesia while thirty-eight encountered near-death experiences (NDE): eighteen experienced the passage of consciousness into a foreign region or dimension (transcendence). Eleven viewed their body and physical surroundings from a detached position of height (autoscopy) and nine both autoscopy and transcendence. When patients with and without NDE were compared, no significant difference in age, sex, race, education, occupation, formal religious affiliation/involvement, or knowledge of similar events from other sources was noted. A definite decrease in death anxiety occurred in most patients encountering a NDE . . . Although adequate explanation of these phenomena is not available, further investigation is needed into the cause and implication of these experiences.'

Dr. Sabom is young, brawny and obviously competent. He is also totally non-eccentric. He looks what he is, a successful and rising practitioner in a highly technical branch of modern medicine which concentrates on repairing and maintaining a muscular pump and the plumbing that goes with it. It is a discipline whose practitioners are not expected to concern themselves too much with their patients' inner experiences. A modern medical training can rather easily produce, as it were, heartless cardiologists. But Sabom is also a good doctor. He can talk to his patients. They trust him, and begin to share what are powerful and intimate experiences.

'I had a lot of difficulty with all this at first', Sabom says. 'My training had not prepared me for this kind of thing.' But he was interested, and realised that he was in a good position, working in a large teaching hospital, to follow up Moody's findings. Furthermore, he could do 'prospective' rather than 'retrospective' research: Moody's own case histories were from people who came forward spontaneously with accounts of near death experiences. Sabom sought out patients who had suffered cardiac arrests, but who had until then said nothing about their experiences. They were mostly local farmers and small-town citizens, quite unaware of Moody's book or of the fact that others had had similar experiences.

Sabom also found that his own medical colleagues were generally unaware that patients may have these experiences. Transcendence and autoscopy are not subjects of general conversation in Gainesville, Florida, either in lay or professional circles.

'I first had to get my patients to trust me', Sabom says, 'They are terrified of being laughed at, or diagnosed as mentally ill. So they don't talk. And their doctors don't hear anything.'

But when trust is established, many patients are deeply relieved to find a sympathetic ear. 'For a lot of these people, it's a great help to know that others have had similar experiences, that they're not alone, and that the doctor is willing to listen to what they say.'

The stories told to Sabom differ in details, but in general character they match absolutely those collected by Moody. The experiences fall into two main groups: *autoscopic* (the patient, experiencing great clarity of consciousness, looks down at his body from outside, often observing exactly the frenzied efforts of the medical team to revive him, and sometimes hearing their conversation); and *transcendent* (where awareness passes into another mode, a 'panorama' of the past life may be seen, friends who have died may be encountered, a figure of light often appears and helps a review and evaluation of the past life, and shows the 'unfinished work' which has still to be fulfilled before dying 'finally').

Here are extracts from stories told to Dr. Sabom by two of his patients. The first is from a forty-nine-year-old male security guard who collapsed at the hospital with an acute heart attack. It took thirty minutes, culminating in two electric shocks, to resuscitate him.

'I just couldn't stand the pain any more . . . and then I collapsed. That's when everything went dark and black. After a little while, I was sitting up there somewhere . . . floating, soft, easy, comfortable, nothing wrong . . . I could look down, and I had never noticed that the floor was black and white tile, but that's the first thing I remember being conscious of . . . I recognised myself down there, sort of curled round in a half-foetal position. Two or three people lifted me onto a stretcher and strapped my legs and moved me on down the hall . . . When they first threw me up on that table, the doctor struck me, I mean he really whacked the hell out of me. He came back with his fist from way behind his head and he hit me right in the centre of my chest and then they were pushing on my chest . . . and they shoved a plastic tube, like you put in an oil can, in my mouth . . .

'It was at that point I noticed another table-like arrangement with a bunch of stuff on it. I knew it later to be that machine they thump you with . . . the cart was making a terrible racket as they were wheeling it down the hall. That caught my attention right away . . . I could see my right ear and this side of my face because I was looking away . . . I could hear people talking . . . it [the cardiac monitor] was like an oscilloscope, just a faint white line running across. It wasn't a big scope like they put a TV monitor on you during cardiac cath (catheterisation) . . . it just made the same streak over and over . . . they put a needle in me, like one of those Aztec rituals where they take the virgin's heart out, they took it two-handed, I thought this very unusual . . . then they took these round discs with handles on them and put one up here, I think it was larger than the other one, and they put one down here [patient pointed to appropriate positions on chest] . . . they thumped me and I didn't respond . . . I thought they had given my body too much voltage. Man, my body jumped about two feet off the table . . .

'It appeared to me in some sort of fashion that I had a choice to re-enter my body and take the chances of them bringing me back around or I could just go ahead and die, if I wasn't already dead . . . I knew I was going to be perfectly safe whether my body died or not . . . They thumped me a second time . . . I reentered my body just like that . . . I've lived with this thing for three years and I haven't told anyone because I don't want them to put the straitjacket on me . . . That was real. If you want to, you can give me sodium pentathol . . . It's a pretty kinky experience.'

The 'transcendent' experiences tend to be more variable, and people often find them difficult to describe. They share some common features, but are more obviously coloured to some extent by the beliefs and attitudes of the person concerned. Here is one such experience (which was preceded by an 'autoscopic' phase), from one of Dr. Sabom's patients, a fifty-six-year-old businessman whose heart stopped in the emergency room of the hospital, where he had been brought with severe injuries after a car accident:

'When I was in the emergency room I seemed to be there but then I wasn't there . . . I seemed to see myself on this gurney or whatever and they moved me to a table . . . I seemed to be one of the participants in there but back further from the table than anyone else . . . in the background . . . I was able to look down . . . I was able to see all this . . . the table was over like at that end of the room and the doctors were on the right side of me and they had a lot of nurses on the left side. There was also a priest there . . . they didn't have to give me pain shots or anything, because I was completely out of it . . . I just kept saying that isn't me . . . but I knew it was me and that something had happened . . . I thought the whole thing was strange, I had never experienced anything like it . . . I wasn't frightened in the least . . .

'I was all black from the road tar . . . I had cuts all over my face that were all bleeding. I remember the way the leg was, all the blood,

I remember one doctor saying "He's going to lose his leg" . . . in the meantime they gave me a tourniquet on my leg . . . the monitor was at the back of my head, in the back of me . . . I was able to see the line on the monitor . . . and all of a sudden it stopped and looked like a TV tube when you reset the tube . . . you see that green line go across and it makes one continuous noise . . . then I heard someone say 'It's stopped' or something like that . . . and I remember one of the doctors banging on my chest, pushing on it . . . that's when they brought this unit out . . . they were rubbing those things together . . . and I was there all this time and I thought "My God, this can't be me" . . . and I came off the table about 9 – 10 inches . . . I seemed to arch . . . and then I was in complete total darkness . . . I didn't know where I was or what I was doing there or what was happening . . . time has no bearing on it all . . .

'I started getting scared and all of a sudden there was a light down at the end, the light got brighter, and all of a sudden I seemed to be floating in air . . . I saw a lot of beautiful blue, I saw the clouds floating by. I was like in a shaft or beam of light and I was travelling through it . . . something stopped me and said I had to go back. And I said "Why me Lord?" and whoever it was said my work wasn't done on earth, that I had to go back. And I felt a great disappointment because it's undescribable what you feel, it's really undescribable, it's so peaceful and restful . . . I really didn't want to go back. I felt like I could float in there the rest of my life, I mean, for all eternity . . . I started back on the way I had come, floating through this light . . . before the accident I had always thought that it [dying] would be very unpleasant . . . I was always frightened of it . . . Now I'm not afraid any more . . . I don't talk to anybody about this. I'm afraid because most people think you're sort of batty . . . they would say, boy this guy really has got marbles loose up there.'

These experiences are for those involved as indubitable, or more so, as those in daily life. Talk of hallucinations, of 'temporal lobe seizures resulting from brain hypoxia', of 'depersonalisation in the face of danger' is to patients concerned mere incantation. They may keep their experiences to themselves, but privately they regard such explanations as mere contortions, as unconvincing as most of us would regard the arguments of a solipsist philosopher who explains that the door in which I have just pinched my finger is only an idea in my mind.

Furthermore, doctors who are prepared to take note of such experiences, especially those with a 'transcendent' dimension, report a consistent and profound change in the attitude to death. The majority of these patients bring back with them an absolute certainty that their eventual physical death will simply be the entry into a mode of further existence that they have already glimpsed. These glimpses are almost always accompanied by a joy and certainty scarcely comparable with anything in ordinary life. But it is remarkable how consistently these individuals return, nevertheless, with determination to complete their unfinished business in ordinary life to the very best of their ability. Glimpses of another world after this fashion do not appear to make for unworldliness (this seems to be rather more common among those who talk of other worlds without having had such experiences).

What are we to make of these experiences? What is their relevance for medical practice, for care of the dying, for counselling of relatives, for training of nurses and doctors? What impact, if any, may they come to have on our scientific culture? I shall pursue these questions next week.

1979

Life After Life

Immediately after the last world war, a young Swiss girl training as a laboratory technician in Berne travelled across Europe to spend her summers doing relief work in Poland. She worked with the sick and hungry among the survivors of Auschwitz. In this ravaged place, two experiences made a deep impression: she met a young girl, whose family had been wiped out, working in the camp without rancour, transfused with a radiance and love which inspired all around her. And she also saw, in the grimmest barracks, children's drawings of butterflies on the walls. The capacity of the human spirit to transcend the living death of the camps, realised by only a few but perhaps potential in all, remained with her when she returned to Switzerland, and forms a kind of signature for her subsequent career.

The girl's name was Elizabeth Kübler. She went on to study medicine, married a young American doctor, and after a short period of country practice in Switzerland, came to the United States with her husband, as Elizabeth Kübler-Ross. There she has become famous for her work with terminally ill patients, their relatives, the bereaved, and with the doctors and nurses who care for them.

She also wrote a foreword to Raymond Moody's best seller, *Life after Life*, which surveys a variety of astonishing 'near death experiences' which I described last week. There she confirms that his findings coincide with her own, which are based on work with many hundreds of dying patients who she has cared for over the years, as they approached death. Indeed, she goes further than Moody himself, and says that these findings 'will confirm what we have been taught for 2,000 years – that there is life after death'.

I spent a morning with Dr. Ross at her home on the outskirts of Chicago, designed by Frank Lloyd Wright, the walls hung with objects of Red Indian art. She is small, brown-faced, wiry and tough, with that aura of well-organised stamina that surrounds people who have been engaged in very hard and very practical work for a great many years. She describes her work with a kind of sober compassion, a blend of inner strength, objective judgement, and deep warmth for her patients that is unforgettable.

For a number of years, while teaching and practising psychiatry, she ran seminars in Billings Hospital at Chicago University, to help improve the care of dying patients. In our society, perhaps more than any other in history, death is surrounded by uncertainties, and above all by taboos which seal patients and hospital staff alike into separate compartments of fear and silence.

Dr. Ross has devoted a good part of her life to breaking this silence. Partly due to her work, there are now many signs of far-reaching change. The 'hospice' movement, partly inspired by the remarkable work in this country of Dr. Cicely Saunders at the St. Christopher's Hospice in London, is spreading rapidly in the United States. There are now academic courses in 'thanatology' at several universities. But Dr. Ross's seminars have pioneered the education of those who care for the dying.

She encountered enormous resistance at first. It is not only patients who deny their terminal illness. Doctors and nurses shy away, hide behind impersonality, technical procedures, and formulae. At one of her earliest efforts, having lectured to a medical audience on dying, Dr. Ross introduced a patient with terminal leukaemia. 'The patient was glad to talk – but the students froze'.

More recently, she has given up her formal appointments. She sees individuals and families, concerning herself particularly with dying children and their parents. She charges no fees for these consultations, but makes what she needs from lectures and broadcasts, for which she is in enormous demand.

While I was with her, I had to withdraw for an hour while she met a patient, a distraught young woman with two children. One had recently been diagnosed as having untreatable leukaemia, whereupon the father had hanged himself in the garage. There he was found by the second child. Her work is with people engulfed in a sea of pain.

When treatment is of no more use, and if the parents can accept this, Dr. Ross tries to get children (and adults, for that matter), out of hospital and home. 'I get them to put a really large bed in the living room. Young children are often sent to bed for a punishment and associate their bedrooms with loneliness and distress.' She describes a recent case: a baby with a brain tumour, a distraught mother, an older brother, neglected and becoming aggressive and disturbed. She got them home and visited them a few days later. The boy had learned to give oxygen to his little sister, and was quiet and confident. The mother was at peace. The child in due course died in her arms in the big bed in the living room.

Apart from her patients, Dr. Ross is continuing with very intensive five-day workshops on death and dying. These are attended by fifty people at a time, all directly involved in some way. She always includes some terminally-ill patients, as well as bereaved relatives, doctors, nurses, social workers and ministers of religion. They are exhausting affairs, in which the participants gradually come to share and work through their deepest anxieties and fears about death and dying. A remarkable mood of mutual support and trust develops. 'We go together to the threshold of the abyss,' Dr. Ross says, 'and then we find we can fly.'

At a recent workshop, there was a mother who had seen her small daughter eaten by a shark, and had been distraught with anguish ever since. She brought the little girl's pink dress with her. At the end of these workshops, there is sometimes a kind of ritual in which the participants 'let go' of their fears by throwing pine cones on to a camp fire. The mother was suddenly able to throw the pink dress into the fire.

During the earlier phases of her work with the dying, Dr. Kübler-Ross began to realise that her patients were often undergoing unusual experiences: they would converse with invisible presences, and the next moment speak with complete lucidity to the doctor by the bed. Then one of her patients described an out-of-the-body-experience of the kind now made familiar by Moody's book. Dr. Kübler-Ross has made her own collection of such stories.

'I was raised as a wishy-washy Protestant,' she says. 'By the time I got to the United States, I was more or less agnostic.' But she has not only the reports of her patients on which to rest her present certainty that there is a 'life after life'. She has now decided to brave the scepticism of colleagues, professional ostracism, and the inevitable questions about her sanity, by speaking publicly of some personal experiences.

In 1969, just before she published her now classic work *On Death and Dying*, she was visited by a patient who had died a short while before, a Mrs. Schwartz, who came to thank her for her care and to encourage her to keep on with this work. Dubious at first, Dr. Ross asked her visitor to write a note to a mutual friend. This letter, on University of Chicago notepaper, is still in her possession, and begins: 'Hello there. Dropped in to see Dr. Ross. One of the two on the top of my "list". You being the other. I'll never find or know anyone to take the place of you two . . . '

The literature of spiritualism and psychical research is, of course, full of such reports of encounters with the newly-dead by close friends and relatives. Here again, this is probably a much more common experience than is generally realised, although a chronicler like Raymond Moody for this type of phenomenon has yet to appear. Such events are, of course, easy to dismiss as projections or hallucination. As Dr. Sabom, the cardiologist who made his own investigation, says, an explanation acceptable to the current scientific frame of reference is 'not at present available'. The fact remains that Dr. Ross, whose focus of interest is undoubtedly on her professional work in *this* world, is satisfied that this and later experiences are entirely real.

Amidst all the stir about death and dying, and about life after life, Elizabeth Kübler-Ross has a unique position. She has behind her a long scientific and medical training, a wealth of professional experience, and has made a great and indisputable contribution to the understanding of the dying and their care. Her own experiences, both personal and professional, have led her to the unshakable conviction that the body is the bearer of our existence during life, but not its cause, and that this existence continues when the body has been laid aside. Others who have systematically investigated near-death experiences have usually come privately to the same conclusions, even if they are unwilling to debate them publicly.

In itself, there is nothing unusual about such conclusions. Through the centuries, far more people have been convinced of an existence beyond death than have not. Even now, the polls say that seventy per cent of Americans believe the same. Only for a very short part of history, and in a very limited part of the world, has any substantial group of people held otherwise.

But our scientific culture is a very curious one, quite unlike any that have preceded it. Within a comparatively short period, science has put into our hands quite unprecedented powers. This gives immense authority to the ideas, the methods, and the people who have produced them. This authority easily hardens into doctrine. A basic proposition of molecular biology is quite unashamedly called 'the central dogma'. Thus a kind of assumption has come to permeate scientific culture, with almost tyrannous force, that most of what earlier cultures thought about the universe was primitive superstition.

Yet it is commonplace among those who have looked into the descriptions of near death experiences that these closely resemble accounts from various older spiritual and religious traditions. The *Tibetan Book of the Dead* matches point for point a number of the events recently described by farmers and small businessmen to Dr. Sabom. For Plato, death was an awakening and remembering of a realm more real than that in which the soul is temporarily incarcerated during life. A purely materialistic conception of birth and death is almost non-existent before our time, and even now does not seem to be held with total conviction by very many people.

During recent centuries, many capable, creative and outstanding individuals have claimed direct experience of other dimensions of existence, if anything more real than that of everyday existence: Swedenborg, Jung, Rudolf Steiner, to name only a few. Steiner is of particular interest in this connection, in that he took scientific degrees in Vienna, a doctorate in philosophy, while by his own account having access from childhood to inner experiences which brought encounters with discarnate human beings, and with other beings of more exalted rank, almost as a matter of course. While he was highly critical of doctrinaire science, he vigorously upheld its essential and original striving, which he regarded as a kind of coming of age of the human spirit.

Science was born, not as a doctrine, but in defiance of doctrine, out of a spirit of resolutely independent inquiry. It is here that rightful resistance lives in the medical and scientific community to simple acceptance of body free existence, of an after life, of mere anecdotes of unusual experiences. Yet through fear of relapse into what are conceived as outgrown systems of belief, alternatives are offered which are themselves rooted in hypotheses which have fossilised into articles of faith. We are then landed in a dreary faith indeed: the ultimate promise of orthodox science-as-doctrine is meaninglessness (for the individual, disintegration a few years hence; and a few aeons hence, the heat death of the universe).

What is the scientific problem in accepting that human beings can watch themselves being resuscitated from several feet above their own bodies? It is the conviction that consciousness is *caused* by brain processes. This conviction assumes that the old mind-body problem has been resolved in favour of the materialist interpretation. This ignores the rather obvious fact that theories are devised by minds, not brains. What can be the meaning of a hypothesis that denies the reality of its own creator? However this may be – and I do not propose to explore further into the tangled thicket – the fact remains that there exist no agreed and coherent scientific accounts of how brains and minds function. There is far more mystery than certainty. So a reasonable humility is in order.

It is nevertheless clear that if the concept of body-free consciousness comes to be seriously entertained in science, the existing conventional framework is due for some drastic reshaping. But it seems likely that such changes will come about, not so much through argument, nor through mere accumulation of anecdotal evidence, but through a shift in what we regard as acceptable experiences to talk about.

Moody's and Sabom's researches have shown that certain 'inexplicable' experiences are widespread among patients in hospitals, and probably in other circumstances as well. These experiences are utterly certain for those who have them, and it is no credit to the medical profession that so many patients should be terrified to open their mouths for fear that they will be either ignored, ridiculed, or instantly diagnosed as psychotic. There are not many with the determination of Dr. Kübler-Ross, whose outspokenness is putting her professional standing at risk.

During the past two or three years she has begun to speak openly about her own transcendental experiences. Until now, her work has brought her enormous renown and respect throughout the US. But there are other taboos in our society besides those surrounding death and dying. Their force has kept thousands of patients silent. By speaking out, Dr. Kübler-Ross risks being disowned by a large part of the established medical and scientific profession. She faces the prospect with determination and equanimity. Her work and her experience carry their own confirmation and strength, both for herself and for those she helps.

The first such experience (apart from the encounter with Mrs. Schwartz) was about four years ago. It was 5 am. A long and intense workshop had just ended. There was a string of demanding appointments lined up for the new day. Dr. Ross was exhausted. As she fell asleep, she became aware of separating from her body. Then it was as though 'a whole group of beings got to work on it, renewing all its parts'. Two hours later, she awoke completely fresh.

This prompted her to look for literature on 'out of the body experiences'. She came across the work of Robert Monroe, a businessman who began to have spontaneous experiences of various kinds, and has set up an institute to explore them. 'I decided that if I was to understand my patients' experiences I must find out for myself,' she says. So she went to visit Monroe, who has been experimenting, using tape recorded sounds, with techniques for inducing these experiences in others.

'At our first session, I went out too fast. Monroe got alarmed and called me back. I was very annoyed. When I decide on something, I want to go all the way. I told him that the next time he was not to interfere. So at our next session, I said to myself "I'm going to go faster and further than anybody has ever gone." I felt myself move sideways out of my body. My scientific mind was watching all this quite clearly. Then I said to myself, "Hey, that's not the right direction. Not sideways – up!" Then I felt myself moving upwards at enormous speed.'

She returned after a while to normal consciousness, with no clear memory of the experience beyond the initial stages, but with the words 'Shanti Nilaya' ringing in her ears. She didn't know what they meant. But she felt completely renewed. 'I was in a glow. I felt like a beam of light.' Later, in California, speaking of this experience, 'Shanti Nilaya' was instantly recognised by Buddhists in the audience as the name of a spiritual region, known as 'the home of peace'.

But there was more to come during the visit to Monroe. That evening, alone in the institute's guest house in the woods, she was restless and apprehensive. Suddenly she was seized by an appalling experience: 'I started to relive the deaths of every one of my patients, one after the other, with all the pains, the dyspnoea, the agony. It went on for hours. Twice I could catch a breath, and I found myself pleading for a shoulder to lean on, a hand to hold. Then I heard a great voice saying, "You shall not be given". The third time I could catch a breath, I found myself thinking: "This time I won't ask". I knew I must go through it alone, and that I would accept whatever I was asked to take. In this moment of real acceptance, all the pain fell away.'

There followed a further psychophysical experience. 'My abdomen started to vibrate very rapidly. I remember looking at it, and my medical training saying "This can't happen. Abdomens don't vibrate like this".' The vibration spread through her body and the surrounding space, and then a luminous form, a lotus flower, opened in front of her with a brilliant light behind it 'like a sunrise'. For a moment she felt complete one-ness with everything around her, and then she fell into a deep sleep.

There have been further experiences since, but they have in no way changed the focus of Dr. Ross's work. She described these events as we sat in her home. She was completely matter of fact, fully in control of her thoughts and feelings, although, as she said, these are powerful and very moving experiences.

How have these 'transcendental' episodes affected her work? Mainly indirectly, it seems, by bringing added conviction and urgency to her insistence that our culture needs a new and more profound comprehension of death. She is no longer concerned to keep the approval of scientific and medical orthodoxy, but to help her desperate patients.

She has long observed that dying children often accept their situation and show more courage than adults. She is also now convinced that in traumatic moments children slip out of their bodies very easily. Not long ago, a child was sexually murdered near Chicago. 'I went onto every radio and TV show I could get on to, to talk about this.' Three days later, the child's mother telephoned to describe how the little girl had appeared to her soon after the broadcast, making a gesture to indicate she was whole and well.

Dr. Ross's work is with situations of this kind. She is struggling to set up a centre for her workshops, a 'Shanti Nilaya'. She has acquired forty acres of land with two small houses in a quiet valley in southern California, where she has begun to work, and she hopes in due course to establish other centres.

*   *   *

There is no doubt in my mind that the ridicule and hostility which themes like 'life after life' so easily arouse in established scientific circles point to fears that certain articles of scientific faith will be called into question. Such things are lamentable in a scientific culture.

All those I spoke to during these researches into life after life remained cautious and uncertain as to the ultimate effect of their investigations. It is too soon to know whether the huge interest in Moody's books, the 'hospice' movement, the development of 'thanatology', and the lifting of taboos on discussion of death and dying, herald a major shift in the whole conceptual framework regarded as publicly acceptable in our culture. In the end, experience, and the fruits of experience, are what will count. The force of humanity which Elizabeth Kübler-Ross and many others are now bringing into the care of the dying is changing the lives, not only of the patients, but of those around them. In such circles, the sense that dying is a journey towards a transition, not an end, seems to be growing with unmistakable strength. In this, the most important teachers may be the dying themselves.

'How many times,' Dr. Ross wrote recently, 'has a patient tried to express something, and no-one has cared enough to listen. Remember that all our work started by listening and caring for those silent voices – the voices that taught us about life and living.'

Case Histories

Wally Cameron

In July 1977, Wally Cameron, a twenty-eight-year-old drummer from Toronto, Canada, returned home from rehearsal. Having forgotten his keys, he climbed a drainpipe to enter an upstairs window. But he fell backwards to the pavement, fracturing his skull in four places. A blood-clot also developed on his brain and he aspirated vomit into his lungs. Cameron remembers nothing after his fall, except the following experience which took place in the intensive-care unit of the Toronto General Hospital during the twenty minutes his heart stopped beating.

'I felt a weird ringing noise in my head. It was really irritating. I felt as if I had woken up; there were people around me, but they couldn't see me, which I thought was strange. But I also thought, what the heck, I just want to get out of bed, walk out of the door and go home. The next thing I knew I was up on the ceiling stepping into a tunnel following a white light. I looked down and saw myself lying on the hospital bed: I looked like an old used car that I didn't want any more. I proceeded into the tunnel following the light. It was all around me, but the major part of it was in front of me, moving. And in front of the light was a very relaxed, overwhelming feeling of release.

'It seemed like I followed the light for quite a while; then it stopped, and I ran up to it. When I got there, the light illuminated a large white door. I put my hand on the door and the light gave me a message: "Maybe you should turn back now." But I didn't know how to get back into myself, and I wanted to know what was on the other side of the door. I pushed it open, and my father was standing in the doorway. (He had died two years ago to the day.)

'I said "Dad!" and rushed into his arms and hugged him. To him it was like he had seen me just last week. The room we were in had a floor like marble, but it had no ceiling. Directly in front of me was another wall with another door and a huge illuminated structure on the other side. I can't describe the structure; it was like nothing I've ever seen. But I could feel the presence of a lot of people. I wanted to go there and said, "Dad, are we going in?" He said, "No, we have to sit down and talk about a few things." He took me to an oblong table. When we sat down somebody from the area beyond the wall came in with a tray holding two silver goblets filled with some sort of blood-red liquid. We drank it, and that's when my life started to flash before me on top of the table. While this was happening, somebody from the other area came in and stood by my father. I felt embarrassed every time a stupid thing I had done came up on the table, and that person said (but it was like a feeling as well), "You did it, but you were learning at the same time." Then he went back and my father and I sat and talked.

'While we were talking, a young couple came in. I looked at the girl and thought, "So you're dead too?" She looked at me and said, "Yes, just like you." Then that person who had been standing by my father came back and went over and said something to them. They got up and went into the area beyond the wall. The same person came out again and whispered in my dad's ear. Then my dad said, "I think you should go back now." I said, "Are you kidding? I don't want to go back. I want to go in there." He said, "Don't you have a lot of work to do?" I suddenly remembered I had an album to do for a friend. I jumped up from the table and ran to the door. "Dad, I'm sorry, I gotta get out of here. I'm late for rehearsal. I'll see you next time, Dad." He looked back at me very calmly and said, "Yes, you will." I went back through the door and wham! I felt a flash of light and came to. I pulled some tube from my throat and sat up in bed and yelled, "I gotta get out of here. I'm late for rehearsal."'

Herb Griffin

During a three-day period in October 1974, Herb Griffin, who is Director of Human Resources for the Ontario, Canada, postal region, suffered a series of heart attacks and clinically 'died' (his heart and breathing stopped) more than thirty times. Before he was resuscitated, Griffin had a number of afterlife experiences. All of them were similar; in each experience, Griffin says, 'I felt a bright radiant light and the sensation of warmth coming around me.' Here is his first afterlife experience.

'I vividly recall a feeling of being approached by a bright light, an extremely brilliant radiance. It was like the afterglow of a lightning flash. But when I viewed it for the first time it was like a locomotive headlamp moving closer to me. As the intense, bright light approached, I had the feeling that it was going to surround me. But between the bright light and me was a black shadow, which was protecting me. I couldn't sense how deep or wide the shadow was. I can't describe precisely what it was like. I have the feeling of a deep river.

'At the same time I could see myself as a curled-up body, as if I was in a foetal position on a white beach and the sun was shining down on me with intense warmth. But I was also floating at the edge of the deep, dark shadow. The brilliant light was moving closer; I shouldn't say it frightened me, but it was awe-inspiring. I wondered what would happen when the light eventually surrounded me, when I was in it.

'Just at that point, a man I had known years before appeared. He was dressed in a grey flannel suit and was so close that I felt I could touch him. He said to me, "Come on across. It is all right." What fear I had disappeared.

'Then I felt a tremendous thump on my chest. I heard a girl's voice saying, "Shall I use the paddle [electric shock]?" Another voice said, "No, not yet. His eyelids are fluttering; I think he's coming round." And I came to in hospital.

'One of the remarkable things about the experience is that the man in the grey flannel suit who spoke to me was a friend who was exactly ten years older than me. We were born on the same day, 30 May – he in 1908, me in 1918. He had died ten years before, so when I saw him we were exactly the same age.'

1979

DISCOVERING HOPE

Many people are living nowadays, more or less consciously, in what the famous psalm calls the 'valley of the shadow of death'.[1] Much of what is called depression is an experience of walking in darkness without any light ahead.

Such a mood of the soul is then filled with imaginings. One picture, which haunts the waking lives of many, is of a final nuclear war which would destroy the earth. Seeing the accumulations of nuclear weapons and the confrontations of power blocs which engender them, it is easy to weave such pictures and treat them as almost inevitable facts of the future.

Much will depend, it seems to me, on human beings distinguishing much more clearly between what they imagine in this way and what we perceive in the world around us in the ordinary way. Only then, without confusion, will we be able to see that there is indeed a sense in which we are living, in our imaginings, in realms which are entirely real. But we are entering realities of the soul world, not yet of the physical world.

Christopher Fry, in his play *A Sleep of Prisoners*, has a wonderful phrase, spoken by Tim Meadowes: 'Affairs are now soul-size'. Later in the speech comes a challenge:

> *Thank God our time is now*
> *When wrong comes up to meet*
> *   us everywhere*
> *Never to leave us till we take*
> *The greatest stride of soul*
> *Men ever took.*

Humanity is standing at a threshold. But to perceive the nuclear arms race as a problem whose essential reality lies in the physical world is to misplace reality. The weapons themselves would be nothing without the forces at work in and through human souls, forces of fear, mistrust, ambition, power-seeking, hankering for security. Our affairs are indeed soul-sized; inside outer life is an inner drama.

To cross the threshold from the physical world into the soul world is also to meet in due course the Lord of Death. He has his rightful task – to destroy old life to make way for new, and to free the spirit from matter. But if he is encountered without adequate recognition of his nature and task, he will be experienced as a being of implacable darkness, of intensely destructive will, of annihilation. Speaking of this encounter in a slightly different context in his book *Occult Science*, Rudolf Steiner describes how it can overwhelm us with 'boundless fear and terror'.[2]

When Christopher Fry can say 'Thank God our time is now . . . ', he is calling on another force in the human soul, a force which prepares us for 'the greatest stride of soul men ever took'. What is he talking about? Nothing could be more important, if we feel ourselves to be walking in the valley of the shadow of death, than to find such a force.

A few years after the second world war, a Viennese psychotherapist, Victor Frankl, wrote a remarkable book.[3] The first part is autobiographical. He was interned at Dachau, one of the Nazi death camps. There, everybody faced, at the physical level, an apparently impossible situation. But some survived. Others did not. Frankl asked why. Physical explanations were quite inadequate. He came to see that those who survived were sustained inwardly by their 'search for meaning'. Here again, this search could take quite ordinary outward forms: A determination to continue a career already begun; a personal relationship to be taken further; a journey to some other part of the world planned by not yet made. Just this speaks of a more mysterious force, of a hidden but inextinguishable will in the soul linked with the future. This will may be clothed in quite familiar wishes, but it can enable the soul to remain upright in the valley of the shadow of death, and see a light ahead.

After the war, Frankl built from his experiences a way of working with his patients which he called Logotherapy. Patients came to him who were meeting crises in their lives – crises connected particularly with finding a way forward. He worked with them in their 'search for meaning'.

This search is echoed in Fry's play, quoted above, when Tim Meadowes cries out:

> *Where are you making for?*
> *It takes so many*
> *   thousand years to wake.*
> *But will you wake*
> *For pity's sake?*

For Frankl, Logotherapy means finding some response to the

question 'where are you making for?'. This is not a therapy *of* the Logos, the Word in man. This Word is beyond sickness and death. It is a therapy to awaken the Word. Rudolf Steiner often described how we have just emerged from 5,000 years of the Kali Yuga, the dark age during which the guiding lights of the heavens receded into the past and became traditions. The question now is whether we can awake to the light which calls from the future.

More recently, I became aware of another remarkable human being, also working with people facing apparently impossible situations, Elizabeth Kübler-Ross, a Swiss-born doctor working in the United States. She has become famous for her work with the terminally ill and the newly bereaved. She has also brought much help for those who work with the dying, doctors, nurses, clergy. In her classic work *On Death and Dying*,[4] she describes five stages, like trials or ordeals, which are experienced by all who approach death in wakefulness.

The first she calls *Denial*. The problem is to accept the thought, the idea, of a terminal illness. She never forces the idea on anyone; her art is to know when they are ready and wanting to talk. All too often, the fears and insecurities of doctors and nurses, their own denials, prevent such conversations.

During the Kali Yuga, death has ceased to be for the human soul a doorway into a spiritual world. For the Romans, it became a gate into the land of shades. More recently, it has become quite simply a 'dead end'. A first transcending of the dead end begins as the soul awakens and grasps clearly the thought of terminal illness. Here is a beginning of a stride of soul into the future.

The second trial is *Anger*. Elizabeth Kübler-Ross describes this as a rebellion against helplessness. In health, we take for granted our control of our own bodies. Indeed this is how we identify so strongly with our bodies. When the body is in the grip of terminal illness, the soul must struggle free. In the struggle, the individual can become for a time extremely difficult. Unable to control the processes in the body, the patient attempts to control and direct everyone else in the surroundings. But inwardly, the soul is taking a new step of self knowledge.

The third trial is *Bargaining*. This may take all kinds of outer forms: Promises to relations, to doctors, to God, to change habits, give something, do something, if only the progress of the illness can be halted.

In an oriental bazaar, there are no fixed prices, and any purchase entails bargaining. If you accept immediately the asking price, you forfeit all respect. It is important to see that it is not the price itself which matters, it is the process of arriving at it. Through the process of give and take in bargaining, two people get to know each other, and in so doing, find a stronger sense of equilibrium in themselves. So the soul, in trying to come to terms with dying, gradually finds a new equilibrium in itself.

The fourth trial is *Depression*. Looking back, there are desires which will never be fulfilled, tasks not completed, hopes unrealised. And there seems nothing to look forward to. Here the soul is living fully in the shadow of death, and the only light is its own. To find this light is the task of this trial. As it is found, a further light can dawn, what Dr. Kübler-Ross calls *Acceptance*. The soul is ready for a stride across the threshold.

When I first met this description of these trials, it reminded me of something else, but I could not at first remember what. Some time later, I realised that I was being reminded of the 'six accessory exercises' described by Rudolf Steiner several times, notably in *Occult Science*, in *Guidance in Esoteric Training*, and in a slightly different form in *Knowledge of the Higher Worlds*.[5] What I shall say here is based on the descriptions in the first two of these publications.

The significance of the exercises is described by Steiner from several points of view: They are a very important adjunct of any form of meditation, enabling us to harvest the good fruits and overcome any ill effects; they build inner confidence; and they are concerned with forming a spiritual centre in the region of the heart.

The first exercise is *Control of Thought*. One might say 'learning to be centred in thought', developing the capacity to grasp thoughts of our choice and move freely on to the next, not gripped by fixed ideas or pulled hither and thither by wisps of reminiscence. Steiner advises that we practise with extremely simple thoughts, for a few minutes each day. We might think about a pin or a match or a ball of string.

The second is *Control of Action*, to be practised, like the first, in very simple ways. We may decide each morning to take a handkerchief out of a pocket at a particular time and transfer it to another. We should choose acts to which we are not prompted by anything other than the decision itself.

The third is *Control of Feelings*. This does not mean suppressing feelings, but learning to live poised within them, neither estranged from nor engulfed by our emotions, but in balance.

The fourth is *Positivity*. In one account of this exercise, Steiner draws on an apocryphal story of Christ, walking with his disciples, passing a dead dog on the road. The disciples avert their eyes from the rotting corpse. Christ pauses and admires the animal's beautiful white teeth. The exercise points to a quality which does not spring from our 'natural man', but calls for an inner activity – an activity which flows into an attentive and loving interest in the world. Then we may see 'white teeth', indestructible in the midst of decay. (The familiar exhortation to seek a silver lining in every cloud contains a similar spirit.)

The fifth exercise is *Readiness to Learn*. This means meeting and overcoming in ourselves that which is unready to learn, the habits of thought, feeling and action to which we are so attached, but which can close us off from the future.

The sixth exercise is to bring the other five into a unity and harmony. Steiner emphasises that the exercises should be undertaken in this order, for example one each month. Those already practised should not be left behind, but continued, if more briefly, as a new one is taken up. It may gradually be felt that these exercises form an organism, and that the sixth exercise is like a kind of life that flows through the other five and unites them. I have summarised these exercises in my own way, but would recommend readers to study Steiner's own descriptions.

Remembering these exercises after Dr. Kübler-Ross's account of the stages or trials of approaching death, they seemed to me to be linked. One can imagine, for example, that the first exercise, developing the capacity to choose freely what thoughts one attends to, could be a significant preparation for meeting the trial of Denial, where the soul shies away from the thought of its own situation.

The second, control of actions, may be seen as related to the trial of Anger, the will's rebellion against helplessness. Through this exercise, the will has to find its strength and direction without the help of the body – which offers all kinds of natural promptings to action – nor of the surroundings, which offer reminders. Such a practice could help the soul come to terms with the helplessness of a terminal illness, and transform anger into more fruitful energies.

The third, control of feelings, could prepare for a freer path through the trial of Bargaining, bringing an emotional poise in moving to a meeting with death, supporting the development of both self-knowledge and world-knowledge.

The fourth, positivity, is clearly a challenge to awaken the soul's own light which can show a way through the shadows of depression.

The fifth, readiness to learn, is perhaps in truth the most demanding of all. The force of our own self love, our attachment to our earthly personalities, our own opinions, feelings, desires, is probably very much greater than we normally realise. At the same time, death is the most far-reaching learning experience of our lives, through

which we learn that much of what we are so attached to must fall
away if we are to go forward to learn more of who we really are or
are to become. What Dr. Kübler-Ross describes as Acceptance is
not passive. It is a quality which can radiate profound peace, but
contains within it a strength and resolve to take the step across the
threshold – a 'readiness to learn' .

After describing these trials, Dr. Kübler-Ross has a short and
mysterious chapter on Hope. This, she says, must always be sustained through every trial. It must live in the one who is dying, and
in those who are caring. This may seem at first to contradict the
'acceptance' of what we might easily describe as a hopeless situation. It cannot mean that we should raise false hopes or cling to
forlorn hopes. The whole meaning of the trials is to liberate the soul
from illusions. If we listen carefully, though, we may recognise that
Dr. Kübler-Ross is speaking, out of long and deep experience, of a
quality which cannot be grasped by the kind of thinking which lives
only on this side of the threshold (just as there was no ordinary
physical explanation for the survival of those who came through
the concentration camps). Hope is in fact that very activity which
brings the soul through the trials, and it can do this because it lives
in itself beyond the threshold. We say 'hope springs eternal', which
means that hope does not belong to the transitory world, where
death is a necessity, but lives both within and beyond it. Hope
already knows resurrection as a reality – not a reality in the future,
but a reality illuminating the present from the future.

In terms of the six exercises, hope may be imagined as irradiating
the five others and making them into one living, guiding star, as
an essence of the sixth exercise. So it can build a source of inner
strength and confidence, a heart centre for the future, so that we are
not discouraged, disheartened or extinguished when we look ahead.
This heart centre was speaking in Christopher Fry when he has
Tim Meadowes say:

> *Thank God our time is now*
> *When wrong comes up to meet*
> *   us everywhere*
> *Never to leave us till we take*
> *The greatest stride of soul men ever took.*

So we can perhaps understand the six exercises and the special
emphasis Steiner gave to them, as a particular preparation for meeting the future in our times, a preparation for the experiences of
crossing the threshold.

*   *   *

I want to emphasise here most strongly that in equating mankind's crossing of the threshold in our own time with a meeting with death, I am *not* implying that a nuclear war, or any other kind of catastrophic or death-bringing experience is to be expected at a physical level, or necessarily forms part of these events. Steiner describes this crossing explicitly as a journey of the *soul*, proceeding at first largely in the unconscious. Our task is to become more awake to this journey, since we shall not otherwise be able to understand or cope with the experiences involved.

Just as our physical death is not our responsibility, but is brought to us at the right time, so it is in no way our task to accelerate the death of the earth. Indeed our task is the opposite, to care for all life, and prepare fruits and seeds for the future. So the inner preparation of the soul for meeting death experiences, whether in life or at the end of life, should in no way divert or detract from whatever actions individuals may decide to take to protect nature, to promote 'green peace' and so on.

At the same time, we need to discover the soul world as *real*, as not merely a personal and private realm, but one in which we all share. Only then can we understand what we call outer events as the face of inner events. It is then not a matter of indifference if large numbers of people come to live in the grip of thoughts of physical extinction through nuclear war or other disasters, and in the feelings such thoughts arouse. At the soul level, this is a kind of reality for all of us. But *what kind of reality?*

Real life is to be found in our actual destinies here and now. These include the destinies of our friends and colleagues, of the communities in which we live, of our cultures and nations and of our times. It is indeed all-important to learn to read the actual events in our lives as an outer expression of inner realities. But this task must not be obscured by a habit of living in dreams of the future, irrespective of whether they are good or bad dreams, and turn out to be true or false.

The times when it was right for human beings to dream what to do next are past. We now have to *decide* what to do next, and take responsibility for it. Suppose we decide for nuclear disarmament in some form and resolve to campaign for it. What drives, motivates, energises such a campaign?

It is easy to call on two main energies – fear of the future; and hostility to 'them', powers-that-be which are perceived as promoting the arms race. This is understandable and real enough. But it is important to look more carefully at the idea of the future which this implies. It is a future created out of the past. We look at present trends – nuclear stockpiles, complexifying technology – and imagine these extending into the future. So we conjure up a spectre which looms ominously over us, growing ever larger with a kind of mechanical inevitability. Then we look at the huge collective forces at work in military and industrial establishment, in governments and nations, which seem to feed on rivalry, distrust and ambition. It is as though we were confronted by huge self-centred beings which have burgeoned out of old social forms. They awaken hostility and anger.

To campaign out of these imaginings alone, to use only these energies, is not really to *decide for a future*. On the one hand, we are thrown back into an older form of relationship to the future, when human beings felt that their lives would be decided by superhuman beings, by gods. On the other hand, we feed the idea of a mechanical universe, whose future unfolds with impersonal inevitability out of the past.

Neither allows us a capacity for what Rudolf Steiner called moral intuitions[6] – intuitions of what it is possible for human beings to become, if they so resolve. Such intuitions are the light of hope. I believe that they do also live in the current campaigns for nuclear disarmament – but they are easily obscured and buried beneath our darker imaginings.

So here again, we are looking into a battle in the soul, which is also a battle *for* the soul. A future simply projected from the past, from the arms race and the forces at work in established social collectives, bring the trials of denial, anger, bargaining and depression, without summoning the only energy which can meet them. Without hope in its deepest sense, we can find only fear and helplessness.

'Where are you making for?' cries Tim Meadowes in Fry's play. 'It takes so many thousand years to awake. But will you wake, for pity's sake?' In the battle for the soul, we are summoned to awaken to the reality of hope, to the intuition of where we are making for, to a discovery of the living Word in the human soul, calling us to our truly human future.

*   *   *

The problem of grasping hope, the quality of resurrection, with ordinary thought, is perhaps the greatest problem of Christianity. Conventionally, it is often treated as a promise of reward after death, or after the end of the world. But the special quality of the Christian religion, which it shares with the Jewish religion, is that it places humanity in a *story in time*. The difference is that for the Christian church, the decisive events in the story happened two thousand years ago, while for the Jewish religion, the Messiah is still to be expected.

In Steiner's work, we find a way of seeing that in a certain sense both views can be true. Steiner was emphatic that the historical and physical events which culminated in Christ's journey through death from Good Friday to Easter Sunday, and which bore a first fruit at Whitsun, were unique, a true and absolute 'turning point of time' for all mankind. We should not look for any repetition of this event in the physical world. Steiner had to part company with the Theosophical Movement shortly before the first world war, because that remarkable individual we now know as Krishnamurti was being hailed at that time as a new incarnation of Christ. It is now clear that this was not true.

At the same time, Steiner had much to say of a second coming of Christ in our time. His Presence, though, is not to be sought in the physical world, but in a realm which becomes accessible only through an awakening in the human soul.

Near the end of his life, Steiner gave a meditation for the re-founding of the Anthroposophical Society. This Foundation Stone, as he called it, has a final section which refers to 'the turning point of time'. It points explicitly to the historical events of two thousand years ago. But it is also a kind of prayer for the present and future. In its essence, it may be felt to live beyond the time of ordinary experience, but within the reality of time itself, which unites past, present and future. Here are the words of this fourth section:[7]

> *At the turning point of time*
> *The spirit light of the world*
> *Entered the realm of earthly being.*
> *Darkness of night had reigned.*
> *Day radiant light streamed into the souls of men*
> *Light that gives warmth to simple shepherds' hearts*
> *Light that enlightens the wise heads of kings*
> *Oh light divine*
> *Oh Sun of Christ*
> *Warm Thou our hearts*
> *Enlighten Thou our heads*
> *That good may become*
> *What from our hearts to found*
> *And our heads to guide*
> *We have the will.*

Out of his own meditations on this verse, the late Zeylmans van Emmichoven wrote a short essay, included in his book *The Foundation Stone*,[8] to which I am deeply indebted. There he points out that five 'lights' are referred to: The 'Spirit Light of the world'; 'Day Radiant Light'; 'the Light that gives warmth to simple shepherds' hearts'; 'the Light that enlightens the wise heads of kings'; and 'Light Divine'. The verse culminates by calling on the 'Sun of Christ'.

Dr. Zeylmans came to see these Lights as expressions of beings, with names, yet also aspects of one whole, like the petals of a rose. In the 'Spirit Light of the world', he saw Sophia, goddess of all heavenly wisdom; in 'Day Radiant Light' the Archangel of the sun, Michael, whom Steiner once called 'the countenance of Christ'; in the Light that warms the shepherds' hearts, the Bhudda, bringer of compassion; in the Light that enlightens the kings, Zarathustra, the great Initiate into the mysteries of light and darkness; and in the 'Light Divine', the original light of the unfallen human soul, which lives in the child of innocence described in the gospel of St. Luke, the being of offering, of sacrifice, of ultimate 'readiness to learn'.

Perhaps we meet here a a higher level something which lives in germ in the 'six exercises'. When we practice control of thought, we are practising to walk rightly in the realm of Sophia. When we practice control of action, we are striving to humanise our will (Michael is the Archangel of courage, of sun-filled initiative). When we practice control of feeling, we are seeking the healing ways of the Bhudda, between egotism and self-denial. When we practice positivity, we can illuminate the darkness and see what is eternal and what is transitory; we can follow the star of Zarathustra who guided the three kings.

When we practice readiness to learn, we have to shed past experience, be prepared to become as little children, souls of innocence in preparation for the greatest learning experience of our lives. The whole is illuminated and united by the Sun of Christ, the being of Hope.

Thus the fourth section of the Foundation Stone may be glimpsed as a great prayer for our time, a prayer for those qualities we need for the trials of crossing the threshold. It is a prayer like a flower, for which the six exercises may be a kind of bud. Together, they can bring light, warmth, strength, for the journey through the valley in which we find ourselves.

The very fact that we can awaken to these Lights means that we must indeed already know something of the Light of Hope, that very Light without which we could not realise that we are in a shadow. But we shall know this Light only in dreams unless we awaken rightly to the inner and outer realities in which we live, learn to know the soul world in which our affairs are soul size, and begin to read what we call the external world as the outer face of our own inner realities.

1983

[1] Psalm 23.

[2] *Occult Science*, chapter 5, p. 293 (Rudolf Steiner Press).

[3] *Man's Search for Meaning: An introduction to Logotherapy* by Viktor E. Frankl (Washington Square Press 1963).

[4] Tavistock Publications 1970.

[5] Rudolf Steiner Press.

[6] See *The Philosophy of Freedom*, especially chapters 9 – 14 (Rudolf Steiner Press).

[7] *The Foundation Stone* by Rudolf Steiner (Rudolf Steiner Press).

[8] *The Foundation Stone* by F.W. Zeylmans van Emmichoven, chapter 11 (Rudolf Steiner Press).

Notes and Literature

I.   This Living Earth
     1. 'Wisdom and the Life of the Earth' from the *Golden Blade*, 1971, pp. 22-34.
     2. 'Man and the Underworld' from *The Golden Blade*, 1980, pp. 45-60.
     3. 'True and False Flames: Reflections on the Energy Crisis' from *The Anthroposophical Review*, Vol. 2, No. 2, Summer 1980, pp. 1-6.

II. Considering Science
     1. 'Bacon, Rudolf Steiner and Modern Science' from *The Golden Blade*, 1962, pp. 36-45 (originally written under the name of John Waterman).
     2. 'Science and Human Rights', from *The Golden Blade*, 1968, pp. 24-40.
     3. 'Scientific Progress and the Threshold' from *The Golden Blade*, 1964, pp. 54-64 (originally written under the name of John Waterman).
     4. 'Responsibility in Science', from *Resurgence*, No. 107, November/December 1984, pp. 16-19.

III. The Evolution of Evolution
     1. 'Evolution: the Hidden Thread' from *The Golden Blade*, 1956, pp. 18-28 (originally written under the name of John Waterman).
     2. 'Epochs of Evolution' from *The Golden Blade*, 1957, pp. 48-59 (as by John Waterman).
     3. 'Darwinism and the Archetypes' from *The Golden Blade*, 1959, pp. 64-73 (as by John Waterman).
     4. 'The Evolution of Evolution' from *The Observer Magazine*, February 8, 1970, pp. 10-20.
     5. 'Do We or Don't We Understand the Secret of Life' from *The Observer Magazine*, February 15, 1970, pp. 17-20.

IV. A Sense For Language
     1. 'Inner Language and Outer Language' from *The Golden Blade*, 1973, pp. 79-93.
     2. 'On Coming to Our Senses' from *The Golden Blade*, 1975, pp. 39-52.
     3. 'Meaning and the Human Soul' from *The Golden Blade*, 1978, pp. 63-70.

V.   Education for Living
     1. 'The Man Who Wants to Scrap Schools' from *The Observer*, October 24, 1971, p. 9.
     2. 'The Social Meaning of Education' from *The Teachers College Record*, Vol. 81, No. 3, Spring 1980, pp. 345-359.
     3. 'Mindstorms in the Lamplight' from *The Teachers College Record*, Vol. 85, No. 4, Summer 1984, pp. 549-558. Also appearing in *Computers and Education*:Critical Perspectives (Teachers College Press, 1985).
     4. 'The Movement That Everyone Tries to Forget' from *The Times Educational Supplement*, March 23, 1973.

VI. Caring for the Planet
     1. 'Prophet of the Convivial Society' from *The Observer*, September 23, 1973.
     2. 'Menace in the Silent Spring' from *The Observer*, February 17, 1963.
     3. 'Polluting the Planet' from *The Observer*, November 10, 1968.
     4. 'Time to Stop the Plunder' from *The Observer*, November 17, 1968.
     5. 'Small and Beautiful World' written in appreciation of Fritz Schumacher, from *The Observer*, November 9, 1977.

VII. After Life
     1. 'The Evidence for Life After Life' from *The Observer Supplement*, April 8, 1979.
     2. 'Life After Life' from *The Observer Supplement*, April 15, 1979.

VIII. 'Discovering Hope' from *The Anthroposophical Review*, Vol. 5, No. 2, 1983.